THE GREAT JAZZ DAY

The Great Jazz Day

by Charles Graham

Additional texts by Dan Morgenstern, Whitney Balliett, Gary Giddins and Ralph Ellison

Rare photographs by Art Kane, Dizzy Gillespie, Milt Hinton and Mike Lipskin

Da Capo Press

DEDICATION

To Charles Delaunay and Hughes Panassie, whose pioneering *Hot Discographie* and *Le Jazz Hot* first encouraged me and countless others to pursue the incomparable music of Louis Armstrong, Roy Eldridge and Coleman Hawkins, thus changing my life.

Panassie's *Hot Jazz: The Guide to Swing Music* came out in France in 1934. Translated by Lyle & Eleanor Dowling, it was published here in 1936.

Delaunay's *Hot Discography*, 1948 English language edition, was edited by Walter Schapp, George Avakian and Delaunay, and was translated by Schapp.

— Charles Graham

ACKNOWLEDGMENTS

Jeff Atterton, historian, critic and discographical expert, who found a publisher for this book. Jeff wrote for England's *Melody Maker* and other important magazines.

Jean Bach, jazz historian, film producer and writer par excellence, and my friend for many years.

Lorraine Gillespie, Dizzy Gillespie's wife of almost 60 years, helped find the proof sheet of Gillespie's pictures taken that day. She also gave me one of his two vintage-fifties Leica M-2 cameras. I have the happy notion it's the one he had with him that day.

Milt Hinton's wife Mona took a home movie, *That Day*, with Milt's 8-mm movie camera. It was that 10-minute movie which propelled Jean into making her movie.

Paul Bacon, our cover designer, belongs to that select circle of jazz fans who are also practicing musicians.

Frank Driggs, whose unique and unparalleled photographic archives supplied pictures not available anywhere else, was also the one to put me in touch with Mike Lipskin.

Art Kane's sons Jonathan, Anthony and Nicholas encouraged me immensely.

Laurence J. Hyman took cornet lessons in his youth from the nonpareil Rex Stewart. I cannot adequately thank him for his encouragement and his incomparable work in editing, designing and producing this book.

—C.G.

Edited and designed by Laurence J. Hyman.
Editorial assistance by Mike Lipskin.

Published by Da Capo Press
A Member of the Perseus Books Group
www.dacapopress.com

Distributed in the United States and Canada by
Andrews McMeel Universal, 4500 Main Street, Kansas City, MO 64111-7701

Printed in the United States.
Cataloging-in-Publication data for this book is available from the library of Congress
ISBN: 0-306-81163-4

Photograph on page 1, Art Kane
Photograph on pages 2-3, Mike Lipskin

Contents

Art Kane photograph from January 1959 *Esquire*.

Preface

THE PHOTOGRAPHS IN THIS BOOK show what happened on 126th Street in Harlem on August 12, 1958, when almost 60 musicians assembled for a portrait—the Big Picture—that had been scheduled to run in *Esquire* magazine.

Esquire wrote letters to every jazz musician whose address could be found and passed the word in jazz clubs, at musicians' bars and at Musicians' Union Local 802, on 52nd Street in Manhattan, following up with telephone calls the day before the shoot.

Nobody knew how many people would show up (at 10:00 in the morning). But at the appointed hour they began coming, by subway at the Lexington Avenue/125th Street stop, by taxi, and some even on foot, to the brownstone apartment building at 17 West 126th Street, between Park and Fifth avenues.

The main photograph, taken by Art Kane, became the centerfold of *Esquire's* January 1959 issue, "The Golden Age of Jazz."

The Big Picture has been reprinted many times, and some years ago Jean Bach got the idea of interviewing the survivors of the main photograph to see what they remembered about that day.

We also chose to reprint a group picture of trumpet players taken by Herb Snitzer for the October 1961 issue of *Metronome*, which was devoted to the trumpet in jazz. Dan Morgenstern was the editor of *Metronome* in 1961 and his story of the trumpet players gathered for their picture in Central Park is presented here, along with candid photographs taken that day by photographer Jack Bradley.

In addition, we are privileged to include many photographs of jazz musicians taken by other accomplished photographers. One of these is a large photograph taken at a book party in 1956 celebrating the publication of *The Story of Jazz*.

This book also presents some excellent writing by Ralph Ellison, Whitney Balliett, Gary Giddins and Dan Morgenstern, setting the stage for the photographs and adding to a greater appreciation of these musicians and their Golden Era.

—Charles Graham
New York City, Summer 1999

HOLIDAY ISSUE / JANUARY, 1959

PRICE 60¢

Esquire

THE MAGAZINE FOR MEN

THE
GOLDEN AGE OF
JAZZ

ROBERT BENTON

I

The Big Picture

Three People

THERE WERE THREE people who created the photograph that became the centerfold of *Esquire's* "Golden Age of Jazz" issue, which came out in January 1959.

First of all, Harold Hayes, the innovative and unconventional features editor of *Esquire* in 1958, was an amateur trombone player and jazz lover who had decided to focus on jazz in that issue. He had been promoting one controversial subject after another, so this one was almost conservative by comparison. But it was close to his heart, and since his boss, publisher Arnold Gingrich, was also an ardent jazz fan, Hayes knew he'd have no opposition from him.

New graphics editor Robert Benton, who would later become a highly successful Hollywood film director ("Bonnie and Clyde," "Kramer vs. Kramer," "Cool Hand Luke"), was the second person at *Esquire* who thought a jazz issue would be a good idea.

Benton had been top graphics man at *Esquire* for less than four months, and Hayes himself had been at the magazine only three years.

They were willing, in Benton's words, "to try lots of new and risky ideas," which in this case meant hiring an unknown (non-)photographer to suggest and take pictures for the proposed jazz issue. The artist they had in mind was a complete wild card since he had never, in Benton's words, "taken any professional photographs, but he loves jazz and has lots of imagination and great ideas."

Thus it was yet another dyed-in-the-wool jazz enthusiast, *Seventeen* magazine's art director Art Kane, who was approached to become the third and most important person responsible for the Big Picture. Kane didn't own any professional cameras at the time and had to borrow two from his friend, the already-established fashion photographer Milton Greene.

In addition to designing *Seventeen* magazine, Kane also taught magazine design at New York's New School (for Social Research), a school primarily for adults interested in furthering their knowledge. Many courses at The New School were taught by people who, like Kane, worked during the day at regular jobs, usually in the fields they taught at night.

One of Kane's students was Benton, whose job at *Esquire* was similar to Kane's at *Seventeen*. Although neither of them could have predicted it, that student-teacher relationship would bring them together to create what became the most important jazz picture ever taken.

Benton was impressed with Kane's ideas and enthusiasm and knew that he was crazy about jazz. Benton himself was not a jazz fan, but he knew his *Esquire* boss, Harold Hayes, was. It made perfect sense for Benton to have his teacher talk to Hayes about ideas for the jazz issue and to take pictures for it.

When young Benton asked Kane if he'd come over to talk with his editor, Kane jumped at the chance. They got together at *Esquire,* and out of their meeting came the ideas that changed Kane's life forever.

Kane proposed getting together as many jazz musicians as possible for a group portrait uptown in Harlem. "That's where jazz was nurtured," he pointed out. Kane saw it, he said, "as a kind of graduation picture, with as many important musicians as we can get, even if there are some vital ones who may not be in town on the day we choose." Those luminaries not pictured included, as it turned out, Louis Armstrong, Duke Ellington and Charlie Parker. (Parker had died three years before. Kane later went to Kansas City and visited Parker's mother, who lent him Bird's saxophone case. Kane photographed it in front of Parker's gravestone.)

Kane and Benton scouted several blocks near 125th Street in Harlem for the right brownstone. "They all looked alike to me," Benton said later, "but this particular brownstone, number 17 on 126th Street, was what Kane wanted, and that's what he got."

Jazz writer Nat Hentoff and others gave them as many names and addresses as they had, and *Esquire* staffers went to work contacting the musicians. Notices were put up in all the jazz clubs, too, and especially at the Musicians' Union Local 802 on West 52nd Street. Everybody on the list was invited to show up at 126th Street, between Madison and Fifth avenues, at 10 AM on Saturday, August 12. The day before the gathering, *Esquire* telephoned as many people as they had phone numbers for.

Esquire asked the traffic department to close that block to vehicles between 10 AM and 2 PM on the picture-tak-

One Photograph

ing day, but all the department could promise was 10 AM to noon. The noon cut-off is probably why we have pictures showing trucks passing on the street in the later hours of the picture session. The *Esquire* staff still had no idea how many musicians would show up. These were night people, used to sleeping until noon or early afternoon, and 10 AM was an early call.

Hayes, Benton and Kane got there ahead of time with a couple of assistants, so there were several people to help direct things and get the musicians into place. Kane also asked an ad agency friend, Steve Frankfurt, to help him load and unload film for the cameras.

Nat Hentoff can be seen in early parts of the home movie taken by Milt Hinton's wife Mona, and also in one of the shots made with Dizzy Gillespie's camera (with Gillespie himself in the picture). Hentoff left, however, once he saw that things were going as planned and that plenty of musicians were showing up.

Soon after 10 AM, the musicians had started drifting in. They had been told to come to the Lexington Avenue subway at 125th Street (or the Metro-North Railroad station at 125th Street), and to walk over to the designated block. Some came by subway, some by taxi. Some even came by Long Island Railroad to Pennsylvania Station and transferred to the subway for the trip to Harlem.

Among those who came by taxi were Thelonious Monk and Gigi Gryce with Bob Altshuler of Riverside Records. Oscar Pettiford came in Mary Lou Williams' car with Elaine Lorillard (who had started the Newport Jazz Festival in 1954).

Many people who were in the final shots did not appear in pictures taken on the first side of the street (in front of the house with two windows). Kane doesn't remember moving the musicians across the street, and later denied that the move had happened at all, until shown the pictures on opposite sides of the street.

Gillespie was there early, on the first side. He's seen sitting with the group on the steps in some pictures, and later seen climbing up to the outside of the stoop railing, holding a small 7-inch tape box. In one of Milt Hinton's pictures, Gillespie is perched up there laughing and holding on to the railing. During this time he does not have his camera, but by the time everyone moves over to the second side of the street he's seen in several other people's photographs taking pictures with his camera.

Where was Gillespie's camera before he started taking pictures, to whom did he give it, and finally, who then shot the rest of the roll? Toward the end of the day Gillespie is again seen holding that tape reel, and appears in pictures made with his own camera. He moved around a lot, taking pictures in the middle of the session on the second side and clowning a bit, interacting with more people than anyone else did.

Other noticeable movements include Willie "the Lion" Smith, who stood next to his short pal Luckey Roberts in the front row most of the day, but who got tired after a while, sat down on a set of steps out of the frame and missed being in the Big Picture.

Roy Eldridge stood to the far left at first, but later went over to the far right to be next to his friend Gillespie for the last few pictures.

Count Basie, standing most of the day at right rear, sat down on the curb, not once but twice.

J.C. Higginbotham moved around to photograph other folks.

When they moved from one side of the street across to the other, a few people took up very different positions from those they had on the first side, but most stayed in the arrangement they had been in earlier.

Rex Stewart was one of the three musicians who had brought their horns there that day in carrying cases. Eldridge and Lester Young were the other two. But only Stewart took his out of its case. He even blew a few notes on it. ●

The jazz greats in the historic Art Kane photograph on the preceding pages are numbered above for ready reference: 1. Hilton Jefferson; 2. Benny Golson; 3. Art Farmer; 4. Wilbur Ware; 5. Art Blakey; 6. Chubby Jackson; 7. Johnny Griffin; 8. Dickie Wells; 9. Buck Clayton; 10. Taft Jordan; 11. Zutty Singleton; 12. Red Allen; 13. Tyree Glenn; 14. Miff Mole; 15. Sonny Greer; 16. Jay C. Higginbotham; 17. Jimmy Jones; 18. Charles Mingus; 19. Jo Jones; 20. Gene Krupa; 21. Max Kaminsky; 22. George Wettling; 23. Bud Freeman; 24. Pee Wee Russell; 25. Ernie Wilkins; 26. Buster Bailey; 27. Osie Johnson; 28. Gigi Gryce; 29. Hank Jones; 30. Eddie Locke; 31. Horace Silver; 32. Luckey Roberts; 33. Maxine Sullivan; 34. Jimmy Rushing; 35. Joe Thomas; 36. Scoville Browne; 37. Stuff Smith; 38. Bill Crump; 39. Coleman Hawkins; 40. Rudy Powell; 41. Oscar Pettiford; 42. Sahib Shihab; 43. Marian McPartland; 44. Sonny Rollins; 45. Lawrence Brown; 46. Mary Lou Williams; 47. Emmett Berry; 48. Thelonious Monk; 49. Vic Dickenson; 50. Milt Hinton; 51. Lester Young; 52. Rex Stewart; 53. J. C. Heard; 54. Gerry Mulligan; 55. Roy Eldridge; 56. Dizzy Gillespie; 57. Count Basie

Harlem Morning

A new film tells the story behind a legendary picture
by Whitney Balliett
The New Yorker
January 23, 1995

AROUND TEN O'CLOCK on a morning in mid-August of 1958, an extraordinary group of jazz musicians began gathering outside a row of brownstones on 126th Street, between Fifth and Madison avenues. They had been invited by *Esquire* to have their picture taken for a special jazz issue, scheduled for January of 1959. Fifty-eight musicians turned up. They included New Orleans, New York, Chicago, Kansas City, and bebop musicians—the whole glorious jazz schmear as it existed in the late fifties in New York. There were megastars (Count Basie, Coleman Hawkins, Lester Young, Roy Eldridge, Dizzy Gillespie and Gene Krupa); future stars (Gerry Mulligan, Thelonious Monk, Sonny Rollins, Charles Mingus, Art Farmer, Art Blakey and Horace Silver); former Ellingtonians (Rex Stewart, Lawrence Brown, Tyree Glenn, Oscar Pettiford and Sonny Greer) and former Basie-ites (Buck Clayton, Dickie Wells, Jimmy Rushing, Vic Dickenson, Jo Jones and Emmett Berry); great teachers and shapers (Mary Lou Williams, Luckey Roberts, Willie "the Lion" Smith, Red Allen and Zutty Singleton); indispensable journeymen (Milt Hinton, J.C. Higginbotham, Joe Thomas, Stuff Smith, Wilbur Ware, Chubby Jackson, Hank Jones and J.C. Heard); an Eddie Condon contingent, minus its leader (Pee Wee Russell, Miff Mole, Bud Freeman, Max Kaminsky and George Wettling); one American woman singer (Maxine Sullivan) and one English woman pianist (Marian McPartland); a ringer (an unknown musician from Buffalo named Bill Crump); and one messup (Willie "the Lion"), who, bored with waiting in the hot sun, had wandered off when the chosen shot was taken, leaving a noticeable gap next to Luckey Roberts. The youngest musician, at twenty-seven, was Sonny Rollins, and the oldest, at seventy-one, was Roberts.

It had been the notion of Robert Benton, then the art director of Esquire, to include a batch of new pho-tographs of jazz musicians for the January issue. He brought in Art Kane, a young hotshot freelance art director, and Kane suggested that a group photograph be taken in Harlem, the cradle of New York Jazz. He also offered to take the picture himself, even though he'd had no experience as a photographer. The word went out on the jazz grapevine, and the musicians began trickling in on time, despite the heavy duty of being anywhere but in bed at 10 in the morning. (Jazz musicians are night creatures; a musician at the shoot said he was astonished to discover that there were two 10 o'clocks in each day.) Because they are peripatetic, jazz players sometimes don't run into one another for years at a time; as the crowd swelled, so did the milling, the pressing of the flesh, the hugs, and the how-ya-beens. Kane started shooting anyway. Milt Hinton, a fine amateur photographer, handed his wife, Mona, his 8-mm movie camera and told her to aim it and press the button. He himself began taking stills; as did a student of Willie "the Lion"'s named Mike Lipskin. Eventually, the crowd formed a ragged line on the sidewalk between two high brownstone stoops. Then, with Kane pleading and shouting from across the street, part of the group, led by Red Allen, rose up onto the stoop in between, so that the assemblage resembled an upside-down "T." Count Basie, tired of standing, sat on the curb, and twelve kids, mostly from the neighborhood, sat next to him, forming an emphatic line under the picture. Some of the musicians were coatless and in sports shirts, but most wore ties and jackets. Some were even in dark suits, and seven had hats on. Except for a few nervous young Turks like Johnny Griffin, Mingus, Sahib Shihab, and Rollins, everyone looked pleased and relaxed about being where he was. Dizzy Gillespie, standing at the far right with his legs crossed, is sticking his tongue out at his onetime idol, Roy Eldridge, who is directly in front of Gillespie

Top: The group is mostly up on the steps for the final photograph, but *Esquire* editor Harold Hayes and art director Robert Benton are still talking it over as a car streaks by. (Mike Lipskin photograph) Above: Getting set up on the second side of the street. Art Kane is at left. In middle Benton gestures toward steps, "Can we get them up there?" Marian McPartland is at right with Oscar Pettiford. (Milt Hinton photograph)

and has turned his head awkwardly toward him. Gillespie-the-irrepressible had obviously just called, "Hey, Roy!"

Kane took a hundred and twenty exposures, and the final selection duly appeared as a double-page spread in Esquire. It caused a small sensation, and soon became a permanent part of jazz arcana. The image also stuck in the head of a pretty, witty, famous New York blonde named Jean Bach. Born in Chicago and raised in Milwaukee, Bach has been a passionate jazz fan since she was eighteen and began hanging out with Duke Ellington and Roy Eldridge. In 1941 she married an Eldridge imitator, Shorty Sherock, and spent seven tumultuous years travelling with Sherock's group. ("It was a strange band," she once said. "It had a floating Basie-type rhythm section and an Italianate trumpet section that played a little sharp and real loud.") Then she got a divorce, moved to New York, married a TV producer named Bob Bach, and, in time, began producing the Arlene Francis show on WOR radio. She retired in the eighties, and several years ago she began brooding about Art Kane's picture. The surprising result is a brilliant, funny, lissome documentary film called "A Great Day in Harlem." It's about the taking of the picture, and it's also about mortality, loyalty, talent, musical beauty and the fact that jazz musicians tend to be the least pretentious artists on earth.

Jean Bach lives in Gertrude Vanderbilt Whitney's old studio on Washington Mews, and the other day she sat in her living room and talked about her film. "I kept asking myself how all these fabulous musicians had got together on somebody's brownstone stoop in Harlem to have their photograph taken. All I knew was that a man named Art Kane had taken it and that it had run in *Esquire*. I started asking musicians I'd run into who were in the picture how it had come about, and I'd generally get these hazy, gee-I-can't-remember-man answers. One day I noticed that only a dozen or so of the fifty-seven people in the picture were still with us, and the electric light went on. It was time for me to interview the survivors, and maybe film the interviews, for the record."

Bach talked to her friend Bill Harbach, who had made some short films, and he put her onto a film person named Kemper Peacock, who found her a cameraman name Steve Petropoulos. Before she knew it, she had fifty or sixty hours of interviews. She talked to Johnny Griffin and Art Farmer, both of whom live in Europe, at New York gigs, and she filmed Bud Freeman in a retirement place in Chicago. She finally caught up with the elusive Art Blakey in "his gorgeous West Side apartment." She shot Gerry Mulligan in his house in Connecticut, and she did several interviews in her living room, placing each musician in a different part of the room to fool the viewer. Sahib Shihab died two weeks after she talked to him, and Blakey three months later, and since then Freeman, Gillespie, Buck Clayton, and Max Kaminsky have gone. Then Milt Hinton told Bach's friend Charles Graham about Mona's 8-mm film, and she decided to combine that footage somehow, if it still existed, with the filmed interviews—in other words, to make a movie.

Bach asked her friend Kathryn Altman, Robert

Jean Bach's living room while famed Canadian photographer Karsh of Ottawa zeroes in on Dizzy Gillespie as he tunes up. (Charles Graham photograph)

Charles Graham, Jean Bach, and, right, Janet (Mrs. Avery) Fisher. (Third Street Music School photograph)

Altman's wife, for advice, and she suggested that Bach get in touch with a producer named Matthew Seig, who works with Altman. Seig said yes, and when Mona Hinton's film was finally found, in Milt's basement in Queens, Seig told Bach that it was time to rent a studio and hire an editor. They hired Susan Peehl, who edited the fine 1993 Billie Holiday documentary "Lady Day: The Many Faces of Billie Holiday," and put her in a studio apartment over on Third Avenue, where she lived the picture night and day for the next year and a half. Seig also came up with the brilliant idea of using footage from "The Sound of Jazz" television show, which aired just six months before the Harlem shoot and included many of the same musicians.

Bach went on, "Then I discovered the joys of getting permission from music publishers to use their music. There are twenty-three songs, or pieces of songs, in the picture, and to date they have cost well over a hundred thousand dollars. I realized early on that I couldn't swing all the costs myself, and I applied to every foundation that exists, and all I could hear was the sound of pocketbooks snapping shut across the country. I finally got a grant from a baby friend in Milwaukee. She and her husband have the Jane and Lloyd Pettit Foundation."

The film was finished last June. It has been shown in London and for a week on the Coast, and is therefore eligible for the Academy Awards, and it won a first prize at the Chicago Film Festival. It opens at the Quad, on Thirteenth Street, on February 17th. "So far, I've only had one real demurrer," she said. "And it came from Artie Shaw. We're old friends, and when we had lunch on the Coast a little while ago I asked him what he thought of the picture, and he said, 'Jean, do you want me to be polite, or do you want me to be honest?' I said the latter, and he had all these niggling criticisms, and then I realized what was really bothering him. In the film, sweet Bud Freeman speculates that in a hundred years Pee Wee Russell might prove to be more highly thought of than Benny Goodman. What rankles Artie is that Freeman said Goodman. If he had said Shaw, Artie would have just laughed and said something like 'Oh, that Pee Wee.'"

Susan Peehl's quicksilver editing of "A Great Day" mixes interviews (she sometimes cuts rapidly back and forth between two musicians talking about the same subject, to give the impression that they are conversing with each other), archival footage, sequences from the astonishing "The Sound of Jazz," Mona Hinton's film, Hinton's and Mike Lipskin's stills, and more than a dozen of Art Kane's alternative shots. She mixes these in such a way that the musicians move and talk and gesticulate: you are on 126th Street in 1958. She also gives us miniature portraits of Thelonious Monk playing (his feet flapping like flounders on the floor beneath the piano) and doing one of his impromptu dances, and of Lester Young in his famous black porkpie hat, his flat eyes peering out of his pale, flat face. Near the end of the film, there is a calm, and Art Farmer says, "We don't think about people not being here. If we think about Lester Young, we don't think he's gone. We think, well, Lester Young is here. Coleman Hawkins is here. They are in us, and they will always be alive." Farmer has a dark, heavy voice, and he makes you shiver.

Remembering That Day Up in Harlem

Art Kane Remembers

IT ALL STARTED in the summer of 1958, at which time I was not yet a photographer. I didn't even have a real camera. I was an art director, a fairly well-known one, at *Seventeen* magazine, and I was also teaching graphic design at The New School.

One of my students was a young guy out of Texas named Robert Benton who had just been taken on at *Esquire* magazine as assistant art director. He was very talented and we got pretty chummy. About that time he learned I was crazy about jazz music, and also that I was getting more and more interested in photography.

A few months later he was promoted to the top graphic editor's spot at *Esquire* and he called me up to ask if I'd be interested in coming up with ideas and taking pictures for a jazz issue of the magazine. It would focus on the four greatest musicians in jazz: Duke Ellington, Louis Armstrong, Charlie Parker and Lester Young.

I told him I'd love to do it, and he told me to come over to the office to meet the editor, Harold Hayes. It turned out Hayes was a big jazz buff and it was his idea to do this special jazz issue.

After I thought about it I came up with the idea of get-ting as many musicians together in one place as we could. It would be sort of a graduation photo or class picture of *all* the jazz musicians. After I thought about it some more I decided they should get together in Harlem. After all, that's where jazz started when it came to New York.

I walked around Harlem for a day and finally found a street up there with a row of houses that looked absolutely typical of the neighborhood, 126th Street, between Fifth Avenue and Madison. It was only a few blocks from the New York Central Railroad at 125th Street and from the subway, and they could easily walk over from there, so that would make a great assembly point.

Then I had *Esquire* call the police department and ask them to close off the block for a few hours, except for people who lived there, so we could take the pictures. I said I wanted no traffic except for actual residents of that street from 10 AM until 2 PM.

So I made my request and a couple of weeks later it began to happen, right in front of my eyes. The next thing you know they all started moving into the block I'd picked out. I couldn't believe it was happening. I mean, I'd made this crazy request and there it was—it was actually happening.

First arrivals on 126th Street, coming from Metro North 125th Street station (seen in background). Mona Hinton with her little movie camera turns to greet Buster Bailey behind her. To the right of Bailey are Vic Dickinson (with umbrella) and, Lester "Pres" Young. Between Bailey and Dickinson are Hinton's mother and J.C. Higginbotham. The man at far left carries Hinton's handbag. (Milt Hinton photograph)

The only thing was that I couldn't control it, because we had all these musicians who hadn't seen each other for a long time, some of them for months or even years.

They were all talking and laughing and shaking hands and paying attention to each other, but not to this idiot kid across the street who had the audacity to set up the whole thing there.

I had never felt so alone before in my life, standing on the other side of the street watching them milling around and paying no attention at all to me. I was thinking, "Okay, Kane, you did it, now it's your job to get them into some kind of formation for a picture."

So I grabbed a copy of *The New York Times* and made it into a sort of megaphone and put it up to my mouth. I yelled and begged, "Please, please get together in some kind of a formation. Move up into those steps up there in front of that house."

Little by little, slowly but surely, they began moving up into the steps and filling up the front of the brownstone. It was like asking a baby to do something. No one was paying any attention to me. But I had one marvelous assistant with me up there that day. He was Steve Frankfurter, and he helped me and Robert Benton in getting them together up there on the steps.

He was also supposed to help load the two cameras I had borrowed, but he was as inept as I was in loading them. First he put the film in backwards, and I yelled at him, "What are you doing? You're putting it in backwards!"

So here you have a non-professional photographer, who's got an assistant who's never loaded a camera before, taking this picture which 30 years later is probably the best-known group photograph ever taken of jazz musicians.

I have no idea how they decided to stand where they did, and with whom, but they did. Slowly they formed themselves into a big group. Slowly they worked their way into position any way they saw fit, and I saw they couldn't have gotten into any better position. So I picked up the paper megaphone and screamed and begged, because I needed 57 pairs of eyes looking at my camera.

As it is, I only got 56 pairs of eyes or maybe fewer, but I got enough eye contact to make it work. It was in maybe only two frames out of the entire set that I got enough eye contact. On top of that I'd noticed Count Basie had sat down on the curb, and then a few kids decided they'd get in the picture by sitting down next to the Count. And finally about 10 or 12 kids in all were sitting down there on the curb next to him.

Dizzy Gillespie was over there sticking his tongue out the way he does sometimes, and Lester Young was looking at me in a sinister way. (I learned the reason for that

Top: More musicians have arrived. Dizzy Gillespie is in the middle taking pictures of Buster Bailey (right), Joe Thomas (hand on cheek) and George Wettling beside him. At Gillespie's right Pee Wee Russell poses. At Gillespie's left is Charles Mingus. (Milt Hinton photograph) Above: Hanging around on the first side of the street. Rear left, is laughing trombonist Miff Mole, then trumpeter Max Kaminsky, then drummer Wettling. In the middle is tenor man Bud Freeman talking to Gene Krupa. Behind him Buck Clayton talks to Rex Stewart and Art Blakey. (Milt Hinton photograph)

Right: Now they're up on the steps, first side. At bottom middle is Stuff Smith and next to him Horace Silver. Above Smith is Pee Wee Russell and at his right, a smiling Chubby Jackson. Count Basie (in hat) is above Russell. (Milt Hinton photograph)
Below: Up on steps on the first side. Rex Stewart is at left, then Count Basie, then Charles Mingus, then Milt Hinton, cleaning camera lens. (Mike Lipskin photograph)

All set for the photograph on first side of street. Five kids are in the photo already (three on curb, two standing). Lester Young is at left, next to Gerry Mulligan. Thelonious Monk (in hat) is at far right, next to Sonny Rollins. (Art Kane photograph)

a few days later when I took his picture alone and we talked a little bit.) You could tell he was an unhappy guy almost at once.

There were a lot of little mini-dramas taking place that day. And when it was all over I packed up my cameras and Steve and I took off. I went back to *Seventeen* magazine and Steve went back to his agency, Young & Rubicam.

Then the contact prints came over to my office, and they looked like real pictures. They were my first *real* pictures! I thought, "Wow, these are actually *great* pictures. It's a lot of real people." And that was it.

We chose the picture, the one in the centerfold. Then I followed up with the four portraits, the four full pages of portraits. I used up my entire two-week vacation to get those shots of the four great jazz musicians that appeared along with the big group portrait in the centerfold.

It was a real feeling of power. I came up with this really outrageous idea, and seeing it unfold the way I'd thought of it was one of the most magnificent moments of my life. That's what changed my career and what changed my life.

I knew from that moment on that this was what I wanted to do with my life. I wanted to be a photographer. That was what did it, the feeling of power from seeing those musicians moving up there onto those steps. And turning that moment into the Big Picture.

Finished on first side, looking to the North, second side. At left is Buck Clayton (in hat), facing him is Red Allen, and to his right are Chubby Jackson, Osie Johnson and Zutty Singleton. Oscar Pettiford holds a newspaper. (Milt Hinton photograph)

Robert Benton Remembers

I GUESS I HAD BEEN working as the art director at *Esquire* two or three months while Harold Hayes was the senior editor or something like that. I forget his exact title. I knew Harold pretty well by then and I knew he was crazy about jazz music. He really loved it. He had this idea to do a special issue dedicated to jazz and got permission from the publisher.

I was still new enough and dumb enough in those days to try all sorts of risky things. I'd known Art Kane's philosophy for a long time, because I'd taken his course at The New School. At the time there were only maybe three or four great young art directors in New York. Henry Wolf and Art Kane and one or two or three other people were really considered the bright young Turks.

I called Art and asked if he would come and talk to Harold Hayes about photographing this jazz issue. I knew he had the kind of conceptual mind that could take in all kinds of ragged information and put it into some kind of dramatic focus. I felt that the photographer's job was to decorate the story, to make a visual border for the piece. I had no idea what it might be. But I knew Art had that kind of mind.

So he came in and started talking to Hayes. Art is very

enthusiastic, has an enormous amount of energy and can sell anybody anything. I don't know who came up with the idea, but somehow they decided to try a double-page spread of as many jazz musicians as they could get. It sounded wonderful to me—I thought it was loosely connected to some pictures Irving Penn had once taken of painters and dancers, so there was a kind of history to it.

But instead of doing it in the controlled situation of a studio, Art said that he wanted to do it up in Harlem. That was the moment when I began to get nervous, because I figured we'd never be able to control things up there. It was a miracle that he made it work at all. The fact that it works is entirely due to Art and to Harold Hayes.

If I remember correctly, we looked at lots of scattered places in Harlem. As far as I was concerned one brownstone looked just like any other brownstone. But Art decided it had to be this particular brownstone. He went to whoever you had to go to to get permission to photograph it at about noon. And he asked the police to close this block from 10 or so in the morning to one or two in the afternoon to any traffic except for residents.

We got there about half an hour early, about 9:30 AM. Art was there already when we arrived, and I forget how long it took for everybody else to arrive. I kept thinking,

"You're not going to get anyone. Maybe about 10 or 12 people. It's not going to work. Nobody will show up."

But suddenly people began to show up. And they came, and kept on coming. It was so astounding that I forget when he actually shot the picture. I know we were there about three or four hours in all, and I don't know how long they were there before the real picture-taking started. I doubt it was very long, but I seem to remember the musicians didn't have very much patience.

It was a great reunion for everybody, and they were very happy to see each other. They were used to seeing one another in small groups, never in a big group of this size.

What made this thing work was that they were so surprised to be together—so many of them. Another thing that made the picture work so well was that they were all so happy to be there.

I have no idea how we managed to get so many peo-ple there so early in the day. It's amazing to me still. And how they decided where to stand is also a mystery to me. I know Art didn't tell anybody where to stand and Harold didn't, and I certainly didn't. They just naturally chose their own spots and who to stand next to.

The little kids on the curb? It was random chance, and Art was smart enough to use it. He taught me something valuable that day, that I've used over and over again in directing my movies since then. Don't tell them what to do. Just let them do it. Don't direct them but let them do what they want to because that's what's going to work.

So instead of shooing the kids out of the way, away from the camera, he was wise enough to say, "Use it. Use its snapshot quality and tell the truth in it." I think it's brilliant for that reason. It's sort of the forerunner of a lot of the documentary nature of photographers since then—like Diane Arbus, for example, who would find people in the street and allow them to pose themselves.

Leaving the first side to cross the street are Count Basie, right, Coleman Hawkins, and behind him, left, Bud Freeman. (Mike Lipskin photograph)

Top: Waiting on the second side. Dickie Wells, smoking, Count Basie in the middle and to his right (barely visible), Coleman Hawkins. (Mike Lipskin photograph) Above: "Almost everyone is here," says Art Kane, far right, white shirt, "but how do I get them up on the steps? They're having too much fun." Moving into the picture at far left is Robert Benton. (Milt Hinton photograph)

Luckey Roberts.
(Mike Lipskin photograph)

The beauty of this is that he didn't tell anybody to stand this way or that. And it wasn't an attempt to show them in any kind of action. These people are standing for a class photograph, the first time this was done as a stylistic device.

Aside from the documentary value of this photograph, its aesthetic value and importance have to do with that radiance. Since I'm not knowledgeable about jazz, for me its primary beauty is as a work of art.

Art took his two-week vacation to go out to Las Vegas to photograph Louis Armstrong and to go to Kansas City and get Duke Ellington and Lester Young.

Those other four pictures for that issue of *Esquire* were almost as fascinating, almost as far-out. He photographed Armstrong in the desert sitting in a rocking chair, looking out into the setting sun—with no trumpet at all!

He took Young up to Rye Playland and got him looking into a fun-house mirror. The distortions of it said

something about Lester's life, which was basically an unhappy one—he died five months later.

Then he got Ellington to pose on the back of an A-Train at 4 AM. They gave him that subway car for just 20 minutes in the middle of the night in a deserted train yard. Billy Strayhorn was there with Ellington, but Art couldn't figure out how to use Strayhorn in the photograph. He *was* in several photographs, but not the one Kane finally selected.

And when he got out to Kansas City to photograph Charlie Parker's grave, he talked Bird's mother into letting him borrow Bird's empty horn case.

Right after Art shot these pictures he quit his job as art director at *Seventeen* magazine and became a full-time photographer.

I'm sure this is the most-reproduced photograph that appeared during my years at *Esquire*. I see it every time I pick up a book on photography in the latter part of the 20th century.

Gigi Gryce, left, Hank Jones, middle, and Horace Silver, all smiling. (Art Kane photograph)

Milt Hinton Remembers

SOME MAGAZINE CALLED and said to be at this place at a certain time. I think they said it would be the seventy-fifth anniversary of jazz, or some such thing. So I brought my wife and my mother, and my wife's mother who was visiting us from Ohio. My wife's mother's sister was also visiting us, so naturally Mona wanted to bring all of them. And we brought our daughter Charlotte along too. We all came along to see this special occasion.

I guessed it was going to be a nice day, a very special day, because all these musicians were going to be there. I had a little Keystone 8-mm movie camera. Mona was not too interested in photography, but I just gave it to her and said, "Honey, just aim it and push the button. And if guys are walking by just move the camera on them slowly."

Well she did. I'm so happy she took these pictures, because nobody else had a movie camera there at all.

Now I've got a few hundred feet of film, and it all came out very well.

I saw Oscar Pettiford there, and Stuff Smith, and Coleman Hawkins and Rex Stewart . . . and Dizzy Gillespie and Tyree Glenn and Charlie Mingus!

There they all were, walking and talking and laughing and smiling. They were so happy to see each other, and so was I. But I was so busy, running around and thinking I've got to get this one and that one. I was just afraid the whole time I'd miss somebody, and I wanted to be in the picture myself when it took place.

I don't know how that can ever be repeated, that picture. I was just hoping to catch those guys all together at the same time. I stepped back a bit because I didn't have a wide-angle lens with me that day but I wanted to get everybody in the picture.

A man was running around and pleading, "Gentlemen, will you please get up there on those steps! Please get up on the top and stand there together!" We

Left: Lester Young and Roy Eldridge (holding the shoulder strap of his trumpet case). (Milt Hinton photograph) Below: Everybody is near "final" position. Rex Stewart takes his horn out of bag. Behind him is Young. To the right are Eldridge and Count Basie. Up at right on the outside of the railing is Dizzy Gillespie (partially visible). At far left is Thelonious Monk. (Milt Hinton photograph)

were paying no attention at all to him. We were shaking hands and shouting, "My *man*! How you *been*? How's your wife and kids?"

In one of my good pictures I had stepped back to get little Jimmy Rushing, "Mr. Five by Five," and next to him a very beautiful young Maxine Sullivan. There was also Joe Thomas, the great trumpet player, and Coleman Hawkins. Oscar Pettiford was looking over at me and smiling because I had the camera. The beauteous Marian McPartland was there, and Sahib Shihab, and Monk right up front. On the left of the picture right behind Jimmy Rushing is my old buddy from school, Scoville Browne. He was standing there looking around because he wanted to see everybody, and in fact I later gave him my other camera with color film in it and he took some shots too.

Next to Monk is Rex Stewart, just standing there. Nobody had gone up on the steps yet. This man was begging us to get up on the steps and nobody had moved. Nobody was paying any attention to him at all. In fact, they were looking down at Basie and the line of kids there next to him on the curb.

I don't know why they chose this particular brownstone but that was the case.

In one of my favorite pictures you can see all these drummers together in one spot. There's George Wettling, who was a famous drummer, with Paul Whiteman. Just above him is Joe Jones, the great drummer with Count Basie, and next to him is Gene Krupa, who was Benny Goodman's drummer. A little above them is Sonny Greer, who was Duke's drummer for so long. Above them is Zutty Singleton, Louis Armstrong's drummer on those great "Hot Five" and "Hot Seven" records, and above him is Art Blakey who had the Jazz Messengers for such a long time.

Bass players like each other, but drummers are different. They're all wood. Even though they're standing together in the picture, they really don't cotton to each other all that much. Bass players, we're all one to a customer, so whenever I'm playing bass, I'm the best bass player in the band. We all share our working together somehow. If I can't make the job, I send one of my buddies. Bass players are like that.

We always have a lot of respect for each other. I know Ray Brown is most respectful of me. He really revolutionized bass playing, he and Jimmy Blanton, who died when he was only 21 years old. I think Ray and Oscar Pettiford took it into a whole new area of jazz playing.

Milling around on the second side. Art Kane's larger camera is on a tripod at the right. Just behind it is Vic Dickenson. At far left is trumpeter Joe Thomas, at his left, Roy Eldridge, at his right, Little Jimmy Rushing, and in front of Rushing is Bud Freeman (in light jacket). Above Freeman is J.C. Higginbotham. Maxine Sullivan faces Sonny Greer and Rushing. Far right (in white suit) is Sonny Rollins. (Milt Hinton photograph)

Everybody is almost in place except Dizzy Gillespie (far lower left with camera). Milt Hinton sprints out for a fast photograph and Coleman Hawkins is walking into the scene from far right, just about in place. Lots of "civilians," including children, gather about. (Art Kane photograph)

We like each other and we try to get together and talk and share our experiences.

To the right of those drummers in the photograph is the great drummer Osie Johnson, and there's Buster Bailey, a fine clarinetist, standing next to another clarinetist, Pee Wee Russell. He looks so sad, you can't take a bad picture of him. There's Miff Mole, the great studio trombone player who was in New York even in the Twenties, before Benny Goodman or anybody. And next to him is J.C. Higginbotham, Red Allen's trombone partner, standing just below Red. There's Buck Clayton, and above him is Tyree Glenn, my buddy from Cab's band.

And there's my own time-keeper, the great bass player Chubby Jackson from Woody Herman's band, and the great bass player Wilbur Ware from Chicago. Down on the street is that poor photographer again, pleading with us, "*Please*, please, get up on those steps."

It was like some great kind of homecoming. I can't think of another time when there was ever such a great gathering of musicians in one spot. They were what we call the *big* dogs. Coleman and Monk and Dizzy and Roy and Basie.

This was before Ray Brown had taken over the bass. I was well on my way and had won a few awards in *Metronome* and *Down Beat*. I'm just glad I was there that day, and that I had my camera with me.

Two clarinetists, Pee Wee Russell and Buster Bailey. Jimmy Rushing is in front and Bud Freeman (left) looks worried.
(Art Kane photograph)

Horace Silver Remembers

IT WAS LIKE a great big reunion, being in the same place with all these great musicians, many of them my idols. To be thrown in with them like this was a great honor and a great blessing.

When I was starting out I had a tenor sax, and I'd get out my old 78 records and put them on the turntable and play Lester Young records. I'd copy his solos off the records and try to play them. I'd get up in a hallway off the living room that went up to the attic and I'd try to get that sound of his up in the hallway. It was like an echo chamber and it would amplify his sound.

Lester replaced Coleman Hawkins in the Fletcher Henderson band when Hawk left for Europe. When Lester took a solo the guys in the band would be laughing behind his back because they were used to that big rough sound of Hawkins'.

Every morning Mrs. Henderson—she played trumpet—would wake Lester up and drag him down to the basement and play the band's records for him and say, "That's what you're supposed to sound like. Like Coleman Hawkins." And he'd say, "No, that's okay for him but this is *me*. This is what I sound like. This is the way *I'm* supposed to sound."

Thank God that he had the strength to stick with the way he was; otherwise the whole train of tenor saxophone playing would be different. There would be no Gene Ammons, no Stan Getz, no Dexter Gordon, no Zoot Sims, no Al Cohn, or so many other tenor players.

I was playing tenor, but I was also a good piano player. When Stan Getz came through town, he needed a rhythm section so we played for him. He liked us so much that he hired us right then and there. I became a full-time piano player and had a band before you knew it.

So I became a leader and moved to New York, because that's where all the clubs and all of the record companies and most of the booking agents were.

Above: J.C. Higginbotham
poses with his favorite,
Maxine Sullivan.
Joe Thomas mugs
beside Sullivan.
(Art Kane photograph)
Right: Marian McPartland,
left, Thelonious Monk at
right (in glasses) and
Milt Hinton entering
picture at far right.
Oscar Pettiford holds paper.
(Art Kane photograph)

Sonny Rollins Remembers

I never thought I would be up there with my idols, Coleman [Hawkins] and Lester [Young]. I was one of the youngest there. Some of them were my idols, and some of them were my contemporaries, in a way.

I started out listening to Coleman. I was playing alto saxophone, but when I heard him I switched to the tenor. I lived on 137th Street and used to hang around in front of his house, the Kinghaven, waiting for him to come home in the morning. I had an 8 x 10 photograph of him, that James J. Kreigsman portrait. I asked him if he would sign it for me.

It was really great that I could ever get to know him and then to play with him. The guys on the block asked me, "Sonny, who's the greatest tenor player in the world?" And I answered, "Coleman Hawkins," and they said, "No he's not." And so I said, "Who's the greatest, then?" And they told me, "Lester Young is." And I said, "Who's Lester

Young?" That's how I found out about Lester, and that's how I started to listen to him. Coleman was still my idol but I found out there was another way of playing the tenor, completely different from Coleman.

I could think of a million stories about Oscar Pettiford, who was one of the greatest. Rex [Stewart] was one of the greatest, too. I never dreamed when I started out that I would ever even get to meet them, much less to play with them.

Lester Young was original in his clothing and in the way he held his horn at 45 degrees, and especially in his sound. The way he carried himself—that hat, that little porkpie hat. And his language. He made up most of his language. He'd just use code words, like "bells" and "eyes" or "big eyes" or "no eyes." Instead of "I feel a draft," he'd just say, "draft."

It's like he came here from another planet and stayed for a short while, and then he went back.

Below: Left to right, bottom, are Stuff Smith (in bow tie), Sonny Rollins and Coleman Hawkins. Bill Crump (in glasses) is behind Smith and, above him, Bud Freeman. To the right of Freeman are, left to right, Pee Wee Russell, Buster Bailey, and Oscar Pettiford (with newspaper). (Art Kane photograph) Opposite, top: Almost ready for final. Jimmy Rushing (biting cheek) next to Maxine Sullivan, then Joe Thomas. Hawkins is next, then Pettiford, then Marian McPartland. Dizzy Gillespie talks to Thelonious Monk (in hat), and Rex Stewart is to the right of Monk. (Milt Hinton photograph) Opposite, bottom: Horace Silver, left, Luckey Roberts, front, and Sahib Shihab. Willie "the Lion" Smith is gone. (Art Kane photograph)

Mike Lipskin Remembers

I MET THE GREAT Harlem pianist Willie "the Lion" Smith when I was thirteen years old, because I desperately wanted to learn how to play in the stride piano style. That was in 1956. Willie and I quickly became close friends and would talk almost every day on the phone. I'd take the subway from Kew Gardens up to his apartment on 151st Street and Eighth Avenue in Harlem for "lessons"—more about his philosophy than about playing the piano—on weekends and holidays.

Willie invited me to accompany him to various functions—private parties for Duke Ellington, jazz concerts, recording dates and charity events at the Savoy and Audabon ballrooms in Harlem. He could be quite ver-

bose when holding forth about his blend of spiritualism, philosophy and astrology.

In contrast, when he talked about things that did not impress him he was a man of few words. For instance, if I asked at a concert who a bass player was, he'd reply, "That's Page," referring to Walter Page of Count Basie Band fame, or, "That's Braud," meaning Wellman Braud, the wonderful bass player with the Ellington band during its first two decades. So one morning Willie called to invite me to join him to have his "picture taken." That's all he said.

I met him at his apartment and we took a cab to the location for the photo session on 126th Street. Since Willie had never described what was to transpire, it was some surprise to see all of these well-dressed folks stand-

At lower left is Roy Eldridge (in hat). Behind Eldridge's left shoulder is George Wettling. Above Wettling is Gene Krupa. To the left of Krupa, laughing, is Jo Jones. To the right of Krupa is Sonny Greer, and above him are Zutty Singleton and (with handkerchief) Art Blakey. (Milt Hinton photograph)

ing around at 10 AM. I only learned later that the art director of *Esquire* magazine, Robert Benton, had convinced most of the jazz musicians in New York, including Willie, to assemble on 126th Street to have their picture taken. Being fifteen at the time and primarily interested in stride and pre-bop, I recognized about half of the greats there but was friends only with Willie, Luckey Roberts (with whom I studied), Maxine Sullivan, Rex Stewart, Max Kaminsky and Zutty Singleton.

About that time I had taught myself photography, from shooting to darkroom technique. I worked with a $20 Japanese imitation of a Rollei twin-lens reflex camera and a $60 enlarger. Those cheap cameras looked great but came with unimpressive lenses that had to be stopped down to get the best resolution. I got in the habit of bringing my $20 camera everywhere I went with Willie, snapping what I thought was history. Not having learned from Willie the significance of this event, I only brought one roll of 12-exposure black-and-white film. Had Willie mentioned what was going on, I would have had several rolls on hand. I stood next to the *Esquire* photographer, Art Kane, and got some of the shots you see in this book. Kane took 120 shots, and I took 12!

At the time this event occurred, jazz had been around long enough so that the musicians milling about that day represented many different eras of this music. In fact, that assembly probably had the broadest representation of jazz styles ever, spanning much of this century. Representatives ranged from Miff Mole, who played with the first white small groups in the early Twenties, to Charles Mingus and Sahib Shihab, young Turks at the forefront of the "modern" sound. The pianists came from four decades and diverse styles, from Luckey Roberts (pre-stride) to Marion McPartland and Thelonious Monk (modern).

Most of the musicians congregated in small groups roughly corresponding to their place in jazz history. This probably occurred because those of certain musical eras played together or hung out as they were growing up. (It would be hard to imagine Pee Wee Russell having a detailed reminiscence with Sonny Rollins, or Luckey Roberts with Thelonious Monk.) But the posed photographs don't reflect chronological grouping. The photographer Art Kane, composition in mind, pleaded with the subjects to position themselves accordingly. Most of them were so enthralled in catching up with one another after years and years that corralling them was no small task and required emphatic urging from across the street.

Willie "the Lion" and Luckey Roberts stood to the left side and, not knowing most of the younger people, kept to themselves. I alternated between walking around the others, snapping shots, and staying with Willie and Luckey. Willie suffered from heat, and it was anything but temperate that August day. He's not in the final shot that appeared in *Esquire* because he got tired and went to rest on the steps of another brownstone, out of range of the camera.

Musicians have an interesting social way about them. They'll become fast friends while playing in a band

Top: With his back to us, in the middle, is Rex Stewart, whose trumpet mouthpiece is just visible at his left. In front of Stewart, Coleman Hawkins and Roy Eldridge are talking. Thelonious Monk is behind them, listening. (Dizzy Gillespie photograph) Above: Lester Young standing next to Gerry Mulligan. (Art Kane photograph)

together. After the job or tour is finished, with some exceptions, the players, so close during the gig, may not be in contact with one another until the next time they're hired together. Maybe not for 20 years. That must be one of the reasons the mood that morning had a joyousness and unique "vibe" I'll never forget. Fifty-eight musicians getting together, in the morning, not for a gig and not for pay!

The session came to an end and people slowly dispersed. I took Willie back to his apartment, my head swimming with the significance of what I'd witnessed, glad at my luck to be there at that time.

Dizzy Gillespie Remembers

When I found out there was going to be this big meeting for a picture in *Esquire* I said to myself, "Here's my chance to see all these musicians without going to a funeral." Usually, whenever you see a lot of them together it's only at a funeral, and here was a chance to get together without anybody being dead or anything.

Most of the time when we got together in New York it would be for a funeral, so instead of that, this was going to be a happy time, and that was nice. I really liked that. And I like this picture a lot—it's a whole lot of people I like a lot.

Mary Lou Williams was there too. It makes me sad to look at these pictures and see how many people are gone. So how long ago was that? Thirty-five years, huh? Whew! I was just a young boy, see. [He was 41].

Twenty years later we were at the White House with our illustrious president. Jimmy Carter, he was running the country then. I had been to the White House before. I played for the Shah and his wife and I met Jimmy Carter there that time.

So at that time Sarah [Vaughan] and I were there together, and Earl Hines was sitting in the audience. Jimmy Carter says to me, "Why don't you ask him to play piano?" And I said, "Say what?" He says, "Why don't you ask him to play?" And I said, "Me ask him? This is *your* house. *You* ask him to play."

So he asked him to come up on stage, and he came up. But Earl Hines never did get to play. He just sat there waiting to play, but he never did get to play.

Almost all in place. Editor Harold Hayes is at far right talking to Lester Young. Count Basie is at his right. Thelonious Monk is to his left (in hat and glasses), then Dizzy Gillespie (also in glasses). Willie "the Lion" Smith is still in place with his arm around Luckey Roberts. (Mike Lipskin photograph)

Dizzy Gillespie gave his camera to someone else in the middle of the day, after shooting about 10 frames. This photograph was taken with Gillespie's camera at the exact instant Art Kane clicked *his* shutter for the Big Picture. (Dizzy Gillespie collection)

Jimmy Carter was there in short sleeves on the lawn with everybody. Mary Lou was there, and Hazel [Scott, former wife of Harlem congressman Adam Clayton Powell].

I had a book to give to Jimmy Carter. I saw him sitting down, and I started to go over to him, and someone said, "Where are you going, sir?" And I said, "I'm going over to give him this book." And he said, "Did you get permission?" And I said, "I know the dude."

So I went over to him, but I could see he didn't recognize me. "This book," I said to him, "is called *The Baha'i World Administration*. It has to do with world government and how they can start a world government." Jimmy Carter says, "Oh, thank you very much." So I put the book down and I left. A little bit later I got on stage with my trumpet, and he recognized me.

After a while somebody mentioned "Salt Peanuts," but everything was all over with. But Max and I decided to do a little encore. I said we would play "Salt Peanuts" if the president would sing it. So he came up on the stage and sang it. I offered him a job to go on the road with us and sing it, and he said, "After this I may have to take you up on that offer." ●

View from the right. Count Basie is sitting, and Willie "the Lion" Smith is still with Luckey Roberts at left. Dizzy Gillespie is next to Marian McPartland. Note "balloon girl" next to Rex Stewart at right. (Mike Lipskin photograph)

An alternate final shot. Willie "the Lion" Smith is still in place next to Luckey Roberts. Eleven kids are in place. The kid next to Count Basie, on the curb, wonders who this man is. (Art Kane photograph)

Art Kane selected this photograph to exhibit at the Staley-Wise Gallery. It was shot with Milton Green's Hasselblad. Willie "the Lion" Smith is still there. Everybody is visible except Sonny Rollins, who is behind Dizzy Gillespie. (Art Kane photograph)

Almost ready for the final shot, except for Willie "the Lion" Smith, who sits on steps at far left with the young Mike Lipskin, nearly obscured by three neighbors. (Art Kane photograph)

Above: Another version of the Big Picture. Rex Stewart is blowing his cornet. (Art Kane photograph) Right: Very near the final shot. Lester Young laughs at something J.C. Heard (right) has just told him. Rex Stewart (left, his back to the camera) holds his horn. On the steps, everybody except Milt Hinton is in place. (Milt Hinton photograph)

Willie "the Lion" Smith and Luckey Roberts sitting on nearby steps. (Art Kane photograph)

After the main photographs were taken. Standing, left to right, are drummer Ronny Free, pianist-singer Mose Allison, Lester Young, Mary Lou Williams, Thelonious Monk's tenor player Charlie Rouse and Oscar Pettiford. (Dizzy Gillespie photograph, courtesy of Father Peter O'Brien)

Biographies for The Big Picture

The musicians shown in the pictures taken on 126th Street in Harlem in August 1958 are listed here alphabetically, with a brief description of each musician's work and place in jazz. The number in parentheses corresponds to the musician's position in the photograph, as indicated on the chart on page 14.

Allen, Henry "Red". (12) Born in Algiers, Louisiana, in 1908, Allen first played trumpet in his father's brass band. In 1927 he joined King Oliver, as had Louis Armstrong before him. After working with the already well-known leader Luis Russell, he worked with Fletcher Henderson, the Mills Blue Rhythm Band, and with Luis Russell's band again, now fronted by

Armstrong. He recorded several wonderful 78s with his own band in the late Twenties and early Thirties. His period of greatest influence was in the late Thirties, when perhaps only Armstrong and Roy Eldridge were more popular and more critically acclaimed. His powerful style, though derived at first from Armstrong, later developed idiosyncratically to the point where his long, melodic lines and original ideas were admired by many modern players as well as devotees of older styles. In the Forties he formed his own sextet and worked at prominent clubs in New York into the Fifties. He was featured in the epochal CBS-TV show "The Sound Of Jazz," which aired not long before the Big Picture was taken.

Jamming at Soundcraft, 1957, are Coleman Hawkins, at left, then drummer Cozy Cole, clarinetist Sol Yaged, trombonist J.C. Higginbotham, trumpeter Red Allen, bassist Milt Hinton and pianist Lou Stein. (Institute of Jazz Studies photograph)

Later he was still a very powerful mainstream player, though he often performed in Dixieland groups. Allen died in 1967.

Bailey, Buster. (26) Born in Memphis, Tennessee, in 1902, Bailey played clarinet. He was a pivotal member of many bands in the early swing days, and was a welcome friend to the young Louis Armstrong when Armstrong joined the Fletcher Henderson Band in 1924. Bailey and Benny Goodman were among the few early academically trained clarinetists, having both studied in their early years with the prominent Chicago symphonic clarinetist Franz Schoepp. By the Twenties, Bailey became well-known in jazz circles through his work in the Henderson band. He toured Europe with Noble Sissle and worked with many other prominent bands, including those of Carroll Dickerson, King Oliver and Lucky Millinder. He then became a long-term member of the phenomenally successful Biggest Little Band in the Land, a sextet led by bassist John Kirby from 1937 through 1946. Thereafter he played in orchestras led by Wilbur DeParis, Red Allen and others. He even made a few symphonic appearances and played in the Broadway pit band for "Porgy and Bess" in 1953 and 1954. Bailey died in New York in 1967.

Basie, William "Count." (57) Born in Red Bank, New Jersey, in 1904, Basie was a pianist, leader, composer and leading figure in the swing era with a long string of successful releases. After studying piano with his mother, he went as a young man to New York where he met and learned from James P. Johnson, Fats Waller (from whom he also learned to play the organ) and other stride piano giants. By the time Basie was 20 he was touring vaudeville circuits as a solo performer and working as an accompanist for blues singers, dancers and comedians. Stranded in the late Twenties in Kansas City with an out-of-work touring group, he decided to stay there, playing piano in a silent-film theatre. In July 1928 he joined Walter Page's Blue Devils, which included another sometime pianist, blues shouter Jimmy Rushing. About two years later Basie left the Blue Devils with others to join the Bennie Moten Orchestra. When Moten died suddenly in 1935, Basie left and organized a band with several former members of the Moten band, including Jo Jones and Lester Young, calling themselves the Barons of Rhythm. It was this band which legendary record producer and talent finder John Hammond heard on the radio. Hammond went to Kansas City to scout, and brought the band to New York for eventual stardom as the Count Basie Orchestra. Basie came to New York in 1936 with a small band which he soon enlarged to the standard swing band size of five or six brass, four or five saxophones, and four rhythm. The band continued to thrive during World War II as one of the greatest of swing bands. Despite many personnel changes, it dropped down to a septet for only two years, 1950 through 1952. The band's recordings and radio broadcasts from New York and other big cities brought Basie international fame for "One O'Clock Jump," "Jumping at the Woodside" and many other classics. The band was particularly successful with its use of arrangements featuring Basie's minimalist piano style (often using only one or two fingers) and the spectacular playing of its stars. Among them were saxophonists Lester Young, Herschel Evans and Buddy Tate; trumpeters Oran "Hot Lips" Page, Harry Edison and Buck Clayton; trombonists Dickie Wells and Benny Morton; and the legendary rhythm section of Jo Jones on drums, Freddy Green on guitar and Walter Page on bass. During and after the War Basie recruited younger, inspired soloists, including saxophonists Don Byas, Lucky Thompson, Paul Gonsalves and Illinois Jacquet; trombone players J.J. Johnson and Vic Dickenson; and trumpeters Al Killian, Joe Newman and Emmett Berry. In 1954 the band made its first tour of Europe. In 1955, Basie's 20th year as a leader, it repeated the European tour. The band featured new stars Thad Jones and Joe Wilder on trumpets; Benny Powell and Henry Coker on trombones; and arrangements by Ernie Wilkins, Neil Hefti, Johnny Mandel and Manny Albam. In September 1957 the band became the first black group to play the Waldorf-Astoria, working there a record-setting 13 weeks. It began to make yearly overseas tours and appeared at major clubs. In addition to the many Basie band recordings, Basie made a number of records as a sideman, starting in 1929 with Walter Page and Bennie Moten and with blues singer Joe Turner. Basie remained a popular and permanent institution on the national and international scene until his death. Even today his band continues to play under the leadership of longtime veteran Frank Foster. The Basie band and its

Count Basie. (Bill Gottlieb photograph)

Count Basie (left, standing) rehearsing his saxophone section. Front row, left to right: Buddy Tate, section leader Earle Warren, Jack Washington and Lester Young on tenor. Buck Clayton plays trumpet, top right, and Jo Jones is on drums. (Institute of Jazz Studies photograph)

stars have garnered many awards, including several from the readers of *Down Beat* and *Metronome*. Basie died in 1984.

Berry, Emmet. (47) Born in Macon, Georgia, in 1915, Berry was a trumpeter who worked in Chicago with the Chicago Nightingales before moving to New York. His first big-time work was with Fletcher Henderson, followed by collaborations with Horace Henderson, Earl Hines, Teddy Wilson, Lionel Hampton, John Kirby and Eddie Heywood. He was with Count Basie for five years in the late Forties and then with other prominent leaders. His broad tone and excellent technique were influenced first by Louis Armstrong and later by Roy Eldridge and Buck Clayton. Berry retired in the Eighties due to illness.

Blakey, Art. (5) Born in Pittsburgh, Pennsylvania, in 1919, this drummer and bandleader was an important figure in the history of modern jazz, particularly hard bop. Blakey was known to many musicians by his Muslim name "Buhaina." Early in his career he was a sideman in the later years of the famous Fletcher

Henderson Orchestra (1939-1944). He also led his own big band briefly in the Boston area. In 1944 he joined the seminal Billy Eckstine band, an incubator of bop which sprang from the Earl Hines big band. It included many innovative musicians, notably Charlie Parker, Dizzy Gillespie, Dexter Gordon and Fats Navarro. In 1947, when the Eckstine group disbanded, Blakey formed a big rehearsal band he called the Jazz Messengers. The many incarnations of Jazz Messengers were proving grounds for a long list of important musicians, including Donald Byrd, Johnny Griffin, Lee Morgan, Freddie Hubbard, Keith Jarrett, Woody Shaw, and Branford and Wynton Marsalis. His later Messenger groups were smaller, usually quintets. Blakey's first band, co-led with Horace Silver, featured trumpeter Kenny Dorham and tenor saxophonist Hank Mobley. When Silver left to form his own band, Blakey took over the group. In 1971-1972 he toured in the Giants of Jazz with Dizzy Gillespie, Thelonious Monk, Sonny Stitt and Kai Winding. Blakey, an innovative and influential drummer, fronted an unbroken series of Jazz Messengers until his death in 1990.

Brown, Lawrence. (45) Brown was a trombonist, born in Kansas in 1905. He was raised in Pasadena, California, where he studied piano, violin, tuba, alto and trombone. At the age of 16 he performed before 6,000 people at Aimee Semple McPherson's temple. He played with Paul Howard's Quality Serenaders from 1927 through 1930, then with Les Hite, Lionel Hampton and Louis Armstrong in 1931. He then joined Duke Ellington in what would be his most important association. Brown later left, with Johnny Hodges, and freelanced in New York until 1956. In 1957 he joined the CBS staff band where he remained for three years. He rejoined Ellington in 1960. Brown won many awards, including Silver Awards from *Metronome* in 1944 and 1945. He had a strong, pure, lyrical tone and was known for his solo on Ellington's "Rose of the Rio Grande." A solemn, taciturn man, Brown was also known throughout his life for his effect on ladies, young and old. He was briefly married to the famous actress Freddie Washington. Brown died in 1988.

Browne, Scoville. (36) Browne was born in Atlanta, Georgia, in 1915. He played saxophones and clarinet, and first worked professionally for Junie Cobb's band in Chicago as a teenager in 1929. He played with the Midnight Ramblers in Chicago for the next two years, then with drummer Fred Avendthorp for two years. In 1933 and 1935 Browne joined a band fronted by Louis Armstrong. He then played for Jesse Stone (1934), Jack Butler (1935), Claude Hopkins (1936) and Blanche Calloway (1937). Browne studied at the Chicago College of Music in 1938-1939 and later played with Don Redman, Slim Gaillard, Fats Waller, Buddy Johnson and Hot Lips Page (1939-1941). In 1942 he joined the Lucky Millinder Blue Rhythm Orchestra, and left in 1958 to form his own quartet. He later returned to play with Page, then Eddie Heywood, and again with Millinder. He continued gigging around New York through the Seventies and Eighties, when he retired from music. Browne died in 1986.

Clayton, Buck. (9) Born in Parsons, Kansas, in 1911, Clayton was a trumpet player, composer and arranger. He learned piano from his father, who taught various instruments. He moved to California at 21, but left shortly thereafter to take a 21-piece band to Shanghai for two years. Back in the U.S. he replaced the prominent Hot Lips Page in Count Basie's band in 1936, when promoter Joe Glaser attempted to make Page into another Louis Armstrong. Clayton is best known for his work with Basie from 1936 through 1943, as well as his excellent arrangements in mainstream swing style. His trumpet work was always inventive and inspired, showing great range and taste. As a result, he was chosen to play on many of the important Teddy Wilson-led Billie Holiday recordings of the late Thirties and early Forties. As an exciting but thoroughly logical and lyrical trumpeter, he was rivaled only by his contemporaries Roy Eldridge and Red Allen. After seven years with the Basie band as it rose to fame in the late Thirties and early Forties, Clayton joined the army in 1943. Discharged in 1946, he

Buck Clayton, right, starred for years with Count Basie. Scoville Browne, on clarinet, is at center. (Bill Gottlieb photograph)

became a member of Norman Granz' Jazz At The Philharmonic, touring France in 1949 and again in 1953. He was member of Joe Bushkin's quartet in New York from 1951 through 1953 and later made numerous records with bands assembled for specific occasions. He worked with Benny Goodman at the Brussels World's Fair in 1958 and with Eddie Condon's groups beginning in 1959. He toured Japan and Australia and made several annual tours of Europe in the Sixties, appearing at jazz festivals. In the mid-Sixties lip problems curtailed his trumpet playing, but he continued to arrange and compose, and fronted his own bands frequently into the late Eighties. Clayton died in New York in 1993.

Crump, Bill. (38) Born in 1919 in Okaloosa, Iowa, Crump was a true mystery man. Even into the 1990s few people except Frank Driggs actually recognized him. Registered from Buffalo in 1958 and 1959 in New York City's Local 802 as a reed and flute player, Crump was actually in New York City looking for work. Not long after the Big Picture was taken he worked in Las Vegas, where his daughter was a dancer. He then moved to Los Angeles, where in 1977 pianist and singer Nellie Lutcher got him admitted to Local 47. He is believed to have died in Los Angeles in the late Eighties.

Dickenson, Vic. (49) Born in Xenia, Ohio, in 1906, Dickenson was a trombonist who came up with midwestern territory bands in the Thirties and Forties. He played with Bennie Moten, Blanche Calloway and Claude Hopkins in the late Thirties, joined the Count Basie Band in 1940, and later toured with Benny Carter. From the Fifties onward he often played with Bobby Hackett and Ruby Braff or led his own groups. In the Sixties he played in The World's Greatest Jazz Band and, later, frequently performed in small groups with Bobby Hackett. Admired for his witty, unusual phrasing and inventive style, he was a major instrumentalist with an individual style who achieved only minimal popular recognition. Dickenson died in 1984.

Eldridge, Roy. (55) Born in Pittsburgh, Pennsylvania, in 1911, Eldridge was a bridge between Louis Armstrong's style and bop, and one of the most significant trumpet players and leaders of the Thirties and Forties. He was self-taught except for some instruction in theory from his elder brother Joe. He started playing semi-professionally at the age of 16, and within a couple of years was on the road with well-known bands, including those of Horace Henderson, Speed Webb, Zack Whyte and Elmer Snowden. Eldridge worked with Teddy Hill's band in New York in 1935, where he teamed up with tenor star Chu Berry (Coleman Hawkins' main challenger). Next, he joined Fletcher Henderson, one of the premier swing bands of its time, where he followed Red Allen as the principal trumpet soloist. Eldridge left Henderson in 1936 to lead his own explosive little band—three saxophones, four rhythm—in a famous extended stay at the historic Three Deuces Club in Chicago. For many months the band broadcast nightly at 1:00 AM. During this period Eldridge says he "left the band business to study radio engineering for eight months," a claim which turned out to be only wishful rewriting of history.

Fletcher Henderson's brass section in 1936. Sitting are, right to left, trumpet star Roy Eldridge, Dick Vance and Joe Thomas. Standing are trombone players Ed Cuffee, left, and Fernando Arbello. (Institute of Jazz Studies photograph)

Roy Eldridge poses with his trumpet before getting on a plane for Europe with the Jazz At The Philharmonic (JATP) all stars. (Norman Granz/Institute of Jazz Studies photograph)

("I know because I was his electronics mentor for the rest of his life," reports Charles Graham.) After a second stint with his band at the Three Deuces, Eldridge went on to national prominence both as horn player and vocalist with Gene Krupa's big band, where he replaced his friend and admirer, the phenomenal trumpet player Shorty Sherock. He made memorable recordings with Krupa, two of which would be identified with him for the rest of his life: "Let Me Off Uptown" and "Rockin' Chair." Later Eldridge formed a larger band which played at the Arcadia Ballroom in New York and at Kelly's Stable. He subsequently worked with many pop-

Nick's in the Village—it was nicknamed "Nicksieland"— was owned by Nick Rongetti. Regulars playing here were Eddie Condon, guitar, Pee Wee Russell, clarinet, Bud Freeman, tenor, and Brad Gowans, valve trombone. (Frank Driggs collection)

ular big bands, including those of Benny Goodman and Artie Shaw, and was on staff at CBS. During this time he toured for more than a year in Europe. In the Fifties he frequently performed with Jazz At The Philharmonic where he teamed with Coleman Hawkins, an association that continued as long as he traveled. Eldridge worked briefly with Count Basie's band but found it too confining. Finally in 1970 he settled, for the rest of his performing life, at Jimmy Ryan's club in New York. Even in this format, he managed to remain the surging, vital swing star he had always been. The Ryan's job lasted for about 10 years, and though the club had been known as a 52nd Street Dixieland stronghold, during Eldridge's long tenure it became a home of swing. Eventually doctor's orders forced him to stop playing the trumpet. However, he continued to appear throughout the Eighties, singing on occasion and playing a little drums and piano (a role he had frequently filled while with Gene Krupa) and at school clinics. In 1991, three weeks after his wife of 52 years died, Eldridge stopped eating and was taken to a hospital where, according to the medical diagnosis, he died of malnutrition. Many who knew him consider loneliness to be the cause of his death.

Farmer, Art. (3) Born in Council Bluffs, Iowa, in 1928, this trumpet and flügelhorn player first worked with Horace Henderson, Floyd Ray and Johnny Otis. Farmer came to prominence as a member of the Gerry Mulligan Quartet in the late Fifties, appearing in the movies "I Want to Live" and "The Subterraneans," and on many recordings with Mulligan. Known as one of the more lyrical of trumpeters, he was elected in *Down Beat* magazine's 1958 poll as the best trumpet player of the year. Still active internationally in the late Nineties, Farmer has lived in Europe for many years.

Freeman, Bud. (23) Born in Chicago, Illinois, in 1906, Freeman was a tenor saxophonist most often associated with Chicago-style jazz. Although the tenor saxophone had previously not been considered a proper instrument in Dixieland music, he made it acceptable. His style derived partly from the sound of prominent C-melody saxophonist Frank Trumbauer, longtime partner of Bix Beiderbecke. Lester Young often cited Freeman as one of his influences. Freeman's solos were usually bouncy, as demonstrated in his original composition "The Eel," which he recorded several times. He was part of the famous Austin High School Gang of Chicago, which often included guitarist, raconteur and promoter Eddie Condon as well as Gene Krupa, Pee Wee Russell and Jimmy and Dick McPartland. As early as 1928 Freeman played in Paris with his close friend, drummer Dave Tough. Later he was part of the saxophone sections of many famous big bands, led by such notables as Paul Whiteman, Ray Noble, Art Kassell, Roger Wolfe Kahn, Ben Pollack, Red Nichols, Benny Goodman and Tommy Dorsey. In 1939 Freeman formed a small recording band which he called the Summa Cum Laude Orchestra. After a relatively brief stint on the road with this group, he worked primarily as a soloist. Beginning in 1969 he played in The World's Greatest Jazz Band. Freeman died in Chicago in 1988.

Gillespie, John Birks "Dizzy". (56) Born in Cheraw, South Carolina, in 1917, Gillespie was a trumpeter, leader and composer. At the time of the Big Picture, he was well on his way to becoming one of the premier jazz musicians in the world. He studied trombone in his early teens but soon switched to trumpet. Gillespie first came to prominence in the late Thirties when he was hired by Teddy Hill to replace Roy Eldridge. Lionel Hampton's first recording for RCA Victor in 1939 starred Coleman Hawkins, Ben Webster, Chu Berry and Benny Carter on saxophones, Cozy Cole and Milt Hinton in the rhythm section, and a 22-year-old Gillespie on trumpet. He was in the Cab Calloway band for more than two years before being fired for cutting up—and also for allegedly *slashing* Calloway with a razor. When he was about 26 or 27, Gillespie, Charlie Parker and Thelonious Monk, along with a few other musicians, began to evolve swing into the complicated music called bebop (later bop). Gillespie worked for a while in the big band of Earl Hines and later with singer Billy Eckstine's band, where he was the musical director. Both bands were strongly influenced by his ideas. After that he led his own groups, several radical large bands in the late Forties and early Fifties. Upon discovering that big bands were economically impractical, he spent the rest of his life leading small groups, although he often fronted big bands on special occasions. He had an unusually outgoing personality that radiated good humor, mimicry and self-parody in equal parts. His humorous stage manner, incredible trumpet improvisations and innovative compositions were the basis of his fame. At the time of his death, Gillespie was the most popular—and the most important—jazz musician in the world. His numerous works include "A Night in Tunisia," "Manteca," "Groovin' High," "Woody 'n You" and many others among today's jazz standards. Although he had joined

Publicity photograph of Dizzy Gillespie for Jean Bach's "The Spitball Story," released in mid-1998. (Jean Bach collection)

the Baha'i religion, his wife Lorraine was a devout Catholic and kept a small Catholic chapel in their home. When he died in 1993, two major memorial ceremonies were held in New York. The first was in St. Peter's Lutheran Church at 53rd Street in Manhattan (where Coleman Hawkins, Roy Eldridge and scores of other musicians' final rites had taken place) attended by an overflow congregation of several hundred mourners. The second, a few days later, was held in the huge Cathedral of St. John the Divine, in upper Manhattan, attended by several thousand people.

Dizzy Gillespie shows kids in Nice, France, how it's done. (Milt Hinton photograph)

Trombonist Tyree Glenn was in Cab Calloway's band for many years. He later worked with Louis Armstrong, then with his own group. (Institute of Jazz Studies photograph)

Glenn, Tyree. (13) Born in Corsicana, Texas, in 1912, Glenn played trombone and vibraphone. His professional career began in Washington, D.C., where he played with the Tommy Mills band from 1934 through 1936. By 1937 he was playing in New York City with Eddie Barefield, then Eddie Mallory and later Benny Carter (1937-1939). He joined Cab Calloway's orchestra in 1940, where he remained until 1946. He toured Europe with Don Redman in 1946, and in 1947 joined Duke Ellington's orchestra for five years. In 1953 he went to WPIX in New York as a staff musician. In 1953 he joined CBS radio, where he appeared daily on the Jack Sterling show and later on Arthur Godfrey's daily radio show. Subsequently he worked at New York studios and again for Ellington. While playing with Eddie Mallory, Glenn accompanied Ethel Walters on her U.S. tour. It was she who encouraged him to take up the vibes by giving him his first set, which he kept and used for the rest of his life. Soon after joining Ellington, Glenn added to his repertoire the growl and wah-wah sounds featured on many Ellington numbers, and used them in all his playing thereafter to great effect. In addition to his exceptionally clear ringing tone, special effects and fine vibraphone solos, Glenn's easy, outgoing personality made him very popular in his frequent night club and radio appearances. During his last years (1965-1968) Glenn performed with Louis Armstrong & his All-Stars. While on the road with Armstrong, Glenn served as the band's musical director, often going on ahead of the group to

rehearse local rhythm sections for the band. Glenn died in New Jersey in 1972.

Golson, Benny. (2) Born in Philadelphia, Pennsylvania, in 1929, Golson is known as a tenor saxophonist, arranger and composer. He first performed in his late teens in Bull Moose Jackson's band and later in bop pioneer Tadd Dameron's band. Golson joined Lionel Hampton's big band in 1953, then worked with other groups before joining Dizzy Gillespie's big band in 1956. Shortly after the Big Picture was made, Golson and Art Farmer joined forces to co-lead The Jazztet, making several recordings. Golson wrote an extended composition, "Portrait of Coleman Hawkins," which he conducted with Hawkins as soloist with the American Symphony Orchestra in 1959 and later recorded for release by Columbia Records. He headed to the West Coast in the early Sixties to work in movies and commercials, returning to New York in the late Seventies. He was a strong tenor saxophonist in the mainstream style. His compositions, many now jazz standards, include "I Remember Clifford," "Stablemates," "Whisper Not" and "Killer Joe." In the Nineties he was still active on the East Coast.

Greer, Sonny. (15) Born in Long Branch, New Jersey, in 1903, Greer was a drummer who worked in local New Jersey bands in his teens. In 1919 he headed to Washington, D.C., where he met Duke Ellington. They first played together as the Washingtonians, with Greer

Duke Ellington, left, posing with Sonny Greer, drummer and nominal leader of the Washingtonians. Greer stayed with Ellington for many years and never played in other big bands. (Frank Driggs collection)

as the nominal leader. The two then went to New York and stayed together until 1951. Ellington's orchestra was featured annually at the Cotton Club in New York from 1927 through 1932. Greer's elaborate percussion set, which included woodblocks, gongs and chimes, was essential to the "jungle" sound of the orchestra. After leaving Ellington he worked with many small groups, including those of Johnny Hodges, Red Allen and Tyree Glenn. Not known primarily as a soloist, Greer was nevertheless an important member of any group he played with. He was a master percussionist and one of the finest swinging brush drummers. Greer died in 1982.

Griffin, Johnny. (7) Born in Chicago, Illinois, in 1928, Griffin played tenor saxophone with Lionel Hampton's big band in the mid-Forties, then moved on to play with Joe Morris and later Joe Jones. After a stint with an army band in the early Fifties, Griffin went to New York to play with Art Blakey's Jazz Messengers and with Thelonious Monk. He later co-led a quintet with Eddie "Lockjaw" Davis. By the mid-Sixties he had moved to Europe, where he has remained, coming back to the U.S. once a year to play.

Gryce, Gigi. (28) Born in Pensacola, Florida, in 1927, Gryce was a composer and arranger who also played alto sax and flute. He studied at the Boston Conservatory before obtaining a Fulbright Scholarship to study classical composition in Paris with Nadia Boulanger and Arthur Honegger. In 1953 he started playing bop with Max Roach, Howard McGhee, Tadd Dameron and Clifford Brown. By the mid-Fifties he had recorded with such notables as Thelonious Monk, Donald Byrd and Lee Morgan. He also co-led the Jazz Lab Quintet with Donald Byrd. His classical compositions include three symphonies and various chamber works. Shortly after the Big Picture was made, Gryce left jazz performing and worked primarily as a teacher. He died in 1983.

Hawkins, Coleman. (39) Born in St. Joseph, Missouri, in 1904, this great tenor saxophonist went on the road with Mamie Smith's Jazz Hounds in 1922 while still in his teens. In 1923 he joined Fletcher Henderson, at that time one of the hottest bands in the country, and stayed there for 10 years. Believing there was nowhere else for him to go in the U.S., Hawkins sent the leading English bandleader, Jack Hylton, a telegram saying, "I would like to come to England." Hylton wired back at once, hiring him. Hawkins intended to stay only a year or so but stayed almost five. By the time he returned to the States, he was widely acknowledged to be one of the best tenor players in the world. In late 1939 Hawkins made his famous recording of "Body and Soul." It was a runaway hit that remains a favorite of musicians. Consisting of a four-bar piano intro followed by several choruses of tenor sax and a protracted ending, it had no vocal chorus and was not arranged. Less than three minutes long, it is arguably the most admired saxophone solo of all time and a true masterpiece. Hawkins was associated with that tune for the rest of his life. After the record's success, he quickly assembled a nine-piece band and went on the road for several years. He never again worked under any leader. At the time of the Big Picture, he was one of the best regarded older jazzmen, reigning as "The Champ" until his decline in the mid-Sixties. Some assume that Lester Young had long ago challenged him and even toppled him from preeminence, but the two were exponents of widely differing schools—Hawkins "hot" and Young "cool"—and were never really in competition. Hawkins died in 1969.

Coleman Hawkins, king of the tenors, in the early Fifties. (Bill Gottlieb photograph)

Heard, J.C. (5) Born in Dayton, Ohio, in 1917, Heard was a drummer who worked for Teddy Wilson, Benny Carter and then Cab Calloway in the mid-Forties. He toured in the late Forties and early Fifties with Jazz At The Philharmonic. In the mid-Fifties he worked in Japan and Australia, and from then on he freelanced with many prominent groups. His drumming was widely admired and often compared to that of his mentors Sid Catlett and Jo Jones. Heard died in 1988.

Higginbotham, J.C. (16) Born in Social Circle, Georgia, in 1906, Higginbotham played trombone in the early Thirties in the bands of Chick Webb, Fletcher Henderson, Benny Carter and others. In the late Thirties, at Louis Armstrong's urging, he joined the Luis Russell band, then fronted by Armstrong. Thereafter he often worked in partnership with his buddy from the Russell band, Red Allen, and played at innumerable recording sessions. His strongly swinging, extroverted trombone style was widely respected by fellow musicians, including Tommy Dorsey and Armstrong. He won many awards from *Esquire* and *Metronome*, among others, and was always busy during his 50-year playing career. Higginbotham died in 1973.

Hinton, Milt. (50) Born in Vicksburg, Mississippi, in 1910, Hinton was an excellent amateur photographer as well as a consummate bass player. Hinton grew up in Chicago and started playing with prominent bands in

Milt Hinton, master bassist and photographer, pictured in 1987. (Holly Maxon photograph)

Milt Hinton with his camera in Queens, New York, about 1950. (Mona Hinton photograph)

the Thirties. In the mid-Thirties he worked for Zutty Singleton at the Three Deuces Club in Chicago, until he was hired away in 1936 by Cab Calloway, with whom he stayed until 1951. From then on he freelanced extensively, working with such top leaders as Count Basie, Louis Armstrong and Benny Goodman. One of the most sought-after bassists in jazz, Hinton has appeared on innumerable recordings, often under his own name. Many of his thousands of photographs, taken over the course of 50 years, have been published in two books co-authored with his friend David Berger, *Bass Line* and *Overtime*, from which some of the pictures in this book are taken. Though active into the Nineties, Hinton was slowing down by 1997. His bass playing and musicianship are widely admired by other musicians, critics and the public.

Jackson, Chubby. (6) Born in New York City in 1918, bass player Jackson was playing bass in popular bands by 1937, including those of Mike Reilly ("The Music Goes Down and Around"), Johnny Messner, Raymond Scott, Jan Savitt and Henry Busse. From 1941 through 1943 he was with Charlie Barnet before starting his greatest association, the first of several stints with various Woody Herman "herds." As a key member of Herman bands, Jackson was widely regarded to be their spark plug. He composed several of the bands' hits, including "Northwest Passage." Jackson went to Europe with his own quintet in 1947 and led a band in New York in 1949. His ebullient personality and great drive made him a valuable addition to any group he played with during the bop era. He won numerous awards, including *Esquire's* New Star award in 1945, its Gold Award in 1946 and 1947, and the *Down Beat* poll in 1945. It is interesting to note that Jackson's son Duffy is an outstanding drummer who worked for years with various Count Basie bands and other bands around the world. At publication Jackson was still alive.

Jefferson, Hilton. (1) Born in Danbury, Connecticut, in 1903, Jefferson was an alto saxophone lead and soloist in many big bands of the swing era, including those of Claude Hopkins (1927-1929), Chick Webb (1929-1930) and Fletcher Henderson (1932-1933). From 1940 through 1951 Jefferson performed with the Cab Calloway orchestra. He also played with King Oliver, Red Allen and Benny Carter and was with the Duke Ellington and Noble Sissle orchestras at various times. Jefferson was an important member of recording groups backing Ella Fitzgerald in 1938 and 1939, and was also in a large band led by Don Redman which backed Pearl Bailey in 1953. Jefferson died in New York in November, 1968.

Johnson, Osie. (27) Born in 1923 in New York City, Johnson grew up in Washington, D.C., and began his professional career as a drummer, singer and arranger at age 18. During World War II he was a member of the famous Great Lakes Navy Band, where his orchestra mates included Clark Terry and famed saxophonist Willie Smith. He arranged recording sessions for Dinah Washington and toured with Earl Hines in 1952-1953, as well as with groups led by Tony Scott, Illinois Jacquet and Dorothy Donegan in 1954. Settling in New York he became a very busy freelance musician, appearing on countless recordings. In 1957 he played at the Newport Jazz Festival with Erroll Garner, performed with the Cleveland Symphony, and appeared on the CBS-TV show "The Sound of Jazz." He was named the *Down Beat* Critics' Poll "New Star" in 1954. Among his arrangements for Dinah Washington were the hit recordings "Fool That I Am" and "It's Too Soon to Know." Johnson died in New York in 1968.

Jones, Hank. (29) Born in Pontiac, Michigan, in 1918, pianist Jones was the elder brother of jazz musicians Thad (trumpet) and Elvin (drums). He started playing in Michigan and later moved to Buffalo, New York. He arrived in New York in 1944 and played in the groups of Hot Lips Page, Andy Kirk and John Kirby, and he also accompanied Billy Eckstine. In addition, Jones worked with Coleman Hawkins, and in 1947 was on one of the first Jazz At The Philharmonic tours. He accompanied Ella Fitzgerald from 1948 through 1953, including a tour of Europe, and made several great recordings with Charlie Parker for Norman Granz. He freelanced in New York until 1956, then joined with Artie Shaw and Benny Goodman. He did more freelancing until 1958, just before the Big Picture was taken. After that he joined the CBS network orchestra and stayed there until it disbanded 17 years later. Jones is the epitome of "session" musicians because he can readily fit into any musical style—old or new, traditional, swing or modern. He can read anything with great precision, a must in top professional work. He performed on the Ed Sullivan Show many times, and has played on hundreds of recordings. In the Seventies he was pianist and assistant to the conductor for the Broadway show "Ain't Misbehavin'." In recent

years he has appeared and toured with innumerable prominent groups and has been a longtime member of a group called the New York Rhythm Section, consisting of Milt Hinton (bass), Barry Galbraith (guitar) and Osie Johnson (drums).

Jones, Jimmy. (17) Born in Memphis, Tennessee, in 1918, this pianist, arranger and composer grew up in Chicago. He started on guitar, then switched to piano in his teens, studying music at Kentucky State College. He first gained notice in Chicago working with Stuff Smith, and later moved to New York with Smith's trio. He became Sarah Vaughan's accompanist in 1947 for five years. After a long hiatus due to illness, he rejoined her in 1952, and they toured extensively. In the Sixties and Seventies he devoted much time to writing and conducting, including work on Duke Ellington's "My People." He toured Europe as Ella Fitzgerald's accompanist in 1966. Thereafter he worked with many prominent musicians, including Joe Williams, Duke Ellington, Coleman Hawkins, Don Byas, Ben Webster, Johnny Hodges, Clark Terry and Rex Stewart. Jones died in California in 1982.

Jones, Jo (Jonathan). (19) Born in Chicago, Illinois, in 1911, Jones was a drummer known primarily for his almost continuous work with the Count Basie band from 1934 until 1948. He was a charter member of the legendary All-American Rhythm Section, which included Basie on piano, Walter Page on bass and Freddie Green on guitar. He advanced the art of jazz drumming considerably with a style he developed early in his Basie career. His drumming innovations helped set the foundations of modern drumming as later exemplified by Kenny Clarke, Max Roach and many others. He rarely soloed at length, in contrast to his famous contemporaries Gene Krupa, Cozy Cole and Chick Webb. After leaving Basie he began a long freelance career which included several Jazz At The Philharmonic tours in the U.S. and Europe. He recorded prolifically with many mainstream stars and leaders, including Benny Goodman, Billie Holiday, Duke Ellington, Teddy Wilson, Lester Young, Johnny Hodges and Art Tatum. Jones died in New York in 1985.

Jordan, Taft. (10) Born in Florence, South Carolina, in 1915, Jordan was a trumpeter in Chick Webb's band for nine years starting in 1933, and became its actual leader when Ella Fitzgerald assumed the front spot after Webb's early death. He then joined popular singing group The Modernaires and was with Steve Lawrence in 1954. Later that year he joined Benny Goodman and toured with him in Europe. By 1964 he was in New York in the pit band backing Carol Channing in "Hello Dolly." On the day of the Big Picture his son and wife were also present. Young Taft can be seen sitting on the curb next to Count Basie. Jordan died in New York in 1981.

Kaminsky, Max. (21) Born in Brockton, Massachusetts, in 1908, this trumpet player was working by the time he was 20 with George Wettling and legendary clarinetist Frank Teschemacher in Chicago. He then played briefly

Max Kaminsky. (Institute of Jazz Studies photograph)

with Red Nichols and recorded with Benny Carter, Eddie Condon and Mezz Mezzrow. In 1936 he joined Tommy Dorsey and later Artie Shaw. Kaminsky is mostly identified with the so-called Chicago jazz school (as exemplified by Condon, Gene Krupa, Pee Wee Russell, et al.), but he was also a good swing trumpeter and a favorite of

Roy Eldridge, for whom he often subbed at Jimmy Ryan's club. He played with a wide variety of leaders, including Sidney Bechet, George Brunis, Willie "the Lion" Smith and Jack Teagarden. Kaminsky died in the mid-Nineties.

Krupa, Gene. (20) Born in Chicago, Illinois, in 1909, Krupa is probably the most famous drummer ever, certainly in the era of swing music, starting with his place in the Benny Goodman band of the late Thirties and later with his own band. Apart from the many records he made with his own band and with Goodman, he was the nominal leader of an extraordinary 1935 recording called "Swing Is Here," featuring Roy Eldridge, Chu Berry and Goodman. Supplementing Krupa's own solid musical style was his superb showmanship. His remarkable work with Goodman at the beginning of the swing era and Goodman's own meteoric rise to stardom combined to propel Krupa to a similar stardom himself. It is unfortunate that he is better remembered for his heavy drumming in "Sing, Sing, Sing" with Goodman than for his superb drumming with his own band. Hollywood made "The Gene Krupa Story" based loosely on his career, with the actor Sal Mineo as Krupa. When the picture failed to include Roy Eldridge, through no fault of Krupa's, he gave Eldridge an expensive set of drums. Krupa's group disbanded permanently in 1951 whereupon he performed with Jazz At The Philharmonic and later with his own small groups. In 1951 Krupa and Cozy Cole started a drum school in New York. He continued

The Gene Krupa band, known as "That Drummer's Band," in 1941. (Institute of Jazz Studies photograph)

teaching, studying classical drumming and playing in small groups intermittently for the next 12 years. Krupa died in 1973.

Locke, Eddie. (30) Born in Detroit, Michigan, in 1930, this jazz drummer joked, "I didn't really belong in the picture that day. I was just following Jo Jones around, carrying his cymbals and stuff like that." He performed in and around Detroit as a duo with fellow drummer Oliver Jackson in a variety act which they called Bop and Locke from 1948 through 1953. Arriving in New York in 1954, Locke worked with pianist Dick Wellstood and later with New Orleans clarinetist Tony Parenti. Afterward, he joined Roy Eldridge for more than a dozen years, then later worked with Coleman Hawkins. He became an important part of the freelance scene in New York, working with Teddy Wilson, Willie "the Lion" Smith and Red Allen. He's still active as a freelance drummer.

McPartland, Marian. (43) Born in Windsor, England, in 1920, this fine pianist came from a family of musicians, including a great-uncle, Sir Frederick Dyson (Mayor of the City of Windsor) who played cello. McPartland debuted as part of a traveling four-piano group, then, just before World War II, she formed a duo with the prominent British pianist Billy Mayerl. She married trumpeter Jimmy McPartland during World War II, and the couple came to the U.S. after the war in 1946 to start a group led by Jimmy. This band broke up in 1951. Marian then formed her first trio and worked at many popular spots, starting with The Hickory House. Gradually that club became a well-known musicians' hangout and was Duke Ellington's regular dining spot whenever he was in New York. McPartland became widely known, continuing to lead her trio as the house band there for a number of years. She also worked at The Composer in New York and at the London House in Chicago. She has appeared widely at jazz festivals and concerts all over the world and has made many recordings on her own label. She is currently known for her weekly radio program, "Piano Jazz," on which she interviews and plays with pianists and other musicians. The program has been heard regularly for many years on hundreds of public radio stations throughout the U.S.

Mingus, Charles. (18) Born in Nogales, Arizona, in 1922, Mingus was an extremely creative and innovative composer as well as a bass player, leader and pianist. His compositions were recorded on his own short-lived labels as well as on Columbia and Atlantic. He first came to national attention as a member of Red Norvo's trio with guitarist Tal Farlow in 1950-1951. He also participated in the memorable Massey Hall concert in Toronto with Charlie Parker and Dizzy Gillespie. In the mid-Fifties Mingus ran the Jazz Composers' Workshop and was a key member, with Max Roach, of the Jazz Composers' Guild, a successor to the Rebels' Festival in Newport in the summer of 1960. He was noted for his egocentric yet generous personality, his habit of admon-

ishing audiences and his self-destructive tendencies. In 1971 he received a Guggenheim Fellowship award and published his autobiography, *Beneath the Underdog.* "Goodbye Pork Pie Hat" and "Better Git Your Soul" are two of the best-known titles among his immense body of original work. His life was stormy, and his legacy, carried on musically by The Mingus Dynasty and other orchestras in the Eighties and Nineties, continues to grow. Mingus died in 1979.

Mole, Miff. (14) Born in Roosevelt, New York, in 1898, Mole was the second-oldest musician in the Big Picture (after Luckey Roberts). He played trombone with many top groups, starting with the Original Memphis Five and Red Nichols & his Five Pennies in 1920. He was the first really influential trombonist, known for his very clean, non-smeary, non-tailgate style. In 1929 he joined the NBC house orchestra and stayed there for most of the Thirties. He played with Paul Whiteman and many other orchestras, including Benny Goodman's in 1943. Returning to small groups after that, Mole worked only sporadically in the Fifties due to illness. He died in 1961.

Monk, Thelonious Sphere. (48) Born in Rocky Mount, North Carolina, in 1917, this pianist, composer and leader moved to New York at a young age. At first a disciple of the great stride pianist James P. Johnson, he later became an early experimenter in what was to become bop, along with Dizzy Gillespie, Charlie Parker, Bud Powell and others at Minton's and other uptown hang-

Thelonious Sphere Monk. (Bill Gottlieb photograph)

outs. He led his own quartet in relative obscurity for years, finally achieving recognition in the Fifties. His eccentric speech and onstage persona, combined with his unique, jagged piano style and offbeat titles for compositions, gained him much notice, even notoriety, for years. He was scheduled to appear on the cover of *Time* magazine in late November 1963, but was bumped from there by coverage of President John F. Kennedy's assassination. (He did make the cover several months later, however.) Monk made many overseas tours with his quartet and travelled around the world with other leaders as The Giants of Jazz in the Seventies. He wrote numerous compositions, including "Epistrophy," "Well You Needn't" and "Crepuscule with Nellie." In the Seventies he gradually faded from public view and became a recluse, living at the home of his most prominent champion, Baroness Pannonica de Koenigswarter. Since his death, his work has attracted ever-increasing attention. Many of his compositions have become jazz standards, most notably "'Round Midnight." Monk died in 1982.

Mulligan, Gerry. (54) Born in New York City in 1927, Mulligan was a baritone saxophonist, composer and arranger. He joined Gene Krupa at age 19, worked with Miles Davis at the Royal Roost in 1946, and wrote several arrangements for the great recording sessions, "Birth of the Cool," led by Miles Davis in 1949. Mulligan recorded with his own groups in 1951, 1952 and 1972. In 1953 he wrote for Stan Kenton's big orchestra, then went to the West Coast where he organized his legendary piano-less quartets from 1955 through the Seventies. He also played with Dave Brubeck's quartet, replacing altoist Paul Desmond. From the mid-Fifties on he dominated jazz polls on baritone, deposing Duke Ellington's Harry Carney. He was one of the central figures in the development of West Coast jazz and cool jazz and was active as a composer until illness in the early Nineties forced him to retrench. Mulligan died in 1995.

Pettiford, Oscar. (41) Born in Okmulgee, Oklahoma, in 1922, this noted bass and cello player, leader and composer was part of a large musical family. He learned to play several instruments at an early age, and by 1943, when he was not yet 20, had worked with Charlie Barnet's big band and Roy Eldridge's quintet. Soon afterward he joined the emerging bop scene in New York as co-leader with Dizzy Gillespie of a group on 52nd Street. From 1944 onward he was in many groups, large and small, including those of Woody Herman and Duke Ellington. By the mid-Fifties he had his own band but was not temperamentally suited to be a leader. A very important musician on bass as well as cello, he introduced much innovation to the playing of both instruments. More than anyone except perhaps the very short-lived Jimmy Blanton (and later Charles Mingus and Ray Brown), Pettiford established the bass as a solo instrument in addition to its role in the rhythm section. Pettiford died in 1960.

Oscar Pettiford, far right on bass, with, left to right, Ellis Larkins on piano, drummer Shelly Manne, clarinetist Andy Fitzgerald (on leave from the Navy), guitarist Al Casey, Bill Coleman and Coleman Hawkins, recording for Bob Theile's Signature Records about 1942, soon after Hawkins, Pettiford and Fitzgerald made several historic records for Theile. (Institute of Jazz Studies photograph)

Powell, Rudy. (40) Born in New York City in 1907, Powell played various reed instruments and was known for his clarinet work with Fats Waller as well as his lead alto saxophone in bigger bands. The records he made with Waller beginning in 1934 were very popular in the middle and late Thirties, as were the frequent late-night radio broadcasts the two made as Fats Waller & his Rhythm Club. After stints with Waller, Powell worked with other, usually full-sized, swing bands in Europe as well as the U.S., including those of Edgar Hayes, Claude Hopkins, Teddy Wilson, Andy Kirk, Fletcher Henderson, Don Redman, Cab Calloway and Lucky Millinder. He also worked with Jimmy Rushing after Rushing left Basie's band to go out on his own, and with Erskine Hawkins, who'd had a big hit record, "After Hours," in the late Thirties. At other times Powell worked with bands headed by pioneering hot violinist Eddie South, Buddy Tate and Ray Charles. Powell died in 1976.

Roberts, Luckey. (32) Born in Philadelphia, Pennsylvania, in 1887, Roberts was a pianist and composer. He was a founder of the stride school of piano playing, along with Willie "the Lion" Smith (who stood next to him almost all day for the Big Picture). Roberts led the orchestra that accompanied Vernon and Irene Castle and was a very successful leader of society bands, as well. He performed at Carnegie Hall in 1939, just after Benny Goodman's historic concert. He was a technically gifted pianist and recorded many player piano rolls. His compositions include a fast display piece, "Moonlight Cocktail," which became a huge hit for Glenn Miller in the early Forties. Duke Ellington declared him, along with Willie "the Lion" Smith, to be among the most important stride pianists. Roberts later owned a popular bar in Harlem called Luckey's. He died in 1968.

Rollins, Sonny. (44) Born in New York City in 1929, Rollins was a tenor saxophonist, leader and composer. By 1947 he was already playing with leading members of the bop movement, including Bud Powell, J.J. Johnson and Art Blakey's Jazz Messengers. By the mid-Fifties he was playing with the Max Roach-Clifford Brown Quintet, after which he started leading; he has led his own groups ever since. Although he frequently mentions Coleman Hawkins and Lester Young as his early influences, he himself had become the leading saxophonist in jazz by the mid-Fifties, following altoist Charlie Parker and preceding tenor player John Coltrane. His often unorthodox appearance, concert demeanor and occasional protracted absences from the music scene threatened, at first, to make more of an impression on the public than his innovations in music. By the Nineties he had curtailed his appearances, but he continues to appear frequently on the concert stage here and abroad. He has probably influenced more post-bop tenor saxophonists than anyone except Coltrane.

Rushing, Jimmy. (34) Born in Oklahoma City, Oklahoma, in 1902, Rushing was a singer and pianist. He began singing in after-hours clubs in the mid-Twenties, and first met with success in and around Kansas City with Walter Page and his Blue Devils (1927-1928) and Bennie Moten's band (1929-1934). In 1935 Rushing joined Count Basie and accompanied him to New York. It was as a member of that orchestra in the late Thirties that he came to national prominence. Known as "Mr. Five-by-Five" because of his girth, he was an entirely original and forceful blues singer and was greatly responsible for the popularity of the Basie band in its early years. Due to the exposure that band gave him, he was able to go out on his own in the Fifties, being replaced in Basie's band by vocalist Joe Williams. Rushing toured and recorded solo and with his own groups, and appeared at many jazz festivals and on overseas tours, including one with Benny Goodman in 1958. He later performed with Eddie Condon and Buck Clayton. He recorded prolifically with the Basie band and one time with Goodman. His distinctive, high-pitched blues-shouting style was as instantly recognizable as Louis Armstrong's. Among Basie's many stars, none was more responsible for its early popular success than Rushing. He died in 1972.

Russell, Pee Wee. (24) Born in St. Louis, Missouri, in 1906, Russell was a clarinetist with the Austin High School Gang in Chicago in the early Twenties, and with numerous Dixieland groups thereafter. During the Twenties he also played with Jack Teagarden in Texas and with Bix Beiderbecke in St. Louis. In 1927 he moved to New York to play with Red Nichols & his Five Pennies, and from 1935 through 1937 he was with trumpeter Louis Prima. From the mid-Forties onward he

Jimmy Rushing. (Isadore Seidman/Institute of Jazz Studies photograph)

Pee Wee Russell. (Bill Gottlieb photograph)

one of the most important founders of the hard bop school. When Stan Getz made an appearance in 1950 in Hartford, Silver's hometown, he heard Horace and his trio play and offered them a job then and there. The job lasted about a year and launched Silver's career. In 1951 he moved to New York and worked with such important and prominent musicians as Lester Young, Oscar Pettiford and Coleman Hawkins. From 1953 until 1955 he was with Art Blakey and the Jazz Messengers. In addition to his importance in establishing hard bop, he fused elements of rhythm & blues, gospel music and jazz, influencing pianists such as Ramsey Lewis, Bobby Timmons and Les McCann. He was largely responsible for setting what would become the standard instrumentation of bop groups in the late Fifties and Sixties: trumpet, saxophone, piano, bass and drums. He also nurtured many important younger players who joined his groups, including Art Farmer, Blue Mitchell, Donald Byrd, Woody Shaw, Benny Golson and Joe Henderson. He carried his piano style, hard "comping" (accompaniment), to a high level of musicianship while developing his own style of composing and arranging. He is one the few musicians in jazz who records his own compositions almost exclusively. He has had numerous hit records and a number of his compositions have become jazz standards, including "The Preacher," "Doodlin'," "Sister Sadie" and "Song for My Father." Since the mid-Sixties he has experimented with large ensembles, including voices, woodwinds, strings and other combinations. Although frequently plagued with arthritis of the hands, he has maintained a busy schedule well into the Nineties.

played most often in groups led by Eddie Condon, frequently at New York Dixieland hangouts like Nick's and Condon's. Russell was famous for his plaintive tone smears, very unusual timbres and wandering melody lines. His unique, complex and inimitable style included a great variety of odd squeaks and growls, alternating soft and hard notes, rasping attacks and soaring, long-held or abruptly terminated phrases and notes. He played greatly contrasting rhythms, often widely varying the time values as well as the notes. Almost no one has attempted to emulate him, nor consciously demonstrated being influenced by his style. Nevertheless Russell was one of the best-known and widely admired clarinet players for years. He died in 1969.

Shihab, Sahib. (42) Born Edmund Gregory in 1925 in Savannah, Georgia, Shihab was a tenor saxophonist and one of the first reedmen to play flute in bop groups, as well as one of the first musicians to become a Muslim. He worked with many prominent bands starting in the late Thirties, was lead alto with Fletcher Henderson from 1944 to 1946 and later played with such modern leaders as Tadd Dameron, Thelonious Monk, Art Blakey and Dizzy Gillespie. From the late Sixties onward he worked in Europe, where he was in the famous Kenny Clarke-Francy Boland big band. Shihab died in 1993.

Silver, Horace. (31) Born in Norwalk, Connecticut, in 1928, Silver has been a pianist, composer and leader of his own quintets since the early Fifties. He started playing tenor saxophone in high school but gave it up when he heard Lester Young on records. He is recognized as

Horace Silver. (Jack Bradley photograph)

Singleton, Zutty. (11) Born in Bunkie, Louisiana, in 1898, this drummer first worked with significant bands in New Orleans clubs and on riverboats. He went to Chicago in the late Twenties and recorded with Louis Armstrong in 1928. In the mid- and late Thirties he became the drummer and leader of the house band at Chicago's Three Deuces Club. He was later featured there on drums in Roy Eldridge's famous broadcasting band. Singleton provided a bridge from the old drumming style of Baby Dodds to the more modern styles of Jo Jones and Big Sid Catlett. He introduced the widespread use of wire brushes, among other innovations. He was a favorite of Louis Armstrong, with whom he worked on many of the seminal "Hot Five" and "Hot Seven" recordings. Singleton died in New York in 1975.

Smith, Stuff. (37) Born in Portsmouth, Ohio, in 1909, Smith learned violin from his father and played for a while in the family band. He earned a scholarship to attend Johnson Smith University but opted instead to join a touring revue. He was with the Alphonso Trent band from 1926 to 1928 and then toured with Jelly Roll Morton. In 1936 he moved to New York where he joined Jonah Jones and Cozy Cole at the Onyx Club on 52nd Street. That group had a nationwide hit with the nonsense tune "I'se A Muggin." When Fats Waller died in 1943, Smith took over leadership of Waller's band. In 1947 he joined Jazz At The Philharmonic. Finally, he settled in Copenhagen in 1965. Well known for a raucous, powerful style with an adventurous sense of melody, he gave added meaning to the word swing. Dizzy Gillespie once said that Smith, along with Roy Eldridge, was one of his strongest early influences. Smith died in 1967.

Smith, Willie "the Lion." Born in Goshen, New York, in 1897, Smith was a pianist. Though he's not in the Big Picture—he was tired and had sat down on steps next door—he appears in many other pictures taken that day. "The Lion" was almost always seen, as he was on that day, with a cigar clenched firmly in his teeth and wearing his derby hat. A most colorful individual, he sometimes bragged that he was Hebrew and even a cantor. He was one of the best known of the Harlem stride school, along with James P. Johnson, Fats Waller and Luckey Roberts. His style was particularly individual in that he adapted the flavor of 19th century impressionist composers Ravel and Debussy, whom he greatly admired, to stride piano. He penned many beautiful miniatures that combined impressionism with stride. In the late Thirties Smith became known to a wider public through several recordings. Artie Shaw and Tommy Dorsey performed memorable arrangements of his compositions, especially "Echo of Spring." Smith was an early mentor to Ralph Sutton, Mel Powell and Duke Ellington, the latter of whom composed and recorded "Portrait of the Lion" in tribute to Smith. In the Fifties Smith performed often at the Central Plaza and elsewhere in New York. He toured Europe several times and appeared at many jazz festivals. His life was documented in an autobiography

Willie "the Lion" Smith at an RCA Records recording session, 1967. (Photograph courtesy of Mike Lipskin)

(with George Hoefer), *Music on My Mind*, published in 1964. Smith died in 1973.

Stewart, Rex. (52) Born in Philadelphia, Pennsylvania, in 1907, Stewart played cornet and trumpet. In his early years he played several instruments, but cornet was always his main focus. His most important early work was with Fletcher Henderson's band as the replacement for Louis Armstrong (at Armstrong's suggestion), who was leaving to form his own band. Initially Stewart felt uneasy about his ability to fill the shoes of his idol, and soon left Fletcher to join the band of Fletcher's younger brother Horace. After a year or so with Horace, the now better-prepared Stewart rejoined Fletcher Henderson. He stayed with Fletcher more than four years this time, until 1934 when he left to join Duke Ellington's band. By that time Ellington was in his golden era, well on his way to becoming what he would be ever after: the most original and longest-playing band leader ever. Stewart, a true master, stayed 10 years with the band for what would be his longest and most important job. There he invented the unique growling, almost human, half-valve sound featured nightly in the extended piece "Boy Meets Horn." This was also the title of Stewart's autobiogra-

Rex Stewart on the CBS-TV show "The Sound of Jazz." (CBS-Sony photograph)

phy, published posthumously by Claire Gordon in 1982. Stewart wrote a number of other well-known Ellington numbers, but he remained forever identified with "Boy Meets Horn." After Ellington, Stewart worked primarily with his own groups and made several U.S. and world-wide appearances, including Jazz At The Philharmonic. In the late Forties he stayed in France long enough to study at the famous cooking school, Le Cordon Bleu. While there, he also delivered several lectures on jazz at the Paris Conservatory of Music. Later he delivered similar ones at the University of Melbourne, Australia. In 1957 and 1958 he became musical director for a festival at Great South Bay, Long Island, celebrating the music of Fletcher Henderson with the Henderson Alumni Orchestra. He also played for two years at Eddie Condon's jazz club in New York. Stewart went into semi-retirement in the Sixties, though he wrote frequently for *Down Beat* magazine and often appeared briefly at night spots blowing his incomparable cornet. A number of extremely interesting articles on music and musicians by Stewart were collected in *Jazz Masters of the 30s*, published by MacMillan as part of a series. Stewart died in 1972 in Los Angeles.

Sullivan, Maxine. (33) Born in Homestead, Pennsylvania, in 1911, Sullivan came to prominence in the late Thirties with the Claude Thornhill band, especially for her Thornhill-arranged hit song, "Loch Lomond." Later she joined the band of bassist John Kirby at the Onyx Club on 52nd Street and married Kirby. In spite of her magnificently cool, clear, perfectly

Maxine Sullivan with the John Kirby band. Clarinetist Buster Bailey is at right. (Institute of Jazz Studies photograph)

pitched voice, Sullivan was forever typecast by her "Loch Lomond" performance. She appeared in at least two movies and made brief appearances on stage. For two years she was heard on the CBS radio show "Flow Gently, Sweet Rhythm." She later sang for varying periods with Benny Goodman, Glen Gray and others. Sullivan left music for some time to study nursing—and the valve trombone!—but around the time of the *Esquire* photograph she had returned to music. She was one of the very best and least egotistical of popular jazz singers. Her clear enunciation and relaxed style notwithstanding, she could swing like mad. Her second husband was stride pianist Cliff Jackson. Sullivan died in 1987.

Thomas, Joe. (35) Born in St. Louis, Missouri, in 1909, this trumpet player should not be confused with the excellent tenor man of the same name who played with Jimmy Lunceford's orchestra. At age 19, Thomas played in Cecil Scott's band and with several lesser-known groups. In 1934 he joined Fletcher Henderson's famed orchestra, later playing with Willie Bryant, Claude Hopkins, Benny Carter, James P. Johnson, Teddy Wilson and Barney Bigard. During the late Forties and early Fifties he freelanced with drummer Cozy Cole, tenor star Bud Freeman and pianist-composer Claude Hopkins, among others, while sometimes leading his own groups. Admired by musicians for his robust trumpet style (influenced directly by Louis Armstrong's sound), he appeared on many recordings, including one in 1937 with Armstrong's first wife, Lil. He was later in a group that produced a memorable recording in 1944, "Thru for the Night," which featured Coleman Hawkins' tenor led by Earl Hines on piano. Thomas died in 1984.

Ware, Wilbur. (4) Born in Philadelphia, Pennsylvania, in 1923, Ware was an extraordinary bass player whose strong tone and harmonic inventiveness made him much sought-after by a wide variety of groups, small and large. Even in his later years he worked with experimental groups while continuing to play in established mainstream and bop groups. Beginning in the mid-Forties he worked with such prominent leaders as Roy Eldridge, Joe Williams and Eddie "Cleanhead" Vinson. By the Fifties he had worked with Johnny Griffin, Art Blakey's Jazz Messengers and Thelonious Monk. Later, as house bassist at Riverside Records, Ware could be heard on many important recordings. In New York he played with John Coltrane in Monk's quartet at the Five Spot. He also led his own small groups and played with the Sonny Rollins trio at the Village Vanguard. Being in great demand, he worked steadily in a wide variety of groups. In the early Sixties he joined Max Roach, Charles Mingus and others in the Newport Rebels, a group formed in protest against the Newport Jazz Festival. A number of significant recordings by this group and associated musicians were released later. In the mid-Sixties illness forced him to return to Chicago, but in the Seventies he returned to New York, where he was active with mainstream as well as avant-garde groups. Ware died in 1979.

Wells, Dickie. (8) Born in Centerville, Texas, in 1909, Wells was a trombonist who worked with many prominent bandleaders, including Count Basie for eight years in the late Thirties and early Forties. In 1959 and again in 1961 he toured Europe with Buck Clayton's band. He was one of the outstanding trombonists of the Thirties and a great favorite in France, where he won numerous awards. A fascinating analysis of his playing style, titled "The Romantic Imagination of Dickie Wells," can be found in jazz critic Andre Hodeir's book, *Jazz: Its Evolution and Essence*. Wells died in 1985.

Wettling, George. (22) Born in Topeka, Kansas, in 1907, Wettling was a drummer. After performing with the U.S. band of visiting English bandleader Jack Hylton in 1935, Wettling stayed in New York and worked in Artie Shaw's first band. He then worked for a succession of other famous leaders, including Bunny Berigan, Red

Trombone star Dickie Wells posing outside the Savoy Ballroom in 1936. (Institute of Jazz Studies photograph)

Norvo and Paul Whiteman. For most of the Forties and into the Fifties he was on staff at ABC-TV in New York. From then on he was in a variety of prominent small combos but played mainly Dixieland with Eddie Condon. He was also a competent abstract painter and a friend of the well-known artist Stuart Davis. Wettling wrote a number of articles for *Down Beat* magazine. He died in 1968.

Wilkins, Ernie. (25) Born in St. Louis in 1922, Wilkins is recognized as a saxophonist, composer and arranger. He is best known for his arrangements for big bands, including those of Dizzy Gillespie, Tommy Dorsey, Harry James and Count Basie. He began playing professionally in a famous Navy band during World War II with such budding stars as Clark Terry, Gerald Wilson, Major Holley and earlier stars like alto saxophonist Willie Smith. In 1949 he was in the last Earl Hines big band. In 1951 he joined the Count Basie band, playing both alto and tenor saxophones. He gained prominence in the Fifties for his compositions and arrangements. He per-

formed and arranged for Dizzy Gillespie's big band and went overseas with it for the U.S. State Department in 1956. He then wrote for Harry James and was greatly instrumental in modernizing that band. His arrangements were largely responsible for the success of the Count Basie band in the Fifties. After that he worked for Earl Hines and others, concentrating mainly on arranging, and served as musical director for A & R Records. In the late Sixties Wilkins went to Europe with Clark Terry's big band as musical director, and he settled in Copenhagen. He has been confined to a wheelchair since suffering a stroke.

Williams, Mary Lou. (46) Born in Pittsburgh, Pennsylvania, in 1910, Williams was a pianist, arranger and composer. She started in a group led by her husband, saxophonist John Williams. When she was 18, she joined Andy Kirk's Clouds of Joy as pianist and arranger. She later arranged for Tommy Dorsey, Benny Goodman, Earl Hines and others, and wrote scores for musicians such as Dizzy Gillespie. In the Fifties she conducted

Pianist Mary Lou Williams was a star and spark plug for Andy Kirk's band of the Thirties and Forties. She is pictured with Kirk (left) and high-voiced singer Pha Terrell. (Institute of Jazz Studies photograph)

From left to right, Dickie Wells, trombone, Joe Newman, trumpet, and Lester Young, tenor, on the CBS-TV "The Sound of Jazz" broadcast in late 1957. (CBS-Sony photograph)

informal piano lessons in her home in Harlem. Thelonious Monk was among the unofficial "students" who gathered there. She was an important influence on Monk, Bud Powell and other pioneers of bop. Williams died in 1981.

Young, Lester "Pres." (51) Born in Woodville, Mississippi, in 1909, Young played tenor saxophone. By 1930 he was playing with various Midwest bands and in 1934 worked briefly with Count Basie. After short stays with several other bands he rejoined Basie, where he remained until he became a solo star. During his time with Basie he developed a very wide following among tenor men. He was perceived as the founder of a new, light, soaring way of playing tenor. It was very different from the husky, aggressive, punchy playing style of Coleman Hawkins, Chu Berry and Ben Webster, the most widely-admired tenor players in the Thirties and early Forties. In the late Thirties Young made a number of historic recordings with Billie Holiday. In late 1944 he was drafted into the Army for what turned out to be a very harsh period in his life. He was released about a year later after months of Army confinement for using drugs. He then returned to playing music, and made his first solo recordings in addition to working every year with Jazz At The Philharmonic. Between his discharge from the Army in 1945 and the taking of the Big Picture, late 1958, he continued to drink and use drugs heavily, and in the late Fifties he was rarely at the peak of his powers. During and after the early years of bebop, Young continued to win admirers, most notably Sonny Rollins, John Coltrane, Stan Getz and Zoot Sims. Ultimately he developed even more adherents to his lyri-

cal style of legato tenor. Although never really a bebop musician, Young was an important transitional figure between swing and bop, along with Roy Eldridge, Charlie Christian and others. He died in early 1959. ●

Lester Young and Ben Webster leaving the CBS studio after playing on "The Sound of Jazz." (CBS-Sony photograph)

Making the Movie
A Great Day in Harlem

by Charles Graham

with additional commentary by Jean Bach

THE MOVIE "A GREAT DAY IN HARLEM" was conceived and created every step of the way by Jean Bach, with the help of several very talented people. Bach is a writer who had also been the producer of the Arlene Francis daily radio show on New York's WOR for 24 years.

She was familiar with the big *Esquire* centerfold in "The Golden Age of Jazz" issue of January 1959 because her late husband, Bob Bach, was one of the world's greatest jazz fans, and he had a large copy of that big picture on the wall in his office. When we met I gave her another big copy of that picture and hung it on the wall in her home.

In the Eighties, Jean Bach and I started going to Denver for the annual Dick Gibson Jazz Party, where we got friendly with bassist (and photographer) Milt Hinton and his wife Mona. When Hinton's first book *Bass Line* came out, I noticed three pictures of musicians in it and realized he had taken them the same day as the Big Picture in *Esquire*.

Suddenly a light went on in my head. Of course! Hinton was *in* the big *Esquire* picture, and he takes pictures everywhere he goes on the jazz scene—had done so for 40 years, in fact. Since he had three pictures in his book taken *that day*, he had probably taken even more the same day!

I grabbed him (almost by the lapels) and said, "Tell me, Milt, please tell me you took lots of pictures up in Harlem that day."

Hinton cheerfully replied, "Sure, Charlie, I took plenty of pictures that day, as well as being in some of them myself. But even better, I gave my little movie camera to Mona and she filmed a reel, and it came out great!"

I wasn't particularly interested in the story about his little home movie, but I was very interested to hear that he did have more still photographs of the events that day.

I told Bach about the pictures, and that I thought I might get hold of them. With photos from Hinton and from Art Kane, I thought maybe I could make a picture book about the Big Picture and that great day.

I also told her about Hinton's short movie. Right away I could see the wheels going around in her head as she asked, "How many musicians do you think are still alive? I want you to make up a list for me. I'm going to make a movie about that day."

And that's how it came about. She thought of it that fast!

Once Bach got started, two professionals were added to the team. Matthew Seig became her co-producer and was particularly helpful with the financial aspects of the movie. He also assisted Bach on almost everything she did apart from the interviews and the artistic decisions.

One of the first things Seig did was to find a gifted editor, Susan Peehl, to whom Bach presented 30 hours of already-filmed footage.

Peehl looked it over and started putting little yellow "sticky" notes on her wall. She organized them by subject matter, with brief synopses of what each fragment of every interview contained—its subject and where it might possibly be used.

In a few days she had several hundred "sticky" notes on the wall. Gaining familiarity with the material, she started tentatively pasting parts of some of the interviews together with others. A few weeks later she had many different little story lines or anecdotes underway.

Bach gratefully told me that Peehl was a genius at making sense out of that jumble.

After several months they had a movie over two hours long which they thought was pretty good. Bach was very happy, continually marveling at Peehl's progress, her inventiveness and her skill in editing by stitching together parts from one interview with parts from another.

Bach's publicist, Virginia Wicks, began to catch the enthusiasm. When the film was entered in the Chicago Film Festival in 1994, to everyone's delight it won first prize there, and went on to receive an Oscar nomination in the full-length documentary division.

Jean Bach picks up the story:

IT WAS ART KANE'S PHOTOGRAPH and vivid memory that originally propelled me into this whole operation. Charles Graham had been obsessed with the picture for years, so I was prompted to seek out Kane and try to learn how the photograph came about. Responding to a letter from me, this important photographer braved a major storm to drive to New York from Cape May, N.J.—more than 100 miles—to tell the improbable story of the group picture that put him on the map. He and his huge dog, both dripping wet, came barreling into my living room and managed to hold me transfixed for the next several hours.

Kane said that single click of the camera shutter changed his life forever. (And mine, too, as it developed.) The success of that photograph propelled him into a new profession. "I decided to switch from being an art director to being a photographer," he explained. "It gave me a feeling of power."

That was enough to get me started on the film. Besides, Milt Hinton had promised to let me have the short home movie his wife Mona shot the day of the picture.

"A Great Day" was on its way.

The idea for the movie was so self-evident you wonder why no one else had ever thought of it. Just deconstruct that famous photograph, zoom in on the subjects one by one, coax some anecdotes out of them and add a bit of appropriate music. Piece of cake, or so I thought.

My first plan was to interview the musicians closest at hand and enjoy the yarns they told me. Hey, this movie was making itself!

It's a good thing I didn't know anything about film-making at the time or I'd never have started it. Who knew you have to *pay* for stuff? Pay for still photos, pay for music, pay for archival footage? Until Matthew Seig came into my life I thought all you needed to make a movie like this was a list of phone numbers.

I met Seig through Kathryn Altman, the wife of movie director Robert Altman. He was Bob Altman's right-hand man and had already worked on several

Jean Bach, Charles Graham, and Dizzy Gillespie relaxing in Bach's kitchen following her interview of Gillespie for "A Great Day in Harlem." (Courtesy of Jean Bach)

At Benny Goodman's book party at the Rainbow Room in 1976 are, from left, Newport Jazz Festival publicity maven Charlie Bourgeois, Charles Graham and Frank Driggs, with Jean Bach, seated. (Courtesy of Charles Graham)

prize-winning documentaries. In addition to helping me find an experienced editor, Seig said he would help me out with the music rights. (Music rights? What did that mean?) Seig was proving he knew his way around the pool.

Another lucky break was an offer from Johnny Mandel to supervise the background music. In addition to having composed and arranged several jazz classics, including "The Shadow of Your Smile," he had brilliantly scored many films. By now, I was batting a thousand. Or so I thought.

I started hitting snags. Some of the stars turned out to be harder to reach than I expected—for instance, Art Blakey didn't have a New York phone number; in fact, he didn't have *any* phone number.

When I heard a local disc jockey announce that Blakey was coming to the city to participate in an all-day Blakey broadcast, I made a calculated decision. This particular DJ had been trying to amass a treasure chest that would enable him to buy his own station, so I decided to become an investor. But the outcome was not what I hoped. Blakey never showed up, and I'm

still not in the radio business. I was back at square one.

My strategy turned toward *cherchez la femme*, because I was told that once I located the woman Blakey was living with at the time, we'd be in business. But Blakey moved around a lot. Some insider would slip me a phone number, and I'd make the call—only to get an angry "No, he's not here." Or "No, I haven't seen him in weeks." Or "No, I don't know where he is." I was always one woman too late.

After a few more calls like that, I was ready to throw in the towel. But somehow the clouds parted, the sun came out, and a charming, beautiful woman welcomed Charles Graham and me into an attractive penthouse. Blakey, deaf as a post, chattered away before my camera. His answers rarely responded to the questions posed—but by then, who cared? He began telling me the story of his life and about his many bands. We were all having a good time. He even insisted that Graham try on a handsome leather jacket we had admired, and for an anxious moment I feared he was going to try to give it to him.

I was determined to film all the musicians still alive, but not only were several maddeningly elusive, others were unable to travel to New York. So we went on the road to bag them.

Then there was the challenge of finding some of those kids sitting on the sidewalk. I placed an ad featuring the photograph in the *Amsterdam News*, the Harlem newspaper, asking, "Do you remember this photo taken on 126th Street in the summer of 1958? Were you there? Do you know anyone who was? If so, please call this number." I hooked up an answering machine, and managed to locate several bystanders from that 1958 photo—even the little boy sitting right next to Count Basie. He was Taft Jordan, Jr., five years old at the time, son of trumpeter Taft Jordan. His memory, some 30 years later, was as good as, or better than, that of anyone else involved in the project.

Memories about the event vary. Blakey thought it took place in front of the building where he was living, on 137th Street. Bud Freeman thought it had something to do with urban renewal. Few remembered how they first heard of it.

Kane remembers that he had the devil's own time getting everyone to pay attention to him. The musicians were so delighted to see one another under those unusual circumstances that they just kept schmoozing, ignoring Kane's pleas to line up and face front.

There are several versions of how the neighborhood kids came to sit down on the curb in front, and innumerable fascinating stories from those who were present that day. There are stories about the horseplay that went on. Stories about how they sorted themselves out (all the drummers together, trumpeters together, the Chicago Austin High School Gang together, etc.). And stories about careers that burgeoned subsequently, or in some cases seemed to fade away.

Among the swing veterans, there was Stuff Smith, standing front and center next to the magnificent Coleman Hawkins. Jazz history boasts only a few violinists—all terrific. But Smith could swing like mad. He was a *wild* man.

Lester Young, Count Basie and Coleman Hawkins are all present in this legendary photograph, but when I make appearances in connection with the movie, I'm invariably asked, "Where is Duke Ellington?" That towering figure, who continues to affect so many of us decades after his death, certainly reigned supreme when the subjects were being rounded up in 1958. I can only conclude that the band must have been on tour when the picture was taken, although there is a full page portrait of Ellington elsewhere in that issue of *Esquire* magazine.

Luckily, some former Ellingtonians *are* in that photo: drummer Sonny Greer, cornet player Rex Stewart and the glorious trombone player Lawrence Brown.

Greer did not read music, but neither did some other great percussion masters—Art Blakey and Buddy Rich, to name but two. Yet Greer grasped the essence of the exquisite Ellington repertoire, back when it was advertised as "jungle music." Greer's light touch, so hip, so fly, completed the mosaic perfectly. Graceful as a Balinese dancer weaving around all his percussion equipment, he made a dazzling picture in the midst of chimes, gong and assorted cymbals and snares—and probably more stuff than he was ever going to need.

From Rex Stewart we learned about the half-valved cornet and all the tricks you could do with it. Ivie Anderson and Stewart conduct a spirited dialogue at the beginning of "I'm Checkin' Out, Goom Bye," with Stewart speaking his lines through the horn. When Anderson answers the phone and asks, "Hello, hello, is this you?" one can actually hear Stewart's cornet pronouncing the words, "Well, who the hell do you think it is?"

When I started making the movie, two of my oldest and closest friends in the photograph, Roy Eldridge and Lawrence Brown, had died just months earlier. Brown was the handsome trombone soloist standing between Marian McPartland and Mary Lou Williams in the picture. He was always suave, self-possessed and wonderfully moving.

You would have thought that by the time this picture was taken, the summer of 1958, there would be more than three women in the group. But there they are, just two pianists and one wonderful singer: Maxine Sullivan, Marian McPartland and Mary Lou Williams.

Jean Bach and Dizzy Gillespie at Fort Adams, Newport, when the jazz festival was moved back there in 1976.
(Charles Graham photograph)

Williams' story continues to amaze me. In her late teens, she played piano and wrote absolutely swinging arrangements for Andy Kirk's Clouds of Joy. Sammy Cahn wrote a song about her which I use in the movie. It's called "The Lady Who Swings the Band," and that title really fits. Williams knew music up one side and down the other and was continually exploring and advancing. She had a kind of salon up in Morningside Heights where all the great progressives like Art Blakey, Thelonious Monk and Bud Powell would gather. They showed each other new ways to approach a musical problem and knocked each other out with crazy chords, just gorging on music, music, music.

Another serious musician is the fellow on the extreme left of the Big Picture, Gigi Gryce. Gryce was a talented genius who studied in Paris with Arthur Honegger and Nadia Boulanger. He died much too young, having spent part of his brief life co-leading the Jazz Lab with Donald Byrd.

This brings us to the illustrious dual-national, Art Farmer. While he's currently on tour in the States appearing with my movie (in which he stars), he's also at home in Vienna, Austria, where he settled years ago.

Farmer has been admired since the early Fifties by

his peers, particularly Dizzy Gillespie, as a consummate artist capable of playing anything. When I did interviews for the film, I asked Gillespie about Farmer, and he told me of being dragged into a recording studio by Duke Ellington to do an impromptu reading on "UMMG" ("Upper Manhattan Medical Group"). Gillespie wasn't entirely pleased with the results, calling it too spur-of-the-moment. He declared, "Art Farmer made a record of it, the way it should be played."

So many of these magnificent beacons have left us, it's good to be talking about those still with us. I think particularly of Horace Silver, whose purity and goodness shine through the music. Like the late Art Blakey, Silver inspires those who play his compositions—it must be heaven to play that fascinating stuff. Farmer once told me how much he appreciated his time with Silver, how forceful he was at the piano, pulling the group along. When Farmer joined Gerry Mulligan's celebrated piano-less quartet, he said it was like one of those dreams where you're walking down the street with no clothes on.

The leaders do pull you along. Benny Golson, shown in the Big Picture between Farmer and Blakey, said that when he teamed up with Blakey he noticed the great drummer played louder whenever he,

On 126th Street in Harlem, Jean Bach with Art Kane, right, and cameraman Steve Petropoulos, left. (Jean Bach collection)

Jean Bach, Charles Graham, Art Kane and the dancer Lorenzo (Mrs. Sahib Shihab) on 126th Street. (Jean Bach collection)

Golson, got a solo. Finally he figured it out: he was too tentative in his playing. Blakey was trying to bring him out of his shell.

Two survivors from the day of the photograph, both stars of the tenor sax, are currently touring the globe, favorites wherever they appear. One, Johnny Griffin, makes his home in France, which required me to wait until he hit New York to film a conversation with him. He was wonderful on the subject of Thelonious Monk, for whom he'd worked. The other tenor, Sonny Rollins, revealed some marvelously sensitive insights during our conversation, and I often think of his comment, "What's the use of living to 100 if you don't accomplish anything?"

We are lucky to still have with us, still playing beautifully, Hank Jones of the celebrated Jones family of Detroit and Eddie Locke, the drummer of choice for so many local groups. Hank never seems to age; he's a perennial favorite of other pianists.

I don't recall if Whitney Balliett said that tap dancers were drummers standing up or drummers were tap dancers sitting down, but since Eddie Locke (as well as his mentor, Jo Jones) has been both, I guess he qualifies either way.

As for the best-loved survivor of all, America's sweetheart Milt Hinton has starred in both of the movies I made, "A Great Day" and "The Spitball Story." Besides being one of the all-time leading bass players of the world, he's a distinguished photographer, and he's responsible for *my* career as a film maker.

I've said nothing about social matters in discussing the black music makers. I don't like dwelling on painful subjects. So many jazz movies today are such downers—it's always raining, the guys are always strung out on dope. I lived through the period when blacks couldn't find places to stay on the road, among other indignities, so I'll just close with one of the con-

versations I had with Miles Davis when he used to phone me at work.

"Miles! Good to hear from you. How're you doing?" . . . Pause.

"Oh, Jean, I'm a black man in a white man's world," he said.

I had to agree.

Miles continued, "You white people find a way to take credit for everything. You treated us terribly on the plantations, so we had to invent the blues. Now you're taking credit for getting the blues invented! Tell me, Jean, what's next?"

Coda

There's a coda to this story of the movie, "A Great Day in Harlem." Copycat photographs similar to the gathering in the summer of 1958 on 126th Street in Harlem have started showing up.

The first one was made by *Playboy* magazine in Hollywood in 1995. Then others began to appear: "A Great Day in Kansas City," "A Great Day in Memphis," "A Great Day in Philadelphia," "A Great Day in Soho (London)," "A Great Day in Chicago," and my favorite, "A Great Day in Haarlem," which appeared in a Netherlands newspaper in 1996.

Other group portraits of musicians inspired by the Big Picture in *Esquire* include a four-page spread in *Life* in 1998, "The Greatest Day in Hip-Hop" (1999), "The Greatest Day in Doo-Wop" (1999) and, finally (also in 1999), "The Greatest Day" in Harlem, showing 156 rappers with their hats on backwards.

The idea just refuses to die. This title, this photograph, this movie—it's like a "Sorcerer's Apprentice" situation.

Or as Virginia Wicks, the film's beautiful publicist explains, "It's like the Energizer Bunny—it refuses to stop!" ●

Another
Jazz Day in Harlem

Life photographer Gordon Parks watches as Charles Graham points out which musicians are no longer living, and who is most likely to appear for *Life*'s re-creation of that "Great Day in Harlem." In the background are the steps where the photo was staged. (Henry Grossman photograph)

Closeup of the survivors. Hank Jones at left, explaining it all. To his right, laughing, is Eddie Locke, followed by Horace Silver (white hat), Marian McPartland, Milt Hinton, Gerry Mulligan and Taft Jordan Jr., who was only five years old in 1958. At top of stairs is Art Farmer, and below him is Benny Golson. Chubby Jackson is standing behind Marian McPartland. Leaning back laughing is Johnny Griffin. (Jack Lind photograph)

Gordon Parks was hired by *Life* Magazine to re-create The Big Picture 40 years later. By then, only twelve original members remained alive, and 11 attended. Since then, Gerry Mulligan and Art Farmer have died.

Life magazine's 1998 re-creation of the 1958 Great Day in Harlem. They assembled 11 survivors on 126th Street for this session. *Life*'s photographer Gordon Parks (white hair) is standing on a ladder at extreme left. Just right of the steps are Gerry Mulligan and Milt Hinton. Left of the stairs are Horace Silver, obscured by flood lights, then Eddie Locke and Hank Jones. At the top of the stairs, resuming their positions from the 1958 photo, are Benny Golson and Art Farmer. To their left is Johnny Griffin, and in front of Farmer is Chubby Jackson. At the bottom of the stairs is Marian McPartland. Sonny Rollins was in Europe and missed the shoot. Sitting on the curb is Taft Jordan, Jr. (Jack Lind photograph)

Dizzy Gillespie with tip-tilted horn, Chicago, 1965. (Raymond Ross photograph)

II
The Trumpet Players
in Central Park

Red Allen and Kenny Dorham. (Jack Bradley photograph)

The Trumpet Players in Central Park, 1961. (Herb Snitzer photograph)

1. Buck Clayton; 2. Roy Eldridge; 3. Dizzy Gillespie; 4. Charlie Shavers; 5. Herman Autrey; 6. Joe Newman; 7. Dizzy Reece; 8. Freddie Hubbard; 9. Red Allen; 10. Don Ferrara; 11. Nick Travis; 12. Bobby Bradford; 13. Joe Thomas; 14. Yank Lawson; 15. Clark Terry; 16. Jimmy Nottingham; 17. Ernie Royal; 18. Johnny Letman; 19. Booker Little; 20. Doc Severinsen; 21. Max Kaminsky; 22. Ted Curson

Dan Morgenstern Remembers

THERE ARE SOME FUNNY THINGS about that big picture of the Trumpet Players in Central Park. Booker Little was eating hot dogs all day, it seemed. He was a sweet guy. Poor Booker. Everybody knew, *he* knew, he wasn't going to live long. So he had a good time. [Charlie] Shavers was another big hot dog eater.

Max Kaminsky—Maxie was sitting all the way in back. We had far too many things to think about, and the guys pretty much arranged themselves. You can see from some of the earlier candid shots the way they sit around.

I don't see Maxie in the earlier shots, but it occurred to me later that Maxie was in a bit of a snit—he had a sizable ego. He's sitting in the back, when he could have been up front. There are several guys up closer to the camera than he is who weren't anywhere near as prominent as he was by then. It's probably because he came a little later than lots of others.

Dizzy [Gillespie] and Roy [Eldridge] seated themselves together as they often did. They always stood or sat together and joked around.

We didn't know who would show up and who wouldn't until it actually happened. We called everyone for noon or one o'clock so we could get plenty of sunlight. And we were delighted, of course. It turned out quite well.

Everybody had a good time. Everybody except Joe Thomas. He looks dour. In fact he *was* a dour fellow. Joe was a great trumpet player, but he certainly wasn't Mr. Sunshine. He always had something bothering him. When he was sober he was in a bad mood because he was sober. And when he was drunk he was even worse.

I have no idea when Jack Bradley took his photographs. We were trying to find a good place to put Herb [Snitzer]. So that's why I'm propping him high up against the wall (see photo, page 82).

We told the musicians to bring horns if they wanted, but if everyone had brought their trumpets there would have been too many. You'll notice that Roy nearly always has his hand on his horn.

Thirty-seven years is a long time, so I can't recall with certainty who came up with the idea—Herb Snitzer, Jerry Smokler or I. What is certain is that we were inspired by the great Art Kane group photograph that had appeared in *Esquire* and still was fresh in our minds. That the Central Park Boat House cafeteria would be an ideal location was Herb's idea, I'm sure, and the idea for the Trumpet Issue, of which the group photograph was to be the centerfold, was mine. I'd always been a trumpet freak—my heroes were Louis Armstrong, Hot Lips Page and Roy Eldridge—and the October 1961 issue of *Metronome* was my first as full-fledged editor.

What I didn't know then was that there would only be two further issues of that venerable periodical, though it was no secret among our tight little staff that *Metronome* was on rather shaky ground. The 78-year-old magazine, which had been mainly devoted to jazz since 1936, had fallen on lean days. During the swing era, it had been in the forefront of jazz journalism, with the upstart *Down Beat* (founded in 1934) as its only serious rival. In the early days of modern jazz (a k a bebop), *Metronome* was the often combative voice of the new—Leonard Feather and Barry Ulanov—doing battle with Rudi Blesh, Gene Williams and other "moldy figs."

In the foreground are Joe Newman, Roy Eldridge, Dizzy Gillespie, Red Allen and Charlie Shavers, at the right. (Jack Bradley photograph)

Metronome polls were taken seriously by the media, and record dates by the *Metronome* All Stars, made up of poll winners, had been annual events since 1939. But the business end of things was not well handled. George Simon had brought what began as a music educators' and then became a rather conservative band musicians' magazine into the world of swing and jazz in 1933. When he decided to quit as co-editor in 1955, the downward slide began in earnest.

When the December 1959 issue of *Metronome* was printed but not distributed, everybody in the business thought the patient had expired. However, the magazine's brilliant young staff photographer, Herb Snitzer, didn't want to see it die. His uncle, Robert Asen, had been a professional clarinet and saxophone player in his youth (he recorded for Gennett with Dink Rendelman's Alabamans). Herb managed to persuade his uncle to acquire what was left of *Metronome*—the famous name, about 5,000 unexpired subscriptions and an inventory that included a treasure trove of photographs. In June 1960, a completely revamped *Metronome* reappeared on the scene.

Some six months later, I asked to join the magazine's staff as assistant editor. There had been some internal upheavals, and my boss would be Dave Solomon, who had come over from *Esquire*. He could play the first eight bars of Bix Beiderbecke's "I'm Coming Virginia" solo on the cornet he kept on his desk top, was as opinionated about jazz as about everything, and was a brilliant but improvident journalist.

I had been employed as editorial assistant in the drama department of the *New York Post*, then still a

newspaper, rewriting press releases and compiling the weekly Neighborhood Movie Guide. I got a very occasional jazz byline, but my night managing editor, Alvin Davis, had just been demoted to columnist by the publisher and my future was uncertain. The temptation of working full time in jazz—I was then the U.S. correspondent for Britain's *Jazz Journal* and had done freelance assignments—with a nice title and more money (if much less security) was too much to resist.

Solomon was determined to turn *Metronome* into not just the best jazz magazine but a significant journal of contemporary ideas. He was tuned into what was about to become the dominant "cult-ture" of the new decade, and quickly brought to the pages of staid old *Metronome* (always less brash and brassy than *Down Beat*) fiction by Williams S. Burroughs, Jack Gelber and Herbert Gold, poetry by Allen Ginsberg and Jack Kerouac—even a little piece by Henry Miller—and cartoons by Lou Myers, Al Swiller and Mike Thaler.

One time, Solomon and I went to visit Lenny Bruce in his famous Times Square hotel room and spent a few hours taping him free-associating about jazz—he was very hip about music. We edited the results into a piece which Lenny polished further; it read very well. There was stuff about hallucinogens and strong editorial attacks on Harry Ansliger's drug policies. Solomon was an early follower of Timothy Leary and involved some of us in very interesting controlled experiments. There was never a dull moment at *Metronome*—or in our pages.

For jazz writers, we had Stanley Dance, Nat Hentoff and Martin Williams; we resurrected Charles Edward

Buck Clayton, Nat Lorber, Red Allen and Kenny Dorham. (Jack Bradley photograph)

Smith and brought in new young voices like LeRoi Jones, A.B. Spellman and Don Heckman. There were great photographs by Herb Snitzer and his colleagues, and great layouts by our greatly gifted art director, Jerry Smokler, who later went on to win awards at *Town and Country*. Solomon engineered a musical encounter between Dizzy Gillespie and Ornette Coleman at his old friend Art D'Lugoff's Village Gate, documented in the magazine by me. Ornette had taken to hanging out at the new *Metronome* offices (we had moved to less costly quarters early in my tenure) and was giving saxophone lessons to Jerry.

Our kind and patient publisher surely flinched at some of the four-letter words (not yet common currency) and odd metaphors in our pages, but he didn't complain. The new *Metronome* was attracting attention.

But we were also courting disaster. It came in the form of the cover of our July issue, which sported a deep-pink tinted photo of a young woman in a bikini, softly focused but with highlights on torso, belly, and upper thighs. It wasn't at all provocative in the *Playboy* manner, but it featured a well-built Coney Island stripper and her audience. We considered it documentary photojournalism, not soft porn. But it sufficed, in 1961, to cause several hundred school libraries to cancel their subscriptions, and since our meager list had just begun to move slowly upward once again, this was a serious blow. The eagle-eyed librarians had, of course, never bothered to read Burroughs, Miller, et al., for if they had, those cancellations would have come much earlier. But our publisher had had enough, and Solomon was shown the door.

Since Solomon had come on board as managing editor under *Metronome* veteran Bill Coss, who was also dismissed, I didn't feel like a traitor in staying on, now as editor. And I must confess that, not long after joining *Metronome*, I had found, in the rejected articles file, a piece I had submitted earlier with suggestions from Coss and Bob Perlongo (the man whose place I took, as he had left along with Coss) that it be accepted. It had received an unconditional rejection from Solomon, though, pointing out that anyone who called Duke Ellington rather than Gil Evans the greatest living jazz composer and arranger was not the kind of writer *Metronome* ought to publish.

In any case, I was now in the driver's seat and I published an editorial in which I stated that *Metronome* would henceforth address itself, once again, primarily to jazz. I had no intention, though, of throwing out the baby with the bath water, and found space for film, theater, photography and literature, in moderation. The October issue, the first without previously committed material, was something on which I wanted my personal stamp.

Hence the trumpets. It being summer, we had faith in the weather. Our subjects being musicians, who can never be quite sure about their availability for a nonpaying gig, we decided to invite more trumpeters than we optimally needed. Among those who didn't show up were Louis Armstrong, who said he'd love to be there but was booked on the road for months ahead, and Miles Davis, who kept us in suspense to the last moment. After Davis saw the published results, he told us he would have come if he had known we would get

Red Allen listens to Joe Newman, at right. Dizzy Reece, left, has his back to the camera. (Jack Bradley photograph)

of the photograph will have observed the range from suit-and-tie to casual, though the black-and-white photos can't do justice to ties and shirts. The general look is surprisingly contemporary, proving that male fashion has remained rather impervious to change.

There was a good feeling to the gathering from the start. There were happy reunions among the elders and happy introductions between generations. Musical styles may change, but certain professional fundamentals remain. Thus it was gratifying to observe Herman Autrey (the oldest player on hand) and Booker Little (the second-youngest; Freddie Hubbard was born five days later) comparing horns.

Booker had a fine time that sunny day; we saw him enjoying his hot dog with kraut. The December issue of *Metronome* published a tribute to this marvelously gifted player and composer, who had become another regular visitor to our office—he relished browsing through old issues of the magazine. Alas, Nat Hentoff's tribute was posthumous. Booker Little died on October 10, 1961, aged 23 years, six months, and three days. Magazines are predated, so Booker did get to see our trumpet spread, and, more importantly, Robert Levin's fine profile of him in that same issue. Booker knew that his days, barring a medical miracle, were numbered (he had an incurable kidney disease). All who had the good fortune to know him remember Booker Little as a man of exceptional qualities. His music, of course, survives.

Roy Eldridge and Dizzy Gillespie—front and center, appropriately—are together here, as always when they shared a scene, and, as always, having fun. These two were more like siblings than mentor and acolyte, the roles so-called jazz history always assigns them. Nor does Roy look like the "link" he is supposed to be between Louis [Armstrong] and Diz. They were friends—and friendly rivals. To Roy, every trumpeter was a potential opponent in a musical joust, and Dizzy, until he himself became a father figure (and maybe even then), also had that competitive spirit. That these two giants should be flanked by Buck Clayton and Charlie Shavers is also appropriate. Charlie (seen consuming a hot dog with the trimmings) had been Dizzy's section-mate in a 1935 Philadelphia band and Roy's sparring partner on Jazz At The Philharmonic, and while each was unique, there were strong stylistic bonds among the three. As for Buck, he, too had been with JATP, and was one of the distinctive swing stylists. Sartorially, however, he and Charlie are contrasts.

Red Allen, though in the second row, is prominent, and that's as it should be; he might as well have been up front. But Red, though not unsociable, wasn't a cat who hung out. He kept to himself when not entertaining fans, didn't drink or indulge, and kept his own counsel. Herman Autrey, off by himself at the other end of row two, was very sociable and did indulge in the grape, but Herb caught him in a pensive moment. Joe Newman, Dizzy Reece and young Freddie Hubbard seem to be sharing something amusing; Bobby Bradford, the most recent arrival in New York,

such a stellar turnout—and if the event had been staged later in the day, though we had set the time for early afternoon.

We had aimed for a good balance of generations and musical styles, and luckily we achieved it. We had been fairly certain that most of the older players would show up, but the youngsters didn't disappoint; most of them were among the first to appear. The weather gods also came through for us—the day was perfect in terms of light and comfort. Herb and I agreed that the musicians should not be coached on how to place themselves for the shoot. We had suggested, but not demanded, that they bring their horns, and a sufficient number did.

Almost everyone was on time, within the half-hour or so we had anticipated for socializing, eating and getting settled. Dress, too, was optional, and viewers is not privy to whatever it was. Sharing his table, Nick Travis and Don Ferrara look, respectively, jolly and bemused. Yank Lawson, Clark Terry and Jimmy Nottingham were all busy in the studios then—Clark had left the Ellington fold in 1959 and was not yet the star he would soon become. Standing behind them, Ted Curson looks remarkably like a young Louis Armstrong. Two other top studio cats, Ernie Royal and Doc Severinsen, flank Johnny Letman, just starting then to make a bit of a name for himself. (Doc's attire is strictly Ivy League, with no hint of things to come.) Booker is in front of Doc, and all by himself in the same row is Joe Thomas, a great unsung trumpeter but not a man at peace with himself or the world. Bringing up the rear, and not looking happy either, is Max Kaminsky.

Two latecomers didn't make it into the main picture. Kenny Dorham looks younger than his 36 years, yet had only little more than a decade of life left; at that, he was luckier than Nick Travis, his junior by a year but gone by the fall of 1964. Kenny was late because a business engagement had held him up. The other culprit, Nat Lorber, had to come all the way from his home near Coney Island and got off to a late start.

Lorber was known to his fellow musicians as "Face," a nickname he tolerated but didn't cherish. If you were close to him, you called him Nat, but his two big heroes (aside from Louis) had special names for him: Hot Lips' [Page] Texas accent produced "Shawty," and Roy Eldridge dubbed him "Space Cadet." Both great trumpeters considered Nat their protégé, but many lesser practitioners of the horn either patronized or ostracized him. Nat's harmonic vocabulary was limited, but he had a great big sound (from Louis and Lips) and could swing and play authentic blues. In a jam session, he could blast most other trumpeters out of the joint, which of course did not endear him to players who considered themselves his musical superiors. But Sidney Bechet, Lester Young and Charlie Parker didn't mind having Nat on the stand with them, and he was always welcome to sit in with Buddy Tate or Tiny Grimes. The paying gigs he had were few and far between, mostly in Harlem (where people took to him) or the Village, but until changing times and advancing age made him stick close to home and his extensive record and tape collection, Nat always found a place to blow. I met Nat when I was 18 and owe most of what I understand about jazz to him.

Among those who came by to kibitz were drummer Oliver Jackson with his fellow Detroit tubman Eddie Locke. The two of them had quickly become first-call guys among the mainstreamers (Jo Jones was their best PR man), and Ollie was an excellent organizer who proved himself helpful in various ways before and during the shoot.

Another welcome visitor was photographer Jack Bradley, already one of the world's foremost Louis Armstrong fans and a key documentarian of aspects of the jazz scene that trendy photographers passed up—or rather, knew little or nothing about. Jack had a

Old-timer Herman Autrey comparing notes about trumpets with Bobby Bradford. (Jack Bradley photograph)

unique approach; he usually clicked the shutter just once when he had his subject in focus. Film was expensive, and Jack was not yet able to support himself as a lensman. So he trusted his eye and made just that one pass. Bless him—most of the time, that single shot sufficed. And Jack saved his stuff, too—it's due to his presence in the park that day that we have his images to flesh out the story.

So that was the day in the park. We thought the shoot and the Trumpet Issue came out pretty well, though I took some lumps from the critical cabal for having asked Hughes Panassie to write a piece about Louis Armstrong. I never had much use for party lines, and certainly was no subscriber to Panassie's peculiar views of contemporary jazz, but he was someone from whom, early on, I'd discovered much great stuff to listen to. And when I started to write, he was among the first to encourage me. And I did think he knew a thing or two about Pops [Louis Armstrong].

Other bylines in that issue included Martin Williams, Nat Hentoff, Dick Hadlock, Stanley Dance and Robert Levin. Hadlock's interview with Benny Harris is, as far as I know, the only published one with that legendary figure.

Two more issues, and then *Metronome* was history. Our patient publisher had not reached the end of his patience, but the nature of his business had changed quite suddenly and in a manner that no longer made the magazine's losses a practical financial proposition. When Bob Asen gave us the bad news, the December issue was ready to go to press, and we begged Bob to

Dan Morgenstern talks to visiting drummer Oliver Jackson. Above Morgenstern is Red Allen and above Jackson is Buck Clayton. Between them is Ted Curson. Left rear is Clark Terry. (Jack Bradley photograph)

As Dizzy Gillespie takes a picture of the others, Dan Morgenstern observes and photographer Herb Snitzer tries to find a better camera angle. (Jack Bradley photograph)

allow it to be printed. He graciously agreed, and thus we were able to let our readers know that the end might be in sight (we still had hopes that someone would rescue the magazine), but no savior materialized.

Though I subsequently was enlisted to start another periodical (*Jazz*; later—without me—known as *Jazz & Pop*) and then went to work for *Down Beat*, the top jazz dog (with which I spent almost a decade, including some six years as editor), the *Metronome* experience was unique. Never again would there be a journalistic environment so free from policy pressures and business constraints and publishers' idiosyncrasies, and the work of our small but dedicated staff reflects that freedom, I think. The day of the trumpeters in the park was a high point during that brief but happy period. But then, as the one and only Mezz Mezzrow so cogently observed: "Them first kicks are killers." ●

Herb Snitzer Remembers Shooting the Picture

THE LATTER PART of 1961 was a trying time for us at *Metronome* magazine. We were desperately trying to keep the business alive and one of our editorial ideas was to do an all-trumpet issue. We wanted to get together as many trumpet players in one big picture as we could.

Undercapitalized when it resumed publication in June 1961, *Metronome* was nevertheless the best jazz magazine being published in the United States, introducing young writers and photographers to a music-reading public. Writers Amiri Baraka, Herbert Gold, Nat Hentoff, as well as photographers Lawrence Shustak, Chuck Stewart and yours truly, were appearing regularly in *Metronome*.

It was literary *and* visual, devoted to jazz and to the artists who make this wonderful music. But no matter how hard we tried, subscriptions and advertising revenues were just not enough to cover the monthly expenses of the magazine. By the end of 1961 publisher Robert Asen was ready to call it quits.

But before he did, editor Dan Morgenstern and I combined our talents to present 22 trumpet players in one image when they all got together one hot August afternoon at the Harlem boathouse in Central Park, New York City. Three major players who were absent were Art Farmer, Miles Davis and Louis Armstrong, with Kenny Dorham arriving too late in the day to be in the main picture.

Louis of course was out of town, and Miles, true to form, didn't bother. Dan eventually titled his story of the meeting, "Pops Couldn't and Miles Wouldn't."

Over the years many people have asked how we were able to get so many wonderful musicians together and our simple answer has always been, "We asked them." It was an event almost unheard of today in the age of megastars, handlers, agents, bodyguards and hangers-on.

Not that there weren't folks like that around in those days. But if you wanted to talk to Dizzy Gillespie or Roy Eldridge you simply rang them up and more times than not they answered the telephone. So we did that. We rang them up, and they agreed to come. After all, it also gave them a chance to be with their peers, and it gave the younger players—Booker Little, Ted Curson, Freddie Hubbard—a chance to mingle with their mentors.

Certainly that's the way I saw it, as these 22 men gathered together. No sooner were they together than the joking and fun-making began. One of the wonderful things about jazz musicians is the humor and joking that goes back and forth. That afternoon was no exception.

Historically this photograph speaks of the changing of the guard. Gathered together were the older players—Roy Eldridge, Charlie Shavers, Max Kaminsky and Joe Thomas—alongside the young Turks. But we weren't thinking about that. We were aiming to get the musicians organized so they wouldn't have to spend a lot of time in the sun, and boy, it was hot!

There was Roy Eldridge in suit and tie, as were Clark Terry, Herman Autrey, Jimmy Nottingham and, in the back row, a young crew cut-sporting white cat by the name of Doc Severinsen. All very formal. And who can forget Red Allen, always correct?

Actually, most of the players wore jackets that afternoon, but not Dizzy. He was front and center, in sports shirt and soft shoes, clowning around with his musical mentor Roy Eldridge. Those two seemed in a world all to themselves—and they were.

Seated right behind Roy is Joe Newman, a favorite player as well as human being. He was a real gentleman—most musicians are. That includes two of my oldest jazz friends, Clark Terry and Ted Curson, also in the photograph.

Buck Clayton and Charlie Shavers were in the front row. How I wished Pops [Armstrong] could have been there. At least he was there in spirit. He was out of town but later said he really wished he *could* have been present.

That time so long ago, the summer of 1961—two years before the free speech movement and only one year after the integration of Southern lunch counters—was a turning point in America's attitudes toward a people long enslaved. And inside jazz it was also a turning point, from the music of Armstrong to the music of Gillespie and Monk, and on to Ornette Coleman, John Coltrane and Cecil Taylor.

It was a different time, needing a different music. And jazz, as always, was there to comment, reflect back and point to the future.

So many of the players seen in the picture are gone now. Those who remain, still playing, are making music and addressing the issues of freedom, individuality, integration and spirit.

I feel privileged, not only to know this picture is mine, but in knowing so many of these men whose music has touched me deeply. They are kindred spirits. I feel part of them and of the music they and I love. ●

Biographies of the Trumpet Players in Central Park

Following are brief biographies of the trumpet players posed together in the summer of 1961 in New York's Central Park for their portrait in the October 1961 issue of Metronome *magazine.*

Allen, Henry "Red." (9) See his entry under The Big Picture.

Autrey, Herman. (5) Born in Evergreen, Alabama, in 1904, Autrey moved to Pittsburgh in 1923 and started performing with local bands. He played with many territory bands until 1933. While working in Harlem for Charlie Johnson at Small's Paradise he was heard by Fats Waller, who hired him. Autrey worked with Fats from 1934 through 1942, and played on most of Waller's recordings. He also worked for Fletcher Henderson, Luis Russell and Claude Hopkins. Later he often played with Stuff Smith, then led his own band in Philadelphia for a long time. A bad car crash in 1954 benched him for a while, but in the Sixties he appeared with the well-known Saints and Sinners band in and around New York. He worked into the Seventies but only as a singer. He was a forceful trumpeter in the style of Armstrong, while his singing derived in great part from the effervescent shouting of Waller. Autrey died in 1980.

Bradford, Bobby. (12) Born in Cleveland, Ohio, in 1934, Bradford began playing cornet in 1949 with groups led by Leo Wright, Buster Smith and others. By 1952 he had worked with Eric Dolphy and Ornette Coleman and in U.S. Air Force bands. Moving to the West Coast in 1964, Bradford first taught school, then started playing with "new jazz" groups, including those of Arthur Blythe, James Newton, John Carter and David Murray.

Clayton, Buck. (1) See his entry under The Big Picture.

Curson, Ted. (22) Born in Philadelphia, Pennsylvania, in 1935, Curson was playing with tenor saxophone star Charlie Ventura by the time he was 18. Encouraged by Miles Davis, he came to New York in 1956 and worked there with major musicians, including Cecil Taylor, Charles Mingus and Eric Dolphy. He also joined the burgeoning "free jazz" school and played often with its exponents. In the early Sixties he moved to Europe as one of many expatriate jazz musicians who found they could get more work there than in the United States.

Eldridge, Roy. (2) See his entry under The Big Picture.

Ferrara, Don. (10) Ferrara was a teacher as well as a trumpet player. His playing is identified mostly with Lennie Tristano's music. He worked with Tristano and Gerry Mulligan as well as with the bands of George Auld and Woody Herman. Lee Konitz said of him, "Don's a real improviser!" In addition to teaching, which became his main activity, Ferrara is a historian of the trumpet who developed the notion of the saxophonist-trumpeter, referring to trumpet players adopting much of the phrasing and speed of the saxophone, as first articulated by Roy Eldridge.

Gillespie, Dizzy. (3) See his entry under The Big Picture.

Hubbard, Freddie. (8) Born in Indianapolis, Indiana, in 1938, Hubbard is one of the most powerful and technically adept trumpet and flügelhorn players of all. Moving to New York at age 20, he worked for many top-flight band leaders, including Art Blakey, J.J. Johnson, Sonny Rollins and Quincy Jones. He has also worked with musicians such as Max Roach and Herbie Hancock in a variety of styles. For many years he was one of the most admired and sought-after trumpeters in jazz.

Kaminsky, Max. (21) See his entry under The Big Picture.

Lawson, Yank. (14) Born in Trenton, Missouri, in 1911, Lawson studied piano and saxophone, switching to the trumpet in his teens. After attending the University of Missouri he worked with Wingy Manone, then joined Ben Pollack's swing band in 1933. When Pollack quit jazz, Lawson and several other members of the band formed what became the Bob Crosby Band (Crosby got the leader's job in great part because of his brother Bing's fame). Lawson played with Tommy Dorsey from 1938 through 1939 and again from 1941 through 1942. He joined Benny Goodman in 1942, then went into studio work for several years. On Louis Armstrong's "Musical Autobiography" (Decca, 1957), Armstrong chose Lawson to play the trumpet parts of King Oliver, Armstrong's mentor. Lawson was an especially powerful lead trumpeter, particularly in the styles of Dixieland and swing, and he continued playing his powerful horn into the Nineties. At publication Lawson was still alive.

Letman, Johnny. (18) Born in 1917 in McCormick, South Carolina, Letman's first "name" job was with Nat "King" Cole in 1943-1944, and his next was with Horace Henderson. Letman went to New York in 1944 and played or recorded with Cab Calloway, John Kirby and briefly with Count Basie. He made records with many leading musicians, including Stuff Smith, Panama Francis, Tiny Grimes, Lionel Hampton, Cozy Cole and Earl Hines, and later appeared at many music festivals.

Little, Booker. (19) Born in Memphis, Tennessee, in 1938, Little started on clarinet but switched to the trumpet at the age of 12. He jammed with Phineas Newborn while still in his teens. He received his Bachelor of Music degree in Chicago and went on to play with sax star Johnny Griffin. Just before the trumpet players' picture was taken, Little was playing with Max Roach. He then started a close collaboration with Eric Dolphy and other avant-gardists. He played with John Coltrane and other precursors of "free jazz" early on. Little died in 1961 shortly after the Central Park photo shoot.

Newman, Joe. (6) Newman was born in New Orleans, Louisiana, in 1922. His father had played piano professionally, and Newman joined Lionel Hampton's band before he was 20 years old. He worked several years with Count Basie while still very young, then worked with the bands of Illinois Jacquet and J.C. Heard. In 1952 he returned to the Basie band to replace of one of its founding members, Harry "Sweets" Edison. Newman toured Europe with Basie in 1954 but left the band in 1961, just before the trumpeters' photograph was taken. He later toured Europe with Benny Goodman, performed at countless jazz festivals and freelanced all around the world. One of the most dependable and powerful trumpeters in jazz, Newman was a heavy smoker and succumbed to emphysema in the late Eighties.

Nottingham, Jimmy. (16) A trumpeter born in New York City in 1925, Nottingham began playing professionally with baritone sax leader Cecil Payne in Brooklyn in 1943. He was in a famous Navy band during World War II, then played with Lionel Hampton's big band as a high-note specialist. Later he played with such notables as Charlie Barnet, Lucky Millinder, Count Basie, Dizzy Gillespie, Quincy Jones and Ray Charles, in addition to performing with several Latin bands. Nottingham died in New York in 1978.

Trumpeter Jimmy Nottingham was in big demand as a studio musician. (Raymond Ross/Institute of Jazz Studies photograph)

Reece, Dizzy. (7) Born in Kingston, Jamaica, in 1931, Reece took up baritone horn before switching to trumpet at age 11. After working with a local swing band in Jamaica in 1947, he moved to London and Paris, where he played with tenor giant Don Byas. In the early Fifties he worked all over Europe with swing bands, returning to London in 1954 to work with Martial Solal, then with Don Byas again, and later with members of the Modern Jazz Quartet. He recorded in London with Victor Feldman, Ronnie Scott and Tubby Hayes. Shortly after the trumpeters' picture was taken, he led a group at the Village Vanguard and took freelance gigs in New York. Reece is fluent in swing and especially bop styles.

Royal, Ernie. (17) Royal was born in Los Angeles, California, in 1921. The brother of well-known lead saxophonist Marshall Royal, Ernie's first big-time work was with the Les Hite band in 1937-1938, which included Lionel Hampton and a number of other later stars. He then joined Hampton's big band from 1940 through 1942. He was in the Navy from 1942 through 1944, then joined Count Basie in 1946 and Woody Herman from 1947 through 1949. Subsequently, Royal became one of the busiest trumpeters on the West Coast studio scene.

Severinsen, Doc. (20) Born in Arlington, Oregon, in 1927, Severinsen first played in the big bands of Charlie Barnet, Tommy Dorsey and Benny Goodman. In 1949 he joined the staff of NBC and stayed with TV for many years. His best-known work started when he became the assistant to Skitch Henderson on NBC's "Tonight Show,"

Doc Severinsen. (Institute of Jazz Studies photograph)

where he later became the leader of the orchestra. His popularity derived not only from his virtuoso trumpet work and quick wit, but also from his colorful attire on camera. In recent years Severinsen has concentrated on numerous concerts of his own and appearances with symphony orchestras like the Boston Pops.

Shavers, Charlie. (4) Born in New York City in 1917, Shavers is the composer of many riff tunes, including the standard "Undecided," and was known as an excellent arranger. He hit the big time at age 19, joining the famous Biggest Little Band in the Land, led by John Kirby. Shavers wrote many of the band's tightly orchestrated arrangements. In 1944, he joined Tommy Dorsey's big band on trumpet and also arranged for the band. Shavers was with Dorsey on and off for more than 10 years, and played in studio bands as well. He had an instantly recognizable bravura style with great control in the highest register. Shavers died in 1971.

Terry, Clark. (15) Born in St. Louis, Missouri, in 1920, Terry played trumpet and flügelhorn in addition to being a band leader. He was in a famous Navy band during World War II before joining Charlie Barnet's band and Count Basie's small band. He then played with Duke Ellington for eight years and later joined the NBC-TV house band. He was also very active in New York studio work for many years. He became widely known for his specialty, "Mumbles," on TV and also for his frequent use of two horns—trumpet and flügelhorn—in "duets" with himself. His easy-to-identify trumpet style shows extraordinary facility, and the humor and camaraderie he projects from the band have made him extremely popular with audiences. He remained very active in appearances all over the world in the Nineties.

Thomas, Joe. (13) See his entry under The Big Picture.

Travis, Nick. (11) Born in Philadelphia, Pennsylvania, in 1925, Travis began playing professionally with Vido Musso in 1942, then with Woody Herman until 1944. While in the service he performed in Paris. Upon returning to the United States, he worked mostly with Ray McKinley in the late Forties, then with Benny Goodman, Gene Krupa and Ina Ray Hutton. He later played with Tommy Dorsey, again with Woody Herman, then with Jimmy Dorsey and others. In the summer of 1950 he toured Europe with Duke Ellington. In 1952 he played with tenorist Wardell Gray, then toured the United States with Stan Kenton. From 1953 to1956 he was lead trumpeter with the Sauter-Finnegan orchestra, and in 1957 he joined the NBC staff orchestra. Travis freelanced in New York from 1957 through 1960. From 1960 through 1962 he was with the Gerry Mulligan Concert Jazz Band and in 1963 became a member of the 10-piece orchestra that played with Thelonious Monk in concerts at Lincoln Center and Carnegie Hall. He later worked with Al Cohn and Zoot Sims and led his own quintet. Travis was an excellent lead man and had a strong, clear tone which was well suited to big bands. He died in 1964.

The Trumpet in Jazz

by Dan Morgenstern, editor of *Metronome* Magazine

It is with some reluctance that I consent to have this November 1961 article from Metronome *reprinted nearly four decades after it was written. There are other things from that early period (I'd started writing professionally about jazz in 1957) that seem to me to wear much better than this rather opinionated survey.*

But since it puts the photograph in that same issue of the magazine in a contemporaneous perspective, maybe it does make sense to reproduce something that now must be taken cum grano salis. *And speaking of perspective, it should be pointed out that the issue also contained articles about Louis Armstrong (by the venerable Hughes Panassie); Clark Terry, who was not yet the household name he was soon to become (by Stanley Dance); Red Allen (by Martin Williams); Benny Harris (by Dick Hadlock); and Booker Little (by Robert Levin). In his column, Nat Hentoff focused on under-recorded trumpeters and singled out Rex Stewart for attention. This writer reviewed live performances by Joe Newman, Bobby Bradford (with Ornette Coleman) and Ruby Braff, and the record reviews included works by Dizzy Gillespie, Freddie Hubbard and Muggsy Spanier.*

So whatever I had to say—in a style inevitable for such overreaching survey articles, which I would no longer attempt to do and certainly not assign to myself today—has to be taken in that context, with apologies for the rather obnoxiously Olympian style common to such "list" pieces. Yet I'm not ashamed of anything I said, though I may have overrated some and underrated others. Two things, however, I would like to amend: I was unfair to Bunk Johnson, and I have no idea why I claimed more jazz chops for Chris Griffin than his Benny Goodman section mates, whom I obviously underestimated; certainly I came to appreciate Harry James as the truly great musician he was.

—D.M.

THE HISTORY OF JAZZ began when the slave ships reached the shores of a not-so-brave new world, but the legend of jazz begins with a trumpet. Buddy Bolden is the first individual to emerge from the anonymous mass of jazz prehistory. There are some who say now that Bolden never really was, or that there were two Boldens and that neither played well, or that jazz really began in West Africa, or Cuba or New York. But legends are not affected by research and facts. Buddy Bolden played the trumpet in New Orleans and on a clear night you could hear him for miles around. He was the first king of jazz and he played a trumpet and it seems right that it should have been that way, for the trumpet is the most brilliant and commanding instrument among the many horns of jazz. Jazz liberated the trumpet from the strictures of brass band music and the limited coloristic role assigned to it in symphonic orchestration. Jazz made the trumpet sing.

In the earliest forms of jazz, the trumpet played the lead part in a polyphonic ensemble, carrying the melody and controlling the pace and volume of the group. A strong tone and powerful lungs were required. Not illogically, trumpet players were often leaders of their own bands. Before the advent of Louis Armstrong, which affected not only the development of trumpets but of jazz as a whole, some of the greatest trumpeters (many of whom actually played the cornet) were Emanuel Perez, Freddie Keppard and Joe "King" Oliver. Bunk Johnson, though a fair enough musician, was not in the same class even in his heyday, according to reliable ear-witness reports. Keppard was famed for his power and drive, Oliver for his subtlety and imagination. He was a master in the use of mutes, used in early jazz for what was then called "freak" or "talking" effects, especially favored for slow blues "preaching." In New Orleans, the famous battles of the bands as often as not became battles of trumpets, and the uncrowned king of jazz was always a trumpeter. Two-trumpet teams were also favored, and a man who could improvise a good second part was much in demand.

Louis Armstrong blows his golden horn for photographer Bill Gottlieb in 1946. (Institute of Jazz Studies photograph)

Thus King Oliver reverted to tradition when he sent for Louis Armstrong, then 22 years old, to come up to Chicago and join his famous Creole Band as second trumpet. The story of Louis' development and impact is discussed in detail by Hughes Panassie elsewhere. Suffice it to say that nothing was quite the same once Louis hit his stride. Those who couldn't keep up muttered that he was playing "clarinet parts" on the trumpet, just as others years later called Dizzy Gillespie a "Chinese trumpet player." Louis' tone, range, speed and unlimited powers of imagination and expression did for the trumpet what Paganini had done for the violin and Liszt for the piano—if not more. For Louis is a creator as well as a virtuoso: a rare combination.

For evidence of this and much of what followed we must trust the phonograph record. It is generally trustworthy, but availability, fashions in music, and later, press agentry and distorted criticism have often inflated reputations and ignored or shortchanged substantial talents. In many cases, it is no longer possible to separate fact from fiction, or to remedy unjust neglect. Nevertheless, the reader may encounter some unfamiliar names in this necessarily concentrated outline. It is

unfortunate that he will not be able to investigate the music behind them, for in many cases there is very little (and in some cases nothing) available on records for reference. But the originals exist, and someday the serious jazz student (and lovers of good music) may be more fortunate.

As jazz developed, the possibilities for the application of a variety of skills broadened. Among trumpeters, there could now be found soloists and section men, sweet players and hot men, mute and growl specialists and men with pretty sounds, high note cats and speed demons. It is probable that a greater variety of sounds and personalities can be found among trumpeters than anywhere else in jazz. At least, this was true up to the period when the saxophone, through the pervasive influence of Charlie Parker, displaced the trumpet as the most glamorous of horns. And the results have been much less variegated and interesting.

Armstrong's genius was sufficiently multi-faceted to allow any number of trumpeters to take their inspiration from it and derive very individual returns. A few, like the late Tommy Ladnier, remained untouched and went their own way. One of these, 64-year-old Ed Allen, has been playing his lyrical, Oliver-inspired horn in a New York City taxi dance hall for the last 16 years, emerging twice from obscurity to record dates released in Europe only. Punch Miller, a contemporary of Allen, was captivated by Louis. After a long illness, he has recently joined the George Lewis band. Two men of Armstrong's age (and inspired by him) still play very well: Bob Shoffner with Franz Jackson's Chicago band, and the legendary Dewey Jackson, active in St. Louis. Other good men of this generation were George Mitchell, master of Louis' "Hot Five" style, and the late Lee Collins. Bubber Miley, with Duke Ellington until three years before his untimely death in 1932, was a wholly original musician who developed the use of growl and plunger effects to a refined art and left an indelible stamp on Ellingtonia.

Miley's equally short-lived contemporary, Bix Beiderbecke, was the great white hope of jazz. His playing was characterized by great beauty of tone, clarity, precision and logic uniquely combined with a yearning lyricism. Red Nichols, greatly influenced by Bix, substituted cleverness for imagination and carried Bix's tendency to play on the beat to an extreme.

Other Bix disciples include the durable Jimmy McPartland, studio man Andy Secrest and the younger Dick Cathcart. To a much lesser extent, the Bix influence can be noted in Rex Stewart (who, like Bix, favors the cornet), Bunny Berigan and Bobby Hackett. These three, however, were more profoundly affected by Louis and each became quite his own man. Rex's speed moved Roy Eldridge, and his humor found echoes in Clark Terry.

Berigan was perhaps the greatest of white trumpeters of an era in regard to which distinctions of race, for whatever they may be worth, can hardly be ignored by the historian. Hackett's very personal style is distinguished by high musical intelligence and superb taste. His admirers range from Eddie Condon to Miles Davis.

A number of interesting trumpeters of the first post-Armstrong generation worked with the bands of Fletcher Henderson: Rex Stewart; the beatific Joe Smith, who was Bessie Smith's favorite accompanist; the explosive and adventurous Bobby Stark, who later worked with Chick Webb; and Red Allen, whose fondness for long lines and strange harmonies made him a precursor of "modern" trumpeting but whose overall conception is nonetheless in a definite Louis mold. Red is one of those who have proven their durability.

A trumpeter who worked with Henderson in the mid-Thirties (when Roy Eldridge was the section's star) has perhaps come closest to approaching Louis' majesty of phrase and purity of conception. This is Joe Thomas, who also possesses one of the most beautiful tones ever coaxed from a brass bell. Joe is still active in New York City, but he hasn't been "discovered" yet.

Also with Henderson was Herman Autrey, who made hundreds of records with Fats Waller and still is a capable and dependable player.

A highly original voice came on the scene in the late Twenties in the person of Jabbo Smith, recently rediscovered and hopefully on his way to a comeback. Jabbo had a smaller sound than Louis, but developed lightning valve action coupled with a leaping, graceful beat and inventiveness of a high order.

An important influence on Roy Eldridge, Jabbo may well be the "link" between Louis and Roy. The playing of Bill Coleman, long a resident of France, resembles Jabbo's in its airy lightness and skipping beat, but Coleman is more lyrical and less prone to pyrotechnics.

At Coleman's side in Cecil Scott's band at the Savoy Ballroom in the Harlem of the late Twenties sat Frankie Newton, later to become one of the best and most original trumpeters of the swing era. Newton's melodic imagination, perfect time and soulful tone were combined with a deeply romantic sensibility which gave his playing, at its best, an emotional depth found only in the greatest jazz. His career was erratic; he was known as a "difficult" man in a time when such characteristics had no commercial value. His name is rarely heard today. Newton was a master of the blues and an accompanist of great sensitivity.

The Midwest produced many great trumpeters. An early member of Bennie Moten's Kansas City band was Lamar Wright, last noted by the general public as featured high-note man in George Shearing's big band. He's still in the business. His two sons, Lamar Jr. and Elmon Wright, are both talented trumpeters. When Moten expanded to two trumpets, Ed Lewis joined the band. Lewis, still active, became Count Basie's lead man for many years. An interesting trumpeter who worked with Moten somewhat later was Joe Keyes, who could sight-read the most difficult parts and was known as a character. According to some, he might well have become a great trumpeter had he been more disciplined in his habits.

The trumpet star of Moten's band at its peak, billed then as "The Trumpet King of the West" was Hot Lips Page. Lips was a great trumpeter, a first-class singer specializing in blues and a consummate showman. But true success passed him by and he died broke. Lips was one of the most powerful trumpeters in jazz history, but he

Lining up to go stompin' at the Savoy, "The Home of Happy Feet," in 1940. (Frank Driggs Collection)

could also play with great restraint and sensitivity. He was the master of the growl and came as close to a *vox humana* quality in his playing as any instrumentalist ever has. He was often classified as a "Louis imitator"—an exceedingly stupid mistake caused by a similarity in voice and theatrical gifts. Though greatly influenced by Louis, Lips' music was steeped in the blues and had a flavor all its own. His conception, adventurousness and fondness for speed all point to Roy Eldridge, with whom he also shared a love for the jam session. Lips did not come East with Basie but left to form his own band.

His replacement was Buck Clayton, who rose to fame with Count and has maintained a position as one of the top trumpets of his generation ever since. Clayton's style has something of Joe Smith's singing grace, Lips Page's acerbity combined with his own clarity of conception and Armstrong's sense of form. He is also among the masters of the mutes, his earlier fancy for the cup mute lately supplanted by a fondness for the Harmon.

Buck is among the finest accompanists (the trumpet, muted or open, is the instrument best suited for commentary behind vocalists), as Billie Holiday well knew.

Another ex-Basie-ite of note is Harry "Sweets" Edison, whose early style resembled Frankie Newton's, though a bit more extroverted. He is among the few trumpeters of the swing generation favored by the contemporary hip audience. His characteristic use of single-note phrases, often bent humorously or pleadingly, has become one of those instantly recognizable trademarks in jazz.

Sweets Edison, Frankie Newton and Lips Page belong to the second generation after Armstrong—the generation whose leading exponent became Roy Eldridge. Before going on to Roy, let us list some trumpeters who, either by age or temperament, belong to the earlier group. A fine mute-man and very original stylist is Sidney dePeris, whose conception is more advanced than he has the opportunity to demonstrate in his elder brother Wilbur's band. On hand to spell Sidney at times is Doc Cheatham, a trumpeter with a golden sound and fine sense of melodic construction.

Benny Carter, better known as one of the finest alto saxophonists and arrangers in jazz, is also a first-rate trumpet with a Louis-tinged style informed with the same grace and elegance expressed in his alto playing and writing.

A group of players associated with traditional and Chicago jazz, all inspired by Louis, include the indestructible and straightforward Muggsy Spanier; Wingy Manone, whose real abilities are often overshadowed by his clowning; Max Kaminsky, steady, reliable and often imaginative; the hard-driving, sometimes surprisingly romantic Wild Bill Davison, who is a jazz original; Charlie Teagarden; Louis Prima, now strictly show-biz, but in the early Thirties a fervent and often excellent Armstrong disciple; the late Sterling Bose; Pee Wee Erwin; Chelsea Quealy, by far the best of the trumpeters associated with early New York white jazz; the capable Yank Lawson; Bob Scoby, who can play very well on occasion; and Johnny Windhurst.

Good swing men are legion: Taft Jordan, a fine all-round talent; Chris Griffin, who always could play more jazz than his Goodman section-mates, Ziggy Elman and Harry James, no slouches either; the durable and excellent Paul Webster of Lunceford fame; England's youngish but well rooted Humphrey Lyttleton, and his senior fellow countryman, Nat Gonella, a true Louis disciple; Irving "Mouse" Randolph; Henry Goodwin, good with mutes; the late Ed Swayzee; Ward Pinkett, another premature death; Sy Oliver, who was a good growler before giving up the horn; Pat Jenkins; Ruben Reeves, once a star sideman with Cab Calloway; expatriate Peanuts Holland; Charlie Barnet's inventive Bobby Burnett; Bernie Privin, now in the studios; Manny Klein, ditto; Walter Fuller with Earl Hines; Johnny Letman, a full-toned, fiery trumpeter long in obscurity but now on the road to well-deserved recognition; Wendell Culley of "Li'l Darling" fame; and Archie Johnson, once with Lucky Millinder and now gigging in Harlem, who's got a story of his own, as does Nat Lorber. Never acclaimed, but nonetheless a fine horn-man, is Frank "Fat Man" Humphries, active in Harlem.

A younger trumpeter who belongs in this group, though he has something quite his own, is Ruby Braff. Often accused of being an anachronism, he is actually a very positive example of the many possibilities still available in jazz for guys with individual ears, as is the Shavers-influenced Don Goldie.

The impact of Roy Eldridge on a whole generation of trumpeters is known to one and all through the example of his most famous one-time disciple, Dizzy Gillespie. Roy is, however, far more than the link between Louis Armstrong and John Birks Gillespie. He is one of the most original and individualistic of jazz trumpeters whose playing today is no less moving and significant than it was when Dizzy picked up his ears and said, "That's for me." In fact, Roy's playing today is at its most mature and expressive, though he has lost none of his love for adventure and experiment. Roy's influence was due to his amazing virtuosity, patterned on Louis' most daring experiments but often more extreme; his harmonic inventiveness, to some extent based on the work of saxophonists Coleman Hawkins and Benny Carter; and the passionate drive and intensity which marks all of his work.

Among the many who fell under Roy's spell were Emmett Berry, whose style is more sober and economical than Roy's and who still has a great deal to say; Joe Newman, influenced also by Sweets and Dizzy, who keeps getting better now that he is on his own; the severely underrated Dud Bascomb, responsible for much of the best trumpet work in Erskine Hawkins' band and still active; Bobby Moore; the phenomenal Charlie Shavers, in some ways the link between Roy and Dizzy and easily one of the most brilliant and imaginative jazz trumpeters alive; Howard McGhee, whose once somewhat exhibitionistic style has changed for the better; Chicago's King Kolax; Billy Butterfield, a very underestimated player; the excellent and versatile Snookie Young, who is finally being featured adequately with Count Basie; Shad Collins; the late Al Killian, noted for his high-note specialties but also a fine straight jazz player; Lunceford's Eddie Tompkins, who died too young;

All-star jam session at Birdland about 1945. The musicians are, left to right, Max Kaminsky on trumpet, Lester Young on tenor sax, Hot Lips Page on trumpet, Charlie Parker on alto sax and blind pianist Lennie Tristano. (Institute of Jazz Studies photograph)

Jimmy Nottingham, much in demand in the studios and also known for stratospheric playing but a fine soloist as well.

There's also the redoubtable Jonah Jones, who stands between Louis and Roy and whose belated good fortune doesn't alter the fact that he is a first-rate jazz trumpeter. Roy also had a host of disciples who became bogged down in imitation or lacked the taste to apply discreetly the technique acquired from the master.

Before going on to Dizzy and the modern school, let us pause to consider a special group of trumpeters associated with the Duke Ellington Orchestra. We have mentioned Rex Stewart. A competent trumpet who worked with Duke in the early days and is still around is Louis Metcalf.

Most famous of all Duke's hornmen is the remarkable Cootie Williams, who was with the band from 1929 to 1940. Gifted with one of the fullest and roundest tones in jazz, Cootie became famed for his growl and mute work, which, though very attractive, is no match for his open horn, dramatic and steeped in the vintage Armstrong tradition. Cootie's playing also exhibits a wonderfully developed sense of time. Oddly enough, he has rarely been able to maintain the high level of creativity reached with Ellington since leaving his fold. Arthur Whetsol, who left the band in 1937, was a trumpeter of great

charm and a perfect delineator of melody. Harold "Shorty" Baker, who originally came to the band as Whetsol's replacement, has a tasty conception and one of the purest trumpet sounds in jazz, but never was given his fair share of solo work. Senior member of the current section is Ray Nance, with Duke since 1940, inheritor of Cootie's plunger role, and a Louis-inspired trumpet with a very moving and personal vibrato, capable of humor and expansive romanticism, and one of the few good jazz violinists around. He is also a singer, dancer and showman par excellence.

Jonah Jones was with Cab Calloway when young Dizzy Gillespie joined Calloway. (In 1998, Jones revealed that it was *he* who threw that famous spitball seen in Jean Bach's new documentary "The Spitball Story". Calloway thought it was Dizzy, who was always cutting up on stage).

The supersonic Cat Anderson is an excellent all-round soloist, section-man and arranger, with a strong Louis tinge.

Clark Terry, inheritor of Rex's half-valve work, is currently specializing on the flügelhorn and is a highly inventive, sparkling and often witty player also capable of glowing lyric feeling. Willie Cook, who has been with Duke on and off since 1951, is not as well known as his considerable talents would merit. His playing combines

Clark "Mumbles" Terry with flügelhorn and trumpet on the Tonight Show at NBC in 1961. (Frank Driggs Collection)

the best elements of mainstream and modern in a most original way. Other good trumpeters who have passed through Duke's ranks were the volatile Freddy Jenkins, now retired from music; Nelson Williams, active in France and sometimes very good; Francis Williams, a fine section man; Andres Merenguito, who briefly replaced Cat Anderson and cut the book in style; and lead man Wallace Jones. Duke's current lead trumpet, Eddie Mullens, is also a good soloist but never gets a chance to show it. While on the subject of lead trumpeting, an unglamorous but highly important specialty, we might mention the powerful Conrad Gozzo; Mario Bauza, now with Machito and once with Chick Webb; Al Porcino; the late Shelton Hemphill; Jimmy Maxwell; and Reunald Jones, long with Basie, who is one of the few lead men who also is a gifted soloist. Ernie Royal also can do both.

With the advent of Dizzy, the problematic period of jazz trumpet begins. Dizzy captured the imaginations of many young players who were quite incapable of matching (or even approaching) his phenomenal virtuosity. Dizzy had come up through the ranks in the "classic" period; he knew his fundamentals. When Dizzy played one of his fabulous runs he knew what he was doing and he knew how to get back home. Dizzy's wit and imagination, bolstered by a phenomenal ear, enabled him to toss off things that perhaps sounded weird to the novice listener, but always made musical sense when checked out. The kiddies didn't know and couldn't do, but they tried. For a while it was possible to hear more bad jazz trumpet playing than ever before. There were notable exceptions.

The late Fats Navarro, with a style based on Dizzy's but with a strong lyrical undercurrent and a richer sound, was well on the way to becoming a contender before the lights went out. It wasn't until a youngster who had once been encouraged by Fats came on the scene that a comparable talent in Dizzy's vein emerged.

That was Clifford Brown, and he, too, was cut down in the midst of life—before maturing fully.

The styles of Navarro and Brown, based on Dizzy's but not quite as demanding technically, in turn inspired a host of young players. Among those influenced directly by Dizzy, however, were Kenny Dorham, who, after a somewhat erratic start, has grown to become one of the best modern trumpets of the day, though lesser men are getting more work; the older Benny Harris and Shorts McConnell; the erratic Red Rodney who can be excellent at times; and Idrees Sulieman, who can play. Doug Mettome, Nick Travis and Conte Candoli are other good men who have been around. Joe Gordon, also subject to ups and downs, could well become a first-rate trumpeter and often is. Don Fagerquist is a fine trumpeter. Of the younger men, Lee Morgan and Donald Byrd are linked to the Gillespie-Navarro-Brown axis. Morgan is somewhat of an *enfant terrible* whose promise has not as yet come true, though he has done more than just indicate it.

Donald Byrd, seriously overrecorded when first arriving in New York, has made great strides. Basie's Lennie Johnson has elements of Dizzy and Roy. Richard Williams, a recent arrival, is strongly under the Clifford Brown spell but may get into something. Like most of the young players in this category, he plays far too many notes far too rapidly. An excellent player who has been around a bit longer but is not well represented on records is Tommy Turrentine.

Blue Mitchell, who has fine tone, is beginning to mature and is worth watching. After Dizzy, as we have

Clifford Brown blowing on stage, 1955. (Frank Driggs Collection)

Miles Davis at Massey Hall, Toronto, 1972. (Frank Driggs Collection)

noted, trumpeting was rough on the youngsters. Not until Miles Davis came along and opened up another venue for innovation did budding trumpeters with more feeling than technique find a place to go.

Miles Davis, originally under Dizzy's spell but also influenced by the late Freddy Webster, who had a beautiful sound and an uncluttered melodic approach, in a sense went back to trumpet playing prior to Roy; i.e., he employed space and sound in a way that may be linked to an aspect of Armstrong rarely utilized by the more aggressive and venturesome late swing players. Miles made it possible once again to play quite simply without the horrors of nonconformity. He was encouraged in St. Louis by Clark Terry.

Miles also brought to the trumpet an air of melancholy which rarely had been in evidence before, except perhaps in some of Frankie Newton's moments of tempered despair. It is curious that Miles' music once was labeled "cool"; in some ways it is warmer than Dizzy's, though less "hot." Miles has developed his instrumental facility greatly since first appearing on wax with Charlie Parker; the musical sensitivity and imagination were there from the start.

Miles' most gifted follower is easily Art Farmer, who has finally come into his own. Traces of Miles are observable in all the younger players cited above, some of whom have altered their styles subtly with Miles' increasing popularity.

Nat Adderley started in a Dizzy bag but now is seasoned with Miles. He is a facile and irrepressible player in search of a truly personal style. Johnny Coles has some of Miles' languor and feeling for space, peppered with occasional humor. The noise about Chet Baker has died down; in retrospect he was neither as good as was once claimed nor as negligible as now felt. If he gets himself together he may yet come through. The little known Webster Young is a sensitive Miles disciple of promise. There are among modern trumpeters several more who stand by themselves.

Most important of these is the greatly gifted Thad Jones, who prefers to stay with Basie but could scare a lot of trumpeters if he ever decided to come out swinging. Joe Wilder is sweet-toned and sensitive. Phil Sunkel is a modernist influenced by Bix Beiderbecke who doesn't play often enough to do more than indicate rare gifts. The late Sonny Berman was an emerging original talent. Two gifted, sensitive trumpeters seemingly incapable of sustained work habits, which is a pity, are Tony Fruscella and Don Joseph.

Doc Severinsen is an extremely competent musician who works so many different gigs that it is difficult to determine what his true style is. Don Ferarra is the only trumpeter who has been affected by the climate of Lennie Tristano's music. Ray Copeland's great gifts have never been fully exposed.

Maynard Ferguson's technical accomplishments overshadow his abilities in a strictly musical vein, which are not inconsiderable. Shorty Rogers isn't playing much these days and it is doubtful if he ever did. Basie's Sonny Cohn is a fine original player who doesn't get enough solo space. Gene Roland, best known as an arranger, and now specializing in the mellophonium with Kenton, is a highly original and attractive trumpet stylist.

Of the up-and-coming youngsters, Ted Curson seems well on the way towards finding a style of his own—not an easy thing these days. Freddie Hubbard, too, is searching—the equipment is there. Booker Little is very gifted and not afraid of trying. Don Ellis' work with George Russell, and more recently on his own, is bright and extremely interesting. Bobby Bradford, Ornette Coleman's new man, seems to think about what he plays, which is refreshing. Willie Thomas has power and guts. Chuck Mangione, just 20, may be a comer.

The future of the trumpet in jazz seems well assured, but if the kiddies want to catch up with the grand old men, from Pops on down, and make the horn boss once more, it will take some hard work and clear thinking. For one thing, it might be well for young trumpeters to consider sound—not one of them can hold a candle there to Joe Thomas.

And then there is the problem of overblowing. Some of the young cats, we're sorry to predict, won't last very long unless they learn the basic fundamentals of proper embouchure. There are few bands today, so it is difficult to acquire discipline. Bands also demand varieties of timbre and dynamics—a problem not properly solved by shoving a mute in the horn.

There was a day, the day of classic swing, when it was fairly easy to tell one trumpet player from another—even though most of them were influenced by the same man. Everybody seemed to have a little something of his own in there.

God bless the child that's got his own. ●

The original Cotton Club in the Thirties, where Duke Ellington and Cab Calloway played to mostly white patrons coming "uptown." (Orrin Keepnews photograph)

III
The Golden Age

Poster for Louis Armstrong's first postwar group at Carnegie Hall, about 1946. (Courtesy of Lucille Armstrong)

Photographer Bill Gottlieb caught this rainy night on
"Swing Street": 52nd Street between Fifth and Sixth avenues
in the early Forties. (Institute of Jazz Studies photograph)

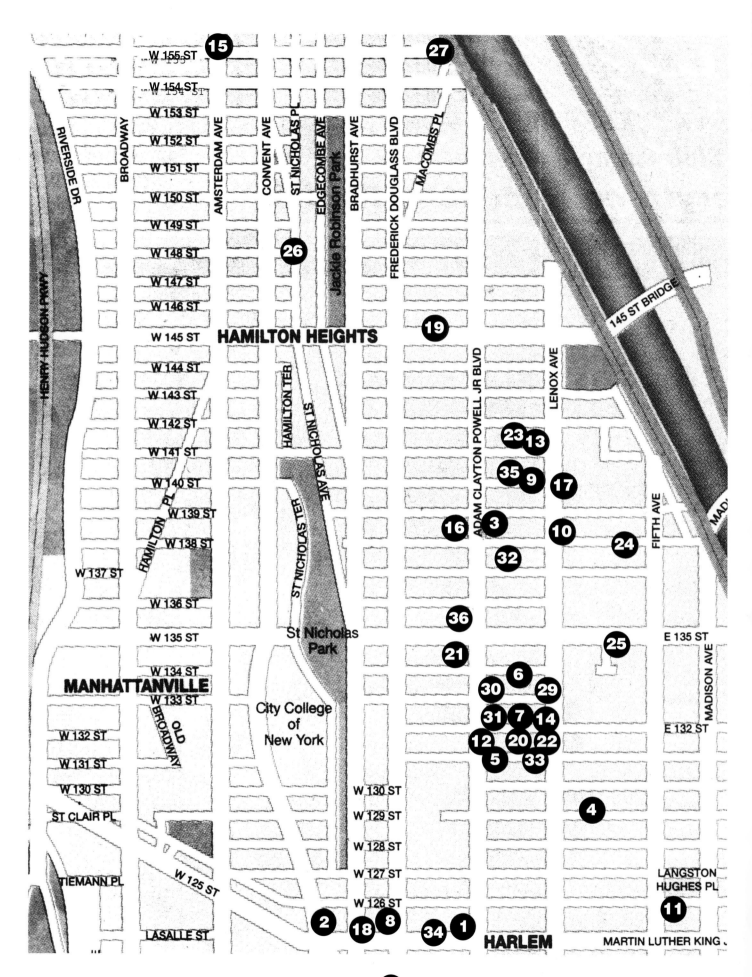

(1) Alhambra Ballroom, 2110 7th Ave. 1929-1945. Opened in 1929 with 15 bands.

(2) Apollo Theater, 253 W. 125 St. 1920s to present. Stage shows included big bands until the 1960s. Continues today with bands about once a month, mostly soul, rock.

(3) Bamboo Inn, 2389 7th Ave. Opened 1923. Bands included Chick Webb's. Closed by fire in 1927. Reopened as Dunbar Palace in 1930 with Fletcher Henderson's Orchestra. Popular Harlem dance spot for many years.

(4) Bamville Club, 65 W. 129 St. 1920-1930. Shrimp Jones headed a band with Coleman Hawkins and Kaiser Marshall, which was taken over by Fletcher Henderson and moved downtown. Next came Elmer Snowden's band. In 1924 a farewell party was held for Sam Wooding's band (Tommy Ladnier, Gene Sedric, Garvin Bushell et al.) just before it went to Europe in 1925. Snowden came back as house band with Bubber Miley , Harry White and Bill (Count) Basie.

(5) Band Box, 161 W. 131 St. Mostly rehearsal rooms. Popular spot for jamming.

(6) Barron's (Wilkins') Club, 198 W. 134 St. Opened in 1915 at 2259 7th Ave., then moved. Luckey Roberts was first house pianist; regulars also included James P. Johnson, Willie "the Lion" Smith and the Washingtonians (with Duke Ellington).

(7) Basie's Lounge, 2245 7th Ave. 1955 onward. Mostly organ trios and small groups. Basie was often seen here when not working on the road.

(8) Braddock Bar, 2342 8th Ave. A bar of great popularity, due to its location at Eighth Ave. and 126th St. ("Sin Street.")

(9) Brittwood Bar & Grill, 594 Lenox Ave. 1932-1941. Many good bands played here during the swing era.

(10) Capitol Palace, 575 Lenox Ave. 1922-1950. Large downstairs room, one of Harlem's first cabarets to feature jazz.

(11) Celebrity Club, 35 East 125 St. Opened in 1935. Large basement space, called Club Selma in the old days, when the neighborhood was still mostly white. For many years Buddy Tate has headed the house band. Dickie Wells frequently appeared.

(12) Connie's Inn, 2221 7th Ave. 1921-1940. Large downstairs cabaret opened as the Shuffle Inn in 1921 with Wilbur Sweatman's Rhythm Kings. One of the three biggest cabarets in Harlem in the late Twenties (with the Cotton Club and Small's Paradise). By 1929 Armstrong had played here with Carroll Dickerson's band. Fats Waller premiered "Ain't Misbehavin'" and "Black and Blue." The Fletcher Henderson band made this its home base briefly. By 1933 Connie's moved downtown; old location renamed Harlem Club, and then Ubangi Club.

(13) Cotton Club, 644 Lenox Ave. Opened as Club Deluxe. Most famous NYC nightclub with largely white clientele until 1935. Bands included Cab Calloway, Duke Ellington and Jimmie Lunceford, plus Louis Armstrong, Ethel Waters.

(14) Covan's Club Morocco, 148 W. 133rd St. 1930-1940. In 1937 guitarist Slim Gaillard and bassist Slam Stewart made their famous song "Flat Foot Floogie." Their scat singing preceded bebop vocalization. It became a national craze and put them both on road to stardom.

(15) Fat Man's Cafe, 450 W. 155th St. 1935 into 1960s. Charles "Fat Man" Turner, a bassist and friend of Fats Waller, started this hangout with Eddie Mallory, at one time Ethel Waters' husband.

(16) Garden of Joy, 7th Ave. at 138th Street. 1918-1924. Open-air, tent-covered dance pavilion atop "Libya Hill." Lit at night with Japanese lanterns. Many piano players met here in afternoons. Acts included Mamie Smith with Bubber Miley, Sidney Bechet, Coleman Hawkins, James P. Johnson.

(17) Golden Gate Ballroom, Lenox Ave. at 142nd Street. 1939-1950. Built to compete with the Savoy Ballroom, but was taken over by the Savoy six months later. Teddy Wilson had the first house band here and innumerable swing bands played here later.

(18) Harlem Opera House, 211 W. 125 St. 1889-1959. Opened as a legitimate opera house by Oscar Hammerstein. Most active period as jazz showplace was mid-Thirties featuring Teddy Hill, Chick Webb, Fletcher Henderson, Don Redman and others. Ella Fitzgerald won her first amateur contest here, not at the Apollo, which did become her launching pad.

(19) Heat Wave, 266 W. 145th St. 1940-1947. This club featured chorus-line floor shows and jam sessions with such (later) stars as "Hot Lips" Page, Ben Webster, Lester Young, Dizzy Gillespie and Charlie Parker.

(20) Hoofer's Club, 2235 Seventh Ave. About 1930 to 1945. Basement of the Lafayette Theater, it was headquarters for the greatest dancers in show biz. The band often had Willie "the Lion" Smith and Benny Carter.

(21) Hotcha Bar & Grill, 2280 7th Ave. 1930-1960. In 1934 Billie Holiday, Billie Daniels and Jimmy Daniels were here. Jam sessions included Roy Eldridge and Chu Berry.

(22) Lafayette Theater, 2227 7th Ave. 1912-1935. Leading Harlem theater into the Thirties, it had 2,000 seats, with segregated sections, before becoming strictly black. Duke Ellington, Fletcher Henderson, Louis Armstrong, Chick Webb and other top acts played there.

(23) Lenox Club, 652 Lenox Ave. 1925-1945. The breakfast dance, starting at 7:00 AM on Sunday morning, was a big feature.

(24) Leroy's (Wilkins') Restaurant, 2220 Fifth Ave. 1910-1923. First cabaret in Harlem to cater to blacks, featuring Willie "the Lion" Smith, James P. Johnson, Count Basie, and a very young Fats Waller.

(25) Lincoln Theater, 58 W. 135th St. 1909 to mid-Sixties. Small at first (under 200 seats,) but expanded in 1915 to a new building. Duke Ellington, Fats Waller, Count Basie, Fletcher Henderson and Don Redman played there.

(26) Luckey's Rendezvous, 773 St. Nicholas Ave. 1940-1950 (formerly Poosepatuck Club 1930-1940). Owner Luckey Roberts was a member of stride piano royalty.

(27) Manhattan Casino, 280 W. 155th St. Opened in 1910. A large hall for more than 5,000 people.

(28) Minton's Playhouse, 210 W. 118 St. Opened in 1938. Famed for jam sessions, it was one of the birthplaces of bop. Located in a dining room of the Hotel Cecil, it was launched by Henry Minton with Teddy Hill as manager. Acts included Thelonious Monk, Charlie Christian, Kenny Clarke, Roy Eldridge, Dizzy Gillespie and Art Blakey.

(29) Monroe's (Clark) Uptown House, 2259 Seventh Ave. 1915 to 1964. See Barron's Exclusive Club (6). Owner Clark Monroe was stabbed to death in front of the exclusive club in 1926. The club was an important incubator of bebop.

(30) Nest Club, 169 W. 133rd St. 1925-1930. Stars were "Tricky Sam" Nanton, Happy Cladwell, Cliff Jackson, Harry Carney, Rex Stewart and Barney Bigard. Gangland atmosphere at times; in 1927 dancer Arthur Bryson was shot in the leg.

(31) Pod & Jerry's (Catagonia Club), 168 W. 133rd St. 1925-1935. Willie "the Lion" Smith was often here; Billie Holiday flopped as a dancer but got her start as a singer here.

(32) Renaissance Casino & Ballroom, 150 W. 138 St. 1915 into the Sixties. It featured gambling, dancing and music. Fletcher Henderson and Chick Webb's bands played, plus Zutty Singleton, Roy Eldridge, Chu Berry and Dickie Wells.

(33) Rhythm Club (Number One), 2235 7th Ave. 1920-1932. Sessions often started after 3:00 AM, and included Louis Armstrong, Sidney Bechet, Fats Waller, Willie "the Lion" Smith, Benny Carter and Johnny Hodges.

(34) Rose Danceland, 209 W. 125th St. 1925-1935. A public ballroom. Stony Spargo was in the first band here in 1927 while the clientele was still all-white.

(35) Savoy Ballroom, 596 Lenox Ave. 1926-1958. "The World's Most Beautiful Ballroom," it opened to a crowd of 5,000 with Fletcher Henderson's Roseland Band (for the night). Battles of bands included Chick Webb vs. Fletcher Henderson, and King Oliver vs. Fess Williams.

(36) Small's Paradise, 2294 7th Ave. 1925-1964. Popular with white patrons, principally for its singing and dancing waiters. In its heyday all the big bands played there; one of the Big Three clubs, along with Cotton Club and Connie's Inn.

(37) Ubangi Club, 2221 7th Ave. (see Connie's Inn)

This (partial) club information is based on the memories and research of George Hoefer, as told in the marvelous Columbia Records album "The Sound of Harlem" produced in 1964 by Frank Driggs.
George Hoefer wrote "The Hot Box," a collectors column in Down Beat for many years. In 1958 he came to New York as *Down Beat*'s New York man and we were close until he died tragically after falling down a flight of stairs on a ferry.

—C.G.

THE GOLDEN AGE/time past

Manners and Morals at Minton's, 1941: The Setting for a Revolution

by Ralph Ellison

That which we do is what we are. That which we remember is, more often than not, that which we would like to have been; or that which we hope to be. Thus our memory and our identity are ever at odds; our history ever a tall tale told by inattentive idealists.

IT HAS BEEN A LONG TIME NOW, and not many remember how it was in the old days; not really. Not even those who were there to see and hear as it happened, who were pressed in the crowds beneath the dim rosy lights of the bar in the smoke-veiled room, and who shared, night after night, the mysterious spell created by the talk, the laughter, grease paint, powder, perfume, sweat, alcohol and food—all blended and simmering, like a stew on the restaurant range, and brought to a sustained moment of elusive meaning by the timbres and accents of musical instruments locked in passionate recitative. It has been too long now, some 17 years.

Above the bandstand there later appeared a mural depicting a group of jazzmen holding a jam session in a narrow Harlem bedroom. While an exhausted girl with shapely legs sleeps on her stomach in a big brass bed, they bend to their music in a quiet concatenation of unheard sound: a trumpeter, a guitarist, a clarinetist, a drummer; their only audience a small, cockeared dog. The clarinetist is white. The guitarist strums with an enigmatic smile. The trumpet is muted. The barefooted drummer, beating a folded newspaper with whisk-brooms in lieu of a drum, stirs the eye's ear like a blast of brasses in a midnight street. A bottle of port rests on a dresser, but it, like the girl, is ignored. The artist, Charles Graham, adds mystery to, as well as illumination within,

the scene by having them play by the light of a kerosene lamp. The painting, executed in a harsh documentary style reminiscent of W.P.A. art, conveys a feeling of musical effort caught in timeless and unrhetorical suspension, the sad remoteness of a scene observed through a wall of crystal.

Except for the lamp, the room might well have been one in the Hotel Cecil, the building in 118th Street in which Minton's Playhouse is located, and although painted in 1946, sometime after the revolutionary doings there had begun, the mural should help recall the old days vividly. But the decor of the place has been changed and now it is covered, most of the time, by draperies. These require a tricky skill of those who would draw them aside. And even then there will still only be the girl who must sleep forever unhearing, and the men who must forever gesture the same soundless tune. Besides, the time it celebrates is dead and gone and perhaps not even those who came when it was still fresh and new remember those days as they were.

Neither do those remember who knew Henry Minton, who gave the place his name. Nor those who shared in the noisy lostness of New York the rediscovered community of the feasts, evocative of home, of South, of good times, the best and most unself-conscious of times, created by the generous portions of Negro-American cuisine—the hash, grits, fried chicken, the ham-seasoned vegetables, the hot biscuits and rolls and the free whiskey—with which, each Monday night, Teddy Hill honored the entire cast of current Apollo Theatre shows. They were gathered here from all parts of America and they broke bread together and there was a sense of good feeling and promise, but what shape the fulfilled promise would take they did not know, and few except the more restless of the younger musicians even questioned. Yet it was an exceptional moment and the world was swinging with change.

Most of them, black and white alike, were hardly aware of where they were or what time it was; nor did they wish to be. They thought of Minton's as a sanctuary, where in an atmosphere blended of nostalgia and a music-and-drink-lulled suspension of time they could retreat from the wartime tensions of the town. The meaning of time-present was not their concern; thus when they try to tell it now the meaning escapes them.

For they were caught up in events which made that time exceptionally and uniquely then, and which brought, among the other changes which have reshaped the world, a momentous modulation into a new key of musical sensibility; in brief, a revolution in culture.

So how can they remember? Even in swiftly changing America there are few such moments, and at best Americans give but a limited attention to history. Too much happens too rapidly, and before we can evaluate it, or exhaust its meaning or pleasure, there is something new to concern us. Ours is the tempo of the motion picture, not that of the still camera, and we waste experience as we wasted the forest. During the time it was happening the sociologists were concerned with the riots, unemployment and industrial tensions of the time, the historians with the onsweep of the war; and the critics and most serious students of culture found this area of our national life of little interest. So it was left to those who came to Minton's out of the needs of feeling, and when the moment was past no one retained more than a fragment of its happening. Afterward the very effort to put the fragments together transformed them—so that in place of true memory they now summon to mind pieces of legend. They retell the stories as they have been told and written, glamorized, inflated, made neat and smooth, with all incomprehensible details vanished along with most of the wonder—not how it was as they themselves knew it.

It was jumping with good times

When asked how it was back then, back in the Forties, they will smile, then frowning with the puzzlement of one attempting to recall the details of a pleasant but elu-

From left to right, Thelonious Monk, Howard McGhee, Roy Eldridge and Teddy Hill at Minton's Playhouse in 1948. Hill, a one-time bandleader, was the manager of Minton's, where Monk was the house pianist during the crucial years. (Bill Gottlieb photograph)

Charlie Parker, sax, and Miles Davis, trumpet, taking jazz into bebop. (Bill Gottlieb/Institute of Jazz Studies photograph)

sive dream, they'll say: "Oh, man, it was a hell of a time! A wailing time! Things were jumping, you couldn't get in here for the people. The place was packed with celebrities. Park Avenue, man! Big people in show business, college professors along with the pimps and their women. And college boys and girls. Everybody came. You know how the old words to the 'Basin Street Blues' used to go before Sinatra got hold of it? Basin Street is the street where the dark and the light folks meet—that's what I'm talking about. That was Minton's, man. It was a place where everybody could come to be entertained because it was a place that was jumping with good times."

Or some will tell you that it was here that Dizzy Gillespie found his own trumpet voice; that here Kenny Clarke worked out the patterns of his drumming style; where Charlie Christian played out the last creative and truly satisfying moments of his brief life, his New York home; where Charlie Parker built the monument of his art; where Thelonious Monk formulated his contribution to the chordal progressions and the hide-and-seek melodic methods of modern jazz. And they'll call such famous names as Lester Young and Ben Webster, Coleman Hawkins; or Fats Waller, who came here in the after-hours stillness of the early morning to compose. They'll tell you that Benny Goodman, Art Tatum, Count Basie, and Lena Horne would drop in to join in the fun; that it was here that George Shearing played on his first

night in the U.S.; or Tony Scott's great love of the place; and they'll repeat all the stories of how, when and by whom the word "bebop" was coined here—but, withal, few actually remember, and these leave much unresolved.

Usually, music gives resonance to memory (and Minton's was a hotbed of jazz), but not the music then in the making here. It was itself a texture of fragments, repetitive, nervous, not fully formed; its melodic lines underground, secret and taunting; its riffs jeering—"Salt peanuts! Salt peanuts!" Its timbres flat or shrill, with a minimum of thrilling vibrato. Its rhythms were out of stride and seemingly arbitrary, its drummers frozen-faced introverts dedicated to chaos. And in it the steady flow of memory, desire and defined experience summed up by the traditional jazz beat and blues mood seemed swept like a great river from its old, deep bed. We know better now, and recognize the old moods in the new sounds, but what we know is that which was then becoming. For most of those who gathered here, the enduring meaning of the great moment at Minton's took place off to the side, beyond the range of attention, like a death blow glimpsed from the corner of the eye, the revolutionary rumpus sounding like a series of flubbed notes blasting the talk with discord. So that the events which made Minton's Minton's arrived in conflict and ran their course, then the heat was gone and all that is left to mark its passage is the controlled fury of the music itself, sealed pure and irrevocable, banalities and excellences alike, in the early recordings; or swept along by our restless quest for the new, to be diluted in more recent styles, the best of it absorbed like drops of fully distilled technique, mood and emotion into the great stream of jazz.

Left also to confuse our sense of what happened is the word "bop," hardly more than a nonsense-syllable, by which the music synthesized at Minton's came to be known. A most inadequate word which does little, really, to help us remember. A word which throws up its hands in clownish self-depreciation before all the complexity of sound and rhythm and self-assertive passion which it pretends to name; a mask-word for the charged ambiguities of the new sound, hiding the serious face of art.

Nor does it help that so much has come to pass in the meantime. There have been two hot wars and that which continues, called "cold." And the unknown young men who brought a new edge to the sound of jazz and who scrambled the rhythms of those who used the small clear space at Minton's for dancing are no longer so young or unknown; indeed, they are referred to now by nickname in even the remotest of places. And in Paris and Munich and Tokyo they'll tell you the details of how, after years of trying, "Dizzy" (meaning John Birks Gillespie) vanquished "Roy" (meaning Roy Eldridge) during a jam session at Minton's, to become thereby the new king of trumpeters. Or how, later, while jetting over the world on the blasts of his special tilt-belled horn, he jammed with a snake charmer in Pakistan. "Sent the bloody cobra, man," they'll tell you in London's Soho. So their subsequent fame has blurred the sharp, ugly lines of their rebellion even in the memories of those who found them most strange and distasteful.

What's more, our memory of some of the more brilliant young men has been touched by the aura of death, and we feel guilt that the fury of their passing was the price paid for the art they left us to enjoy unscathed: Charlie Christian, burned out by tuberculosis like a guitar consumed in a tenement fire; Fats Navarro, wrecked by the tensions and needling temptations of his orgiastic trade, a big man physically as well as musically, shrunken to nothingness; and, most notably of all, Charlie Parker called "Bird," now deified, worshiped and studied and, like any fertility god, mangled by his admirers and imitators, who coughed up his life and died—as incredibly as the leopard which Hemingway tells us was found "dried and frozen" near the summit of Mount Kilimanjaro—in the hotel suite of a Baroness. (Nor has anyone explained what a "yardbird" was seeking at that social altitude, though we know that ideally anything is possible within democracy, and we know quite well that upper-class Europeans were seriously interested in jazz long before Newport became hospitable.) All this is too much for memory; the dry facts are too easily lost in legend and glamour. (With jazz we are yet not in the age of history, but linger in that of folklore.) We know for certain only that the strange sounds which they and their fellows threw against the hum and buzz of vague signification that seethed in the drinking crowd at Minton's

and which, like disgruntled conspirators meeting fatefully to assemble the random parts of a bomb, they joined here and beat and blew into a new jazz style— these sounds we know now to have become the cliches, the technical exercises and the standard of achievement not only for fledgling musicians all over the United States, but for Dutchmen and Swedes, Italians and Frenchmen, Germans and Belgians, and even Japanese. All these, in places which came to mind during the Minton days only as points where the war was in progress and where one might soon be sent to fight and die, are now spotted with young men who study the discs on which the revolution hatched in Minton's is preserved with all the intensity that young American painters bring to the works, say, of Kandinsky, Picasso and Klee. Surely this is an odd swing of the cultural tide. Yet Stravinsky, Webern, and Berg notwithstanding, or more recently, Boulez or Stockhausen—such young men (many of them excellent musicians in the highest European tradition) find in the music mad articulate at Minton's some key to a fuller freedom of self-realization. Indeed, for many young Europeans the developments which took place here and the careers of those who brought it about have become the latest episodes in the great American epic. They collect the recordings and thrive on the legends as eagerly, perhaps, as young Americans.

This shrine, too, has its relic

Today the bartenders at Minton's will tell you how they come fresh off the ships or planes, bringing their brightly expectant and—in this Harlem atmosphere— startlingly innocent European faces, to buy drinks and stand looking about for the source of the mystery. They try to reconcile the quiet reality of the place with the events which fired, at such long range, their imaginations. They come as to a shrine; as we to the Louvre, Notre Dame or St. Peter's; as young Americans hurry to the Café Flore, the Deux Magots, the Rotonde or the Café du Dôme in Paris. For some years now, they have been coming to ask, with all the solemnity of pilgrims inquiring of a sacred relic, to see the nicotine-stained amplifier which Teddy Hill provided for Charlie Christian's guitar. And this is quite proper, for every shrine should have its relic.

Perhaps Minton's has more meaning for European jazz fans than for Americans, even for those who regularly went there. Certainly it has a different meaning. For them it is associated with those continental cafés in which great changes, political and artistic, have been plotted; it is to modern jazz what the Café Voltaire in Zurich is to the Dadaist phase of modern literature and painting. Few of those who visited Harlem during the Forties would associate it so, but there is a context of meaning in which Minton's and the musical activities which took place there can be meaningfully placed.

Jazz, for all the insistence of the legends, has been far more closely associated with cabarets and dance halls than with brothels, and it was these which provided both the employment for the musicians and an audience initiated and aware of the overtones of the music; which knew the language of riffs, the unstated meanings of the blues idiom, and the dance steps developed from and complementary to its rhythms. And in the beginning it was in the Negro dance hall and night club that jazz was most completely a part of a total cultural expression; and in which it was freest and most satisfying, both for musicians and for those in whose lives it played a major role. As a night club in a Negro community then, Minton's was part of a national pattern.

But in the old days Minton's was far more than this; it was also a rendezvous for musicians. As such, and although it was not formally organized, it goes back historically to the first New York center of Negro musicians, the Clef Club. Organized in 1910, during the start of the great migration of Negroes northward, by James Reese Europe, the director whom Irene Castle credits with having invented the fox trot, the Clef Club was set up on West 53rd Street to serve as a meeting place and booking office for Negro musicians and entertainers. Here wage scales were regulated, musical styles and techniques worked out, and entertainment was supplied for such establishments as Recot's and Delmonico's, and for such producers as Florenz Ziegfeld and Oscar Hammerstein. Later, when Harlem evolved into a Negro section, a similar function was served by the Rhythm Club, located then in the old Lafayette Theatre building on 132nd Street and Seventh Avenue. Henry Minton, a former saxophonist and officer of the Rhythm Club, became the first Negro delegate to Local 802 of the American Federation of Musicians and was thus doubly aware of the needs, artistic as well as economic, of jazzmen. He was generous with loans, was fond of food himself and, as an old acquaintance recalled, "loved to put a pot on the range" to share with unemployed friends. Naturally when he opened Minton's Playhouse many musicians made it their own.

Henry Minton also provided, as did the Clef and Rhythm clubs, a necessity more important to jazz musicians than food: a place in which to hold their interminable jam sessions. And it is here that Minton's becomes most important to the development of modern jazz. It is here, too, that it joins up with all the countless rooms, private and public, in which jazzmen have worked out the secrets of their craft. Today jam sessions are offered as entertainment by night clubs and on radio and television, and some are quite exciting; but what is seen and heard is only one aspect of the true jam session: the "cutting session," or contest of improvisational skill and physical endurance between two or more musicians. But the jam session is far more than this, and when carried out by musicians, in the privacy of small rooms (as in the mural at Minton's) or in such places as Hallie Richardson's shoeshine parlor in Oklahoma City— where I first heard Lester Young jamming in a shine chair, his head thrown back, his horn even then outthrust, his feet working on the footrests, as he played with and against Lem Johnson, Ben Webster (this was 1929) and other members of the old Blue Devils orchestra—or during the after hours in Piney Brown's old Sunset Club in Kansas City; in such places as these with only musicians and jazzmen present, then the jam session is revealed as the jazzman's true academy.

It is here that he learns tradition, group techniques and style. For although since the Twenties many jazzmen have had conservatory training and were well-grounded in formal theory and instrumental technique, when we approach jazz we are entering quite a different sphere of training. Here it is more meaningful to speak, not of courses of study, of grades and degrees, but of apprenticeship, ordeals, initiation ceremonies, of rebirth. For after the jazzman has learned the fundamentals of his instrument and the traditional techniques of jazz—the intonations, the mute work, manipulation of timbre, the body of traditional styles—he must then "find himself," must be reborn, must find, as it were, his soul. All this through achieving that subtle identification between his instrument and his deepest drives which will allow him to express his own unique ideas and his own unique voice. He must achieve, in short, his self-determined identity.

In this his instructors are his fellow musicians, especially the acknowledged masters, and his recognition of manhood depends upon their acceptance of his ability as having reached a standard which is all the more difficult for not having been rigidly codified. This does not depend upon his ability to simply hold a job but upon his power to express an individuality in tone. Nor is his status ever unquestioned, for the health of jazz and the unceasing attraction which it holds for the musicians themselves lies in the ceaseless warfare for mastery and recognition—not among the general public, though commercial success is not spurned, but among their artistic peers. And even the greatest can never rest on past accomplishments for, as with the fast guns of the old West, there is always someone waiting in a jam session to blow him literally, not only down, but into shame and discouragement.

By making his club hospitable to jam sessions even to the point that customers who were not musicians were crowded out, Henry Minton provided a retreat, a homogeneous community where a collectivity of common experience could find continuity and meaningful expression. Thus the stage was set for the birth of bop.

A musical dueling ground

In 1941 Mr. Minton handed over his management to Teddy Hill, the saxophonist and former band leader, and Hill turned the Playhouse into a musical dueling ground. Not only did he continue Minton's policies, he expanded them. It was Hill who established the Monday Celebrity Nights, the house band which included such members from his own disbanded orchestra as Kenny Clark, Dizzy Gillespie, along with Thelonious Monk, sometimes with Joe Guy, and, later, Charlie Christian and Charlie Parker; and it was Hill who allowed the musicians free rein to play whatever they liked. Perhaps no other club except Clarke Monroe's Uptown House was so permissive, and with the hospitality extended to musicians of all schools the news spread swiftly. Minton's became the focal point for musicians all over the country.

Herman Pritchard, who presided over the bar in the old

days, tells us that every time they came, "Lester Young and Ben Webster used to tie up in battle like dogs in the road. They'd fight on those saxophones until they were tired out, then they'd put in long distance calls to their mothers, both of whom lived in Kansas City, and tell them about it."

And most of the masters of jazz came either to observe or to participate and be influenced and listen to their own discoveries transformed; and the aspiring stars sought to win their approval, as the younger tenor men tried to win the esteem of Coleman Hawkins. Or they tried to vanquish them in jamming contests as Gillespie is said to have outblown his idol, Roy Eldridge. It was during this period that Eddie "Lockjaw" Davis underwent an ordeal of jeering rejection until finally he came through as an admired tenor man.

In the perspective of time we now see that what was happening at Minton's was a continuing symposium of jazz, a summation of all the styles, personal and traditional, of jazz. Here it was possible to hear its resources of technique, ideas, harmonic structure, melodic phrasing and rhythmical possibilities explored more thoroughly than was ever possible before. It was also possible to hear the first attempts toward a conscious statement of the sensibility of the younger generation of musicians as they worked out the techniques, structures and rhythmical patterns with which to express themselves. Part of this was arbitrary, a revolt of the younger against the established stylists; part of it was inevitable. For jazz had reached a crisis and new paths were certain to be searched for and found. An increasing number of the younger men were formally trained, and the post-Depression developments in the country had made for quite a break between their experience and that of the older men. Many were even of a different physical build. Often they were quiet and of a reserve which contrasted sharply with the exuberant and outgoing lyricism of the older men, and they were intensely concerned that their identity as Negroes place no restriction upon the music they played or the manner in which they used their talent. They were concerned, they said, with art, not entertainment. Especially were they resentful of Louis Armstrong whom (confusing the spirit of his music with his clowning) they considered an Uncle Tom.

Another misconception: How to be truly free

But they, too, some of them, had their own myths and misconceptions: That theirs was the only generation of Negro musicians who listened to or enjoyed the classics; that to be truly free they must act exactly the opposite of what white people might believe, rightly or wrongly, a Negro to be; that the performing artist can be completely and absolutely free of the obligations of the entertainer, and that they could play jazz with dignity only by frowning and treating the audience with aggressive contempt; and that to be in control, artistically and personally, one must be so cool as to quench one's own human fire.

Nor should we overlook the despair which must have swept Minton's before the technical mastery, the tonal authenticity, the authority and the fecundity of imagination of such men as Hawkins, Young, Goodman, Tatum, Teagarden, Ellington and Waller. Despair, after all, is ever an important force in revolutions.

They were also responding to the non-musical pressures affecting jazz. It was a time of big bands, and the greatest prestige and economic returns were falling outside the Negro community—often to leaders whose popularity grew from the compositions and arrangements of Negroes—to white instrumentalists whose only originality lay in the enterprise with which they rushed to market with some Negro musician's hard-won style. Still there was no policy of racial discrimination at Minton's. Indeed, it was very much like those Negro cabarets of the Twenties and Thirties in which a megaphone was placed on the piano so that anyone with the urge could sing a blues. Nevertheless, the inside-dopesters will tell you that the "changes" or chord progressions and the melodic inversions worked out by the creators of bop sprang partially from their desire to create a jazz which could not be so easily imitated and exploited by white musicians to whom the market was more open simply because of their whiteness. They wished to receive credit for what they created, and besides, it was easier to "get rid of the trash" who crowded the bandstand with inept playing and thus make room for the real musicians, whether white or black. Nevertheless, white musicians like Tony Scott, Remo Palmieri and Al Haig who were part of the development at Minton's became so by passing a test of musicianship, sincerity and temperament. Later, it is said, the boppers became engrossed in solving the musical problems which they set themselves. Except for a few yet sympathetic older musicians it was they who best knew the promise of the Minton moment, and it was they, caught like the rest in all the complex forces of American life which comes to focus in jazz, who made the most of it. Now the tall tales told as history must feed on the results of the efforts. ●

SON
CHARLES PARKER, JR.
AUG. 29, 1920 - MAR. 23, 1955

Charlie Parker's grave marker and saxophone case. (Art Kane photograph from January 1959 *Esquire)*

Charlie "Bird" Parker

CHARLIE PARKER DIED at the age of 34 in 1955, one of the wonders of 20th century music. Like his all but interchangeable spiritual brother, Dylan Thomas, who died a year earlier, Parker was labyrinthine. He was a tragic figure who helplessly consumed himself, and at the same time he was a demon who presided over the wreckage of his life. He was an original and fertile musician who had reached the edge of self-parody, an irresistibly attractive man who bit almost every hand that fed him. He lived outside the pale of his own times, yet he indirectly presaged, in his drives and fierce independence, the coming of Malcolm X and Eldridge Cleaver. And he was, albeit succored by a slavish cult, largely unknown during his life.

Parker was born in a Kansas City suburb to a knockabout vaudevillian, Charles Parker, and a local 18-year-old, Addie Boyley (or Bayley). When he was 8 or 9 his parents moved to Kansas City proper, and when he was 11 his father, who had become a Pullman chef, disappeared almost completely from his life. Grammar school went well, but after he had spent two years in high school as a freshman he dropped out. By the time he was 16 his life had already begun to accelerate dangerously. He had got married, he had become a professional, self-taught alto saxophonist, he was a member of the musicians' union, he was a neophyte figure of the teeming Kansas City night world, and he had begun using drugs. When he was 18, he went to Chicago and then to New York, where he became a dishwasher in a Harlem restaurant and fell under the sway of its pianist, Art Tatum. He also played in a couple of taxi-dance-hall bands and jammed tentatively around Harlem. In 1939, he went home and joined Harlan Leonard's band, then Jay McShann's Kansas City band. John Lewis, then a student at the University of New Mexico, has noted the effect that McShann's radio broadcasts had on him: "The altos' solos on those broadcasts opened up a whole new world of music for me. I'd known Jay McShann from the time he used to barnstorm in the Southwest . . . but the alto saxophone was new and years ahead of anybody in jazz.

He was into a whole new system of sound and time. The emcee didn't announce his name [and] I didn't learn it was Charlie Parker until after the war." The effect of McShann broadcasts on the black members of Charlie Barnet's band was no less electric. Somebody played 10 spectacular choruses of "Cherokee" during a McShann broadcast they heard backstage at the Newark theater where they were working, and when their show was over they rushed to the Savoy, found out who the soloist was by asking McShann to play the tune again, and took Parker out to dinner. Parker quit McShann in 1942 and, after a period of rootlessness and semi-starvation in Harlem, joined Earl Hines' big band, a crazy, warring group made up almost equally of old-line musicians and young beboppers. He then passed briefly through the brilliant, short-lived avant-garde big band led by Billy Eckstine, and by 1945 had settled down with the many small bands he would lead and/or record with until his death.

He had also settled, irreversibly, into the role of Gargantua. He was divorced and remarried when he was 22, and the new marriage was, as far as anyone knows, the last legal liaison of the four he had. He lived in hotels and boarding houses. He had become a baffling and extraordinary drug addict—one who, unlike most addicts, was also a glutton, an alcoholic, and a man of insatiable sexual needs. He would eat 20 hamburgers in a row, drink sixteen double whiskeys in a couple of hours, and go to bed with two women at once. At times he went berserk and would throw his saxophone out a hotel window or walk into the ocean in a brand-new suit. His sense of humor was equally askew. Early one morning he took a cab to trumpeter Kenny Dorham's apartment (Parker spent a good part of his life in cabs, using them as his office, as rendezvous points, as places to sleep, as compact, mobile fortresses), got Dorham out of bed, asked for a light, and went on his way. In 1947 he collapsed and spent six months in a state mental hospital in California. (He had gone to the coast the year before with the first bebop band to travel west of the

Mississippi; it also included Dizzy Gillespie, Al Haig, Milt Jackson and Ray Brown.) During his stay in the state hospital, where his astonishing recuperative powers soon became evident, Parker was cared for by a doctor who was also a fan. Ross Russell, Parker's first biographer, has set down the doctor's thoughts about him: "A man living from moment to moment. A man living for the pleasure principle, music, food, sex, drugs, kicks, his personality arrested at an infantile level. A man with almost no feeling of guilt and only the smallest, most atrophied nub of conscience. Except for his music, a potential member of the army of psychopaths supplying the populations of prisons and mental institutions. But with Charlie Parker it was the music factor that makes all the difference. That's really the only reason we're interested in him. The reason we're willing to stop our own lives and clean up his messes. People like Charlie require somebody like that."

Parker's wild excesses never seemed—at least until the very end of his life—to interfere with his music. It is now agreed among jazz musicians that drugs dislocate and dilute their improvisations; it was just the other way with Parker. The only times he could not function were when he was strung out and needed a fix. His style had matured completely by the time he made his first small-band records, in 1945. Parker's playing did not, as has often been claimed, spring magically from the virgin soil of the Southwest. Other musicians had a hand in its creation. When he was a teenager, Parker bathed night after night in the unique, rocking music of Kansas City. No matter where he went, he heard the blues—the heavy, sad, windblown blues of Hot Lips Page, Pete Johnson, Joe Turner, Herschel Evans and Buddy Tate, and the light, rolling, new-coin blues of Count Basie and Lester Young. Young became his idol, and when Parker first went on the road he took along all Young's records and committed his solos to memory. Parker also worked in Kansas City with Buster Smith, a saxophonist whose style bears a speaking likeness to Parker's early playing. He picked up technical advice from a well-trained local band leader, Tommy Douglas, and when he got to New York he studied Art Tatum, who unwittingly showed him how to play at lightning speeds and how to devise wholly new harmonies. Some of these early wingings into the blues were disastrous. When he was 15 or 16, he blustered his way onto the bandstand during one of the tough, endless Kansas City jam sessions, and, trying some fancy stuff in a roaring "I Got Rhythm," lost his way. The drummer, Jo Jones, stopped playing, grabbed a cymbal, and threw it on the floor at Parker's feet—he had been "gonged off" the stand. From such embarrassing acorns Parkers grow.

Parker had a unique tone; no other saxophonist has achieved as *human* a sound. It could be edgy, and even sharp. (He used the hardest and most technically difficult of the reeds.) It could be smooth and big and somber. It could be soft and buzzing. Unlike most saxophonists of his time, who took their cue from Coleman Hawkins, he used almost no vibrato; when he did, it was only a flutter, a murmur. The blues lived in every room of his style, and he was one of the most striking and affecting blues improvisers we have had. His slow blues had a preaching, admonitory quality. He would begin a solo with a purposely stuttering four-or-five-note announcement, pause for effect, repeat the phrase, bending its last note into silence, and then turn the phrase around backward and abruptly slip sidewise into double time, zigzag up the scale, circle around quickly at the top, and plummet down, the notes falling somewhere between silence and sound. (Parker was a master of dynamics and of the dramatic use of silence.) Another pause, and he would begin his second chorus with a dreaming, three-note figure, each of the notes running into the next but each held in prolonged, hymn-like fashion. Taken from an unexpected part of the chord, they would slip out in slow motion. He would shatter this brief spell by inserting two or three short arpeggios, disconnected and broken off, then he would float into a backpedaling half-time and shoot into another climbing-and-falling double-time run, in which he would dart in and out of nearby keys. He would pause, then close the chorus with an amen figure resembling his opening announcement.

But there was another, quite different Parker—the Parker who played extraordinary slow ballads, such as "Embraceable You" and "Don't Blame Me" and "White Christmas." Here he went several steps further than he did with the blues. He literally dismantled a composer's song and put together a structure ten times as complex. New chords and harmonies appeared, along with new melodic lines that moved high above the unsounded original. (He would, however, always inject pieces of the melody as signposts for the listener.) He could do anything he liked with time, and in his ballads he would lag behind the beat, float easily along on it, or leap ahead of it; he would do things with time that no one had yet thought of and that no one has yet surpassed. His ballads were dense visions, glimpses into an unknown musical dimension. Although they were perfectly structured, they seemed to have no beginnings and no endings; each was simply another of the fragmentary visions that stirred and maddened his mind. Thus his 1947 version of "Embraceable You" (first take), which, so intense, so beautiful, remains one of the sensations of music. Parker's fast 32-bar tunes were meteoric. He used multitudes of notes but never a superfluous one. His runs exploded like light spilling out of an opened doorway. His rhythms had a muscled, chattering density. He crackled and roared.

Parker turned the world of jazz around, and the effects are still felt. One hears him in the work of such saxophonists as Charlie McPherson and Phil Woods and Sonny Stitt and Sonny Criss, and less openly in the playing of Sonny Rollins and John Coltrane and Ornette Coleman. One hears him in almost every guitarist, pianist, trumpeter, bassist, drummer and trombonist over 40, and he is still audible in the instrumentalists of the present generation, although most of them may not know it. But Parker's legion of admirers have, by and large, missed his main point. He widened the improvisational boundaries of time and harmony and melody, but he did not reject what had come before him, for at

Charlie Parker playing at the Three Deuces Club, New York, 1947. (Frank Driggs collection)

bottom he was a conservative who found new ways of expressing the same things that King Oliver and Louis Armstrong and Sidney Bechet had said earlier. His admirers donned his form and ignored his content. Countless players appeared who used a thousand notes in every chorus, who had hard, smart tones, and who indulged in fancy rhythmic patterns. Yet they side-stepped the emotions that governed all that Parker played. The ironic results were the hard-boppers of the late Fifties and the cul-de-sac avant-garde of the early Sixties. Fortunately, most of this happened after he was dead, so he did not suffer the horrors that Lester Young endured during the last decade of his life—the musical claustrophobia of hearing oneself reproduced again and again in the work of almost every young saxophonist and of knowing, at the same time, that your own powers have dwindled to the point that the new men are playing better than you are.

Planning music at the Monterey Jazz Festival are, left to right, Benny Carter, altoist Willie Smith, Nat "King" Cole, Charlie Parker and organizer Jimmy Lyons. (Jean Bach collection)

For a time after his release from the hospital in California, Parker cooled it. But the pace of his life quickened again, and by the early Fifties it had got completely out of control. He collapsed on the street, he got into fights, he tried to commit suicide. He slept, when he slept at all, on floors or in the bathtubs or in beds of friends. He cadged drinks and he panhandled. His horn was usually in hock and he missed gigs. And at last his playing faltered—he began to imitate himself. One reason was physical; he no longer had the stamina to sustain his brilliant flights. The other was more subtle. Like Jackson Pollock, he felt that he had reached the end of his explorations. The blues and the 32-bar song no longer were challenges. He had, he thought, discovered every chord change, every rhythmic turn, every adventurous harmony. He talked of big orchestral works, and he considered studying with the composers Stefan Wolpe and Edgard Varese.

But there were expectations, and one of them was the famous concert given in May 1953 in Massey Music Hall, in Toronto. On hand with Parker, who arrived without a horn and had to borrow one from a music store, were Dizzy Gillespie, Bud Powell, Charles Mingus and Max Roach. Parker had long had ambivalent feelings about Gillespie. He admired him as a musician, but he resented Gillespie's fame—the story in *Life* about Gillespie and bebop, in which Parker was not even mentioned; the profile of Gillespie written for *The New Yorker* by Richard O. Boyer. Gillespie, though, kept life in sharp focus. Parker was the opposite—a closed, secret, stormy, misshapen figure who continually barricaded himself behind the put-on (using his deepest voice, he announced at the concert that Gillespie's "Salt Peanuts" was by "my worthy constituent"). Gillespie was a chal-

lenge that night, and so was the rhythm section, which played with ferocity and precision. Parker responded, and in "Wee," "Hot House" and "A Night in Tunisia" he soloed with a fire and a brilliance that match anything in his earlier work.

Parker's death was an inevitable mixture of camp, irony and melodrama. He had been befriended by the Baroness Pannonica Koenigswarter, a wealthy, intelligent eccentric who lived in the Stanhope Hotel and drove herself to jazz clubs in a silver Rolls Royce. Her apartment had become a salon for musicians. In March of 1955 Parker secured a gig at George Wein's Storyville in Boston, and on his way out of New York he stopped at the Stanhope to say hello. The baroness offered Parker a drink. To her astonishment, he refused and asked for ice water. His ulcer was acting up, and cold water would, he said, quench its fire. Suddenly he started vomiting blood. The baroness' doctor examined him and said that he would have to go to the hospital at once. He refused, so he was put to bed and given antibiotics. Several days passed, and he seemed to improve. On a Saturday night, he was allowed to sit in the living room and watch Tommy Dorsey's television show. He was in good spirits. During a juggling act involving bricks, which he remembered having seen in Kansas City as a child, he started laughing, choked, and slumped in his chair. He died a minute or two later. At that instant, according to the baroness, she heard a single huge clap of thunder. The official cause of death was labor pneumonia, but Parker had simply worn out.

The tenor saxophonist Buddy Tate had run into Parker not long before. "I first knew him in Kansas City in the Thirties, when I was with Andy Kirk," Tate has said. "He hadn't gotten himself together yet, but he was admiring Buster Smith, who always played Kansas City style. When he first came to New York, we'd hang out together some. He didn't have any work, and nobody knew who he was yet, but he'd be up at Monroe Clark's Uptown House every night. I'd have him over to the house, and my wife would put on a pot, but he would never eat. I tried at the time to get him into Basie's band, but Basie wouldn't have him, and he never forgot that. But he was always nice and kind and soft around me. I never saw him mad at anybody.

"One morning a week before he died, I was walking down 42nd Street toward Grand Central. It was about 10 o'clock, and I'd been on some sort of big-band record date, just playing clarinet. I saw this man way down the sidewalk, and it was Bird. He was hard to miss, with those out-of-style suits that didn't fit, and those big, old wide granddaddy suspenders he always wore. When I got close, I saw he was all swollen up. I knew he'd been very sick and in the psychiatric part of Bellevue. He said, 'I'm so glad to see you. How you been?'

"I told him fine, and he said, 'Take me for a taste.'

"We went into a bar, and I thought he'd settle down for a few, but he only had two shots. I'd heard he was so strung out he was sleeping on the string section that had been backing him up $2,500, which he didn't have."

—G.G.

Dizzy Gillespie

IN THE EARLY EVENING of June 18, 1978, near the end of a concert on the South Lawn of the White House, Dizzy Gillespie had just finished a funny, rambunctious duet with drummer Max Roach (who said, "I understand where he's going before he does, and he understands the same about me"). Gillespie walked the few feet to where President Carter was standing and listening, and, using a couple of "Your Majesty's" asked the president if he would sing the bebop tune "Salt Peanuts" with him. Gillespie demonstrated its tricky melody, and he and Carter sang it. Gillespie thanked him, and asked him if he would like to go on the road with his band, and Carter said, "I might have to after tonight."

Gillespie—master trumpeter, marvelous mimic, comic dancer, rocketing scat singer, lyrical composer, and a founder, with Charlie Parker, of bebop—was irrepressible. His famous trumpet style was at once a streamlining of Roy Eldridge's fireball playing of the late Thirties and a deft translation of Parker's. His trumpet runs, delivered from his high register to his middle register, were downhill racers. He liked to blare, filling a note to bursting and letting it float smartly away. His breaks, in a number like "A Night in Tunisia," momentarily blinded you. He played later with a mute more often than he used to and sounded as if he were humming in the next room. His ballad numbers, once leaning this way and that, became steady and majestic. He was unmistakable—the hurrying silver tone, the sly, jumping attack, the epigrammatic melodic fills, the rhythmic bobbing and weaving.

He was born John Birks Gillespie in Cheraw, South Carolina, the youngest of nine children of James and Lottie (Powe) Gillespie. He was a devilish child, who fought a lot and was whipped a lot. When he was 9, his father, a discontented man, died; when he was 12, he took up the trombone and the trumpet; and when he was 18 he was in Frank Fairfax's Philadelphia band and was nicknamed Dizzy. He went to Europe with Teddy Hill's band in 1937, and two years later he joined Cab Calloway, who fired him after they got into a fracas over a spitball that Calloway mistakenly thought Gillespie had shot at him. He married a dancer named Lorraine Willis in 1940 in Boston ("Dizzy didn't fool around with all that other stuff," she once said. "He just asked me to get married, and I said, 'O.K.'"), and she long acted as his guide and his ballast.

Gillespie discovered Charlie Parker around the same time, and Parker changed his life. By 1945 he had the first bebop band on 52nd Street, had made the first bebop recording (with Coleman Hawkins), and had taken the first bebop band to California. In 1946 he formed a big bebop band, and in 1948 he took it to Europe. It played in Scandinavia, then foundered, and was rescued by the French critic Charles Delaunay. Gillespie, who rarely dwells on dark things, remembered this about the trip: "We were in a bus somewhere in Denmark, and I looked out the window and saw this guy riding along on an ice scooter. I stopped the bus and asked him if he'd like to get in and let me ride his scooter, and we swapped." He gave up his big band in 1950 and, three years later, played in the Toronto concert that turned out to be *the* crowning bebop event with Charlie Parker, Bud Powell, Charles Mingus and Max Roach. In 1955, Parker died, and the great bebop revolution was over. Gillespie, lending himself to the establishment for the first time, took a new big band to the Middle East for the U.S. State Department in 1956, and he lived more or less within the establishment after that, as an eccentric, brilliant musician and a subtle comic figure who wanted you to laugh at him because he had been laughing at you all along.

Gillespie spent most of his life on the road. During his early years, he traveled to make money. But during the last 10 or 15 years of his life, traveling had become an obsession. Like Duke Ellington and Louis Armstrong, who never stopped going in their last decades, he was in constant motion. ("I think in terms of degrees of latitude rather than miles," he said. "I look at being on the road like it's an education.") In 1990 he appeared in Japan, France, Puerto Rico, Cuba, Newfoundland, Namibia, Spain, Holland, Italy, Sweden, Germany, Czechoslovakia, Russia, Greece, Scotland, Denmark, Switzerland and Israel, as well as at dozens of dates in the United States.

When American worthies reach their 70s, honors and awards begin falling on them like snow. In 1991, Gillespie received his fourteenth honorary degree, was made a Commander d'Ordre des Arts et Lettres by the French, received a Grammy Lifetime Achievement Award, was given the National Medal of Arts by President George Bush and received a Kennedy Center award.

Virginia Wicks, who had done publicity for Gillespie in New York in the Fifties, came out of retirement to do Gillespie's Berlin-Moscow-Prague tour in 1990. She said, "I live in Los Angeles now, and I ran into Dizzy eight or nine months ago at a concert he gave in Santa Monica. I hadn't seen him in a long time, and we hung out backstage. Three or four months later, he called me out of the blue—'Hi, Wicks!'—and asked me if I'd like to do advance work on a benefit concert he was going to give in East Berlin in May. He said he was on his way to Cuba—or "Cooba," as he calls it—and he'd get back to me soon. A month after that, he called from Nova Scotia and said there would be two more concerts—one in Moscow, the day after the Berlin concert, and one in Prague, the day after the Moscow concert. The concerts were being sponsored by the Baha'i community, which Dizzy has been deeply involved with for many years. I was out of practice and a little scared of the whole project, but I said yes, I'd do it. The concert in East Berlin was held at the Palast der Republik, and, thank God, it was a huge success. We flew to Moscow the next morning—it's a much longer flight than you'd think—and on the way from the airport Dizzy said he had a sore throat and wanted to find some lemons and garlic to treat it. We stopped at a free market where there aren't any queues because everything is so expensive. The lemons were tiny and cost three dollars apiece. I warned Dizzy about the garlic because we had a press conference before the concert, but, whatever he did, he never smelled. And he never got a cold. The concert was electric. There was a palpable hush of anticipation before each number, and when the audience recognized a tune it screamed its approval. And the applause at the end was astonishing.

"After, we were taken to a restaurant in an old house where there was an immense horseshoe-shaped table covered with long-stemmed roses and bowls of caviar. Then they drove us in this silent black limousine through alleyways and around Red Square. There was a full moon, and it was like a dream. I said something to Dizzy when we got to Red Square, but he was sound asleep.

"Václav Havel and Shirley Temple Black, who was our Ambassador to Czechoslovakia, were both at the Prague concert, which was in the Palác Kultury. The con-cert was very long, but no one left. Dizzy got a standing ovation that lasted literally 10 minutes. It went on and on, but he didn't reappear. That wasn't like him, and I began to worry that something might have happened to him. I sent word, and it turned out that he had gone to his dressing room way downstairs and hadn't heard a thing. He came on stage and played an encore, and everything was all right."

One May evening in 1990, Gillespie was scheduled to play a one-night stand with his quintet at the Lone Star Roadhouse on West 52nd Street. His old friends Cynthia and Donald Elwood were taking him to dinner at Tout Va Bien, the venerable bistro on West 51st Street. He had finished a six-day stint at Blues Alley in Washington, D.C., the night before and, just before *that*, had spent three days in Spain acting in a film called "Winter in Lisbon." Before that, he had spent three days giving those concerts in East Berlin, Moscow and Prague.

The Elwoods arrived at the restaurant with Gillespie in tow. They were small and tweedy and full of moxie. They lived in Boston and had first met Gillespie there in the mid-Sixties. It was a cool evening, and Gillespie, who is not a clotheshorse, was wearing a Sherlock Holmes hat, a houndstooth jacket, rumpled striped brown pants, a navy-blue T-shirt and a couple of medallions suspended from a long gold neck chain. He had not changed much in the last 10 years. He had a medium-length grayish Afro and he looked grizzly. His huge and celebrated cheeks were broadsides in repose and spinnakers in action, and he had a scimitar smile and a thousand tiny, even teeth. He liked to smile and roll his eyes in mock surprise, but most of the time his eyes were narrowed; they took in much and sent out little, and when he put on his dark-rimmed, two-tone glasses they disappeared.

No one talked like Gillespie. His voice was potatoey, blurred, edgeless. His consonants and vowels were indistinguishable, a gumbo. His laughter barked. In the Seventies, he began taking on a formidable front porch, but he had since lost much of it, allowing him once more to hip-hop around the stage between solos, do his funny dances, pop his eyes, stick out his tongue, and make some of his listeners put him down as an Uncle Tom—this wily, powerful, relentless anti-Tom.

Virginia Wicks and Cynthia Elwood sat against the wall, and Donald Elwood and Gillespie sat across from them. Gillespie said he hadn't had anything but a cup of coffee all day and he was hungry. The waitress, who was French, recognized him, gave a little shriek, and asked him for his autograph. He obliged, and asked her for a menu. Then she asked him if he had a photograph of himself to add to the gallery of notables on the wall. He shook his head and looked at Virginia Wicks, and she said she would send one to Tout Va Bien. Gillespie bent his head to study the menu, and his trumpeter's bottom lip, heavy as a plate, slid forward. He decided on mushroom soup and frogs' legs. Donald Elwood looked up from his menu and said, "What did the waiter say when he was asked what the soup du jour was?"

"He said, 'I don't know. They change it every day,'" Gillespie barked, and ate a piece of French bread.

Virginia Wicks told the Elwoods that Dizzy had just finished shooting a movie in Spain. "I play an old American musician who gets fed up with America and moves to Copenhagen. I wash cars, then I meet this young French piano player and he gets me playing again. There's a gangster, and I have an attack and end up in the hospital. I saw the attack later, and, you know, I was surprised—it really looked like an attack.

Dizzy Gillespie, King of the Street, in the late Forties. (Bill Gottlieb photograph)

I die at the end of the movie. I fall all over, and they catch me before I hit the floor."

Cynthia Elwood asked Gillespie about his house in Englewood, New Jersey. "Lorraine and I have been there 25 years!" he said. "I probably enjoy it more by being away so much and coming back for little visits. We've got a young boy from Texas working for us who did some jobs for my cousin. He's like an overseer. He doesn't overcharge us, and sometimes he works four or five days and won't take any money. He just finished building what we called a porch back home but I guess is what you call a deck up here. It's so nice I'd like to put a bed on it."

Gillespie ate his frogs' legs with his fingers, and the bones, as clean as toothpicks, began to pile up on his butter plate. Like most road-hardened jazz musicians, who often subsist on junk food, Gillespie ate food with relish and great concentration. He said little until he had finished his frogs' legs and a salad. Then he talked at random, moving from subject to subject as it pleased him.

Some of Gillespie's Reminiscences

ON CHARLIE PARKER:
"I haven't seen the movie. I think it would just make me feel sad. I've heard from musicians that it doesn't delve into his music, that it doesn't talk about all his women. And the guy who plays me—he never met me, he doesn't know me, so how could he play me? Bird didn't use drugs in front of me. I saw him shoo guys away when I was around—the people who used to hang around musicians with coke and all. I'd laugh at that. One time, I ran into him at Basin Street West, and he looked so forlorn. He said, 'Dizzy, save me.' I didn't know what do do, but I told him, 'You've got to do that yourself, Bird.'

"I first heard him in 1940 in Kansas City, when I was on the road with Cab Calloway. A young trumpet player in Jay McShann's band named Buddy Anderson told me, 'I want you to hear this alto player.' Well, I'd played with Don Byas and Chu Berry and Coleman Hawkins and Ben Webster, and I didn't think there was anything else to hear in that line. But I heard him, and we jammed together all day at the Booker T. Washington Hotel. Roy Eldridge had been our cup of tea—all us trumpet players—but Charlie Parker turned everything upside down. He was a great blues player, and all his music was bluesy. I always liked to hear him talk, particularly when he used his cultured-professor accent. We worked together awhile in the early forties in Earl Hines' band, and one time we played a white dance in Pine Bluff, Arkansas. This white guy threw some money up on the bandstand during intermission when I was sitting there by myself at the piano. He said would I play such-and-such, and I ignored him. After the dance, I was coming out of the men's room—the only time we were allowed in there was after the whites had left—and someone came up behind me and hit me on the head with a bottle. It was the same guy. I started to go for him, the blood all over me, and five guys grabbed me. Charlie Parker was one of them, and he looked at the guy and said, 'You took advantage of my friend, you cur.' "

ON GOING HOME:
"Almost everybody is nice to me in Cheraw. They had a Dizzy Gillespie day there a while back. The ex-mayor gave a cocktail party for me, and I asked him if it would be all right for me to bring my cousin. I needed a haircut first, so I told my cousin to take me to a white barbershop. The owner was alone, sitting in a barber chair and reading the paper. 'What can I do for you?' he said. I said I wanted a haircut, and he said, 'Sorry. We don't cut colored hair.' Then he said, 'I know you,' and he started talking about my family and such, but I walked out. Later, I got a letter from Cheraw asking me if I would mind if they put up a sign on the outskirts saying Dizzy Gillespie was born there. I said I would mind—it would embarrass me if someone I knew came through and wanted a haircut and couldn't get in. But later I relented."

ON IMPROVISING:
"The hardest part of the music is improvising, and it gets harder the older you are. Improvisation is a gathering together of all the evidence you have of how to resolve going from here to here to here. It's similar to painting. You add colors in your mind, you build colors. Bright yellow is generally loud, green is soft. I'm a more melodious player than I used to be but rhythm is still my business. I see rhythm when I play, I understand rhythm, my best shot is rhythm. Harmony is next. The most difficult thing for me is playing in obtuse keys like A-natural and F-sharp and E. A long time ago, I found out that you've got to learn some piano to do the job as a horn player. You can only play one note at a time on a horn, but there are all the notes in the chord spread out before you on the piano. When Miles Davis first came to New York from St. Louis, he'd be at my house all the time. Lorraine would put a plate out for him. He was very inquisitive. 'Man, where did you get such-and-such a note from?' he'd ask. I'd sit down at the piano and show him.

"The only trumpet lesson I ever took was from that Grupp, used to teach here in New York. I paid him for three lessons, but I never went back after the first one so he owes me."

ON BILL WHITWORTH:
"Back in the early Sixties I played Little Rock, and at that time you couldn't stay in a hotel—you stayed at people's houses. I stayed with Bill Whitworth, who used to play some trumpet. He's the editor now up there in Boston at the *Atlantic* magazine. I stayed at Bill's house with him and his mother. She greeted me: 'Come upstairs and let me show you where you're going to sleep.' I saw this sofa bed in the living room all made up, and I said that would be fine; I didn't want to take anybody's bed. But she said, 'Oh, no! I sleep down here all the time!' I got a letter from Bill later telling me, 'You should know that your being a guest in our house was a crowning achievement. I'm so famous I'm thinking of running for public office in North Little Rock. The sheets you slept in haven't been washed, and all the brass players come from miles around to kiss them.'"

ON RETIREMENT:
"I'll never stop playing as long as I can do physically on the trumpet what I want to do. Look at Doc Cheatham. He's 85 and playing as good as ever. Cheatham never drank much, never took coke, never used grass. He's a perfect example of what to do for longevity."

At 8:30 PM, Gillespie, in company with the Elwoods and Virginia Wicks, walked up Eighth Avenue and turned east onto 52nd Street. The Lone Star Roadhouse was just up the block. Virginia Wicks and the Elwoods took a table down front, and Gillespie went backstage to find his musicians. A jump band called Bob's Diner was holding forth at ear-blasting volume and was being filmed by a Japanese television crew. Bob's Diner finished its set with a thunderous riff blues, and Gillespie's quintet came on stage to warm up. But it wasn't easy. Bob's Diner had left behind a loud, steady electronic hum, and no one seemed to know how to get rid of it. Gillespie, not looking upset, *was* upset, and at first he refused to play. Then, a resilient and kindly man, he decided to turn up his amplifiers and go ahead. He had Ron Holloway on tenor saxophone, Ed Cherry on guitar, John Lee on bass and Ignacio Berroa on drums. It was bulging, 3-D Gillespie. Everything was exaggerated—the volume, the length of the sidemen's solos (Gillespie had never been a garrulous soloist), the force of the ensemble passages. Gillespie himself was utterly professional. He played with a smooth doggedness, with the patience and care of someone who gives good value, no matter the distractions. He played a long "Manteca," a long, slow blues, and a long "A Night in Tunisia." He took a nice muted solo in the first number and in the blues, but he opened up in "A Night in Tunisia," making the famous break explode. The crowd, made up mostly of people in their late 20s and early 30s, seemed to know who Gillespie was, and gave him shouts and whistles; he responded with some dancing, a few eye-rollings, and a jowl-shaking.

A week later, Donald Elwood faxed Virginia Wicks a drawing that Gillespie had done on a manila Elwood had on the table at Tout Va Bien. Here it is:

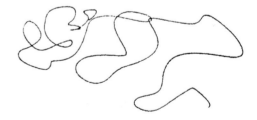

Elwood told Wicks he couldn't remember what Gillespie had said the drawing was of and wondered if she would mind asking him, since he was playing at the Vine Street Bar & Grill in Los Angeles. Gillespie studied the drawing, and said that he couldn't remember what it was supposed to be either, but that it looked to him like three seals on a sled. Of course, it isn't. If you look care-

Dizzy Gillespie at the Savoy Ballroom in New York, 1947, with John Lewis on piano and Teddy Stewart on drums. (Frank Driggs collection)

shows a night. A lot of young musicians came to play with him. He had to push himself hard, but I think he felt he wasn't coming up to where he should be. Anyway, he was very tired when it was over, and he was looking forward to taking a week off. But he rarely checked his schedule—he liked to be surprised about where he was going next—and it turned out that he had to go directly to Washington for a night and do two weeks of one-nighters somewhere out West. He ended up in Emeryville, near Oakland, and I went up from L.A. to be with him. During a long photo session the afternoon of his opening, he told me, 'Wicks, I don't feel so good. I must have eaten something bad.' Well, he was an eater, he loved food. After his first set that night, he sat more heavily in his dressing room than usual, and his color wasn't right. When Whale, his road manager, told him it was time for the second set, he said, 'I can't.' It was the first time in his life."

He was taken to a hospital, and the doctors found that his diabetes had got out of hand. He stayed two nights, then finished the gig. He was scheduled for a week in Seattle, and when everybody told him not to go he said, "Don't tell me what I have to do." ("Not mean, just stubborn," Wicks said.) He went home to Englewood after Seattle and had a six-hour operation for an intestinal blockage, and, though he seemed to improve, he never really recovered. "He used to say that he knew everybody and everybody knew him," Wicks went on. "And it was true. He had a little book filled with the names of people he knew all over the world, and when he arrived at such-and-such a place, he'd call—'Hi, this is Dizzy'— and they'd come and hang out with him. He never took advantage of who he was, and he never acted like a star. I don't know how stars get from here to there, but Dizzy walked down the street."

—W.B.

fully, Gillespie's initials, JBG, emerge from the squiggles. So much for asking a busy man a foolish question.

Gillespie died three years later. Virginia Wicks was with him when he became sick. She later said, "Last January, there was a month-long 75th celebration for Dizzy down at the Blue Note—six nights a week, two

President Jimmy Carter, left, after singing "Salt Peanuts" with Dizzy Gillespie, center, and Max Roach at the White House. (White House photograph)

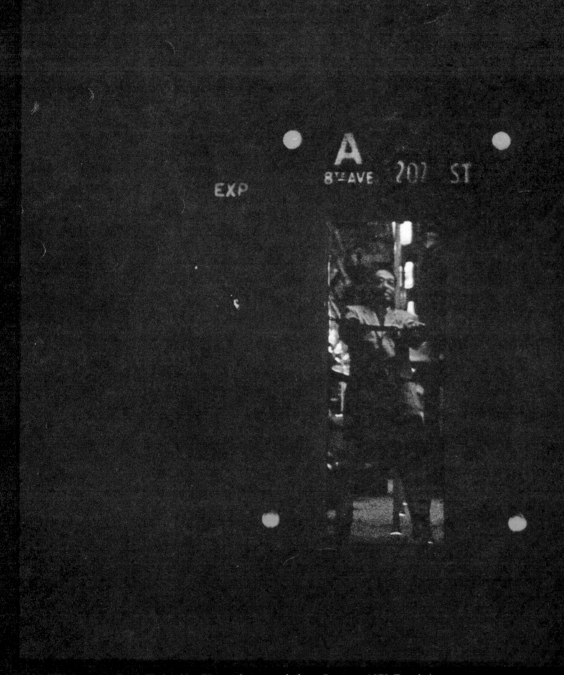

Duke Ellington on the A-Train. (Art Kane photograph from January 1959 *Esquire*)

Edward Kennedy (Duke) Ellington

REFUSED ADMITTANCE to the Broadway musical stage except for the short-lived *Beggar's Holiday*, done with John Latouche in 1946, Duke Ellington created his own musical theatre. This was not surprising, for he was, with his ornate courtesy, his cool, sharp humor, his sometimes arcane dress and his tinted, mocking speech, intensely theatrical—and so was his often programmatic composing. "Jump for Joy," produced in Los Angeles in 1941, and "My People," produced in Chicago in 1963, were elaborate revues in which the music dominated the acts. (That was also the case in "Sophisticated Ladies," despite the highly touted dancing and singing.) "A Drum Is a Woman" was a fantasy written in the mid-Fifties for television. "The River" was an almost Bunyanesque allegory done for American Ballet Theatre in 1970. And his so-called Sacred Concerts were unique extravaganzas that premiered at San Francisco's Grace Cathedral in 1965, at New York's Cathedral of St. John the Divine in 1968, and at Westminster Abbey in 1973, not long before he died. Ellington came to see the Sacred Concerts as the most important things he had written.

"I am not concerned with what it costs," he wrote of the first Sacred Concert in his autobiography, *Music Is My Mistress*. "I want the best of everything possible. I want the best musicians, the best singers and coaches— amateurs or professionals—and I want them to give the best they have. I want all the help I can get and to say that I hope I am good enough because this is the performance of all performances—God willing." Ellington's Sacred Concerts never matched the dimensions of Berlioz's Requiem (four brass bands, full orchestra with 16 kettledrums, a 500-voice choir), but he did his best to fill the empyreal spaces of the cathedrals and churches and temples where he worked. His band was the base, and to it he added choirs, the cathedral organ, male and female vocal soloists, narration, and dancers, tap and ballet. The results were uneven. Some of the songs had the density and fervor of religious music. Others were romantic, and even lachrymose—they sentimentalized God, possibly making Him an adjunct of Ellington's revered mother. Some of the dancing was showy and superfluous, and so were some of the band instrumentals with their long drum solos. The performers were erratic and varied from the sublime (the Swedish soprano Alice Babs, the tap dancer Bunny Briggs, the band itself) to the melodramatic (the singers Jon Hendricks and Tony Watkins and the dancer-choreographer Geoffrey Holder). But it was spectacular when everything came together.

This happened in "David Danced Before the Lord" at the Fifth Avenue Presbyterian Church in December 1965. There, in full aural and visual flower, was Ellington's vision. The number, which was recorded during the concert, begins with a short, annunciatory band chord immediately followed by Briggs dancing fast, light steps. He continues by himself for 16 measures, drops into rangy half-time steps, and keeps dancing throughout the number, which lasts six minutes. The saxophones play the lovely, steplike 32-bar melody (originally "Come Sunday") which, like a lullaby, covers less than an octave and a half and is built on sequential notes. It is played in half time to the dancing, and this sets up an exhilarating rhythmic tension. A choir chants the words over the band, which further enriches the rhythms, and in the next chorus the choir hums the melody while the band plays countermelodic figures—beautiful little flags of the sort that Ellington ran up again and again in his best work. The band falls silent, and the choir chants for a chorus, backed by Ellington and the rhythm section. (Don't forget the continuing rattling, clicking, stomping drone of Briggs' feet and how, every once in a while, he throws in wild, offbeat, two-footed steps, which jar everything around him.) The choir rests, and Ellington and Briggs do a charging duet for a chorus. Then the choir hums the melody again, there's a pause, and Briggs gives an electrifying shout, which is answered by 16 bars of ensemble band shouts. At the same time, the drummer Louis Bellson solos, the choir chants and a clarinetist sails into the stratosphere. This mad five-tiered float careers along for eight bars, and—bang!—Briggs dances out into the sun by himself for several easy measures, and the piece comes to rest with a final band chord.

Part of Ellington's third Sacred Concert was given a trial American run at Queens College in 1975. But, for whatever reasons, the concert was limited to snippets from all three concerts, which were done by a troupe that included the Mercer Ellington band; the Byrne Camp Chorale; the soloists McHenry Boatwright, Alpha Brawner-Floyd, Anita Moore, Tony Bennett and Phyllis Hyman; the tap dancer Honi Coles; an Alvin Ailey group; and Douglas Fairbanks, Jr., as narrator. (Fairbanks' Hollywood-English accent fitted Ellington's New York biblical words uncommonly well.) Nine numbers from the third Sacred Concert were played (about half of the whole), and they sounded much like the earlier concerts. But there were good moments: David Young's tenor saxophone solo backed by the chorale in "The Brotherhood"; the chorale singing "Alleluia" softer and softer, accompanied by only a bass; Joe Temperley's a cappella baritone saxophone solo on "The Majesty of God" (Temperley's tone is strikingly close to Harry Carney's, but it lacks Carney's great *bottom*); and the succeeding quiet, ascending organ chords from the band. "David Danced Before the Lord" was among the 10 numbers taken from the earlier concerts, but it was short and choppy. Coles never had a chance to get his momentum going, and the towering last chorus was omitted. Boatwright and Brawner-Floyd were lugubrious and often off pitch, while Hyman and Moore, who did gospel songs, and Bennett, who did a fine Ellington song called "Somebody Cares," swung.

It was strange not having Ellington there. He was at his best at his Sacred Concerts, and he somehow managed to make their disparate parts blend. In *Music Is My Mistress*, he unwittingly told us how: "As I travel from place to place . . . taking rhythm to the dancers, harmony to the romantic, melody to the nostalgic, gratitude to the listener . . . receiving praise, applause and handshakes, and at the same time doing the thing I like to do, I feel that I am most fortunate because I know that God has blessed my timing, without which nothing could have happened." He left us his music, but he took the timing.

Ellington's Sacred Concerts were, in their way, sometimes ludicrously inflated imitations of the 30 or more masterpieces he set down between 1940 and 1942 for Victor Records. It is still not altogether clear why this exuberant flowering took place. The surrounding musical soil was sandy, and the Ellington band itself had been going through dry times. The rhythm section was inert, the arrangements often had a staccato, old fashioned sound (toy soldier muted trumpets, ornate saxophone writing), and the ensemble playing was imprecise. Even such fine numbers as "Riding on a Blue Note," "Blue Light," "Barney Goin' Easy" and "Portrait of the Lion" seemed inconclusive.

In 1939, things began to stir. The composer and arranger Billy Strayhorn joined the band, and by the end of the year he began to take hold. Ellington left his old, tenacious manager, Irving Mills, and went with the William Morris agency. He also left Brunswick Records, whose sound was closed and soupy, and signed with Victor, whose sound was clear and open.

The band made a heartening European tour (black jazz musicians were already going to Europe to be revitalized; indeed, they were often overwhelmed by applause and kindness), and bassist Jimmy Blanton and tenor saxophonist Ben Webster became part of the band. Blanton, who was just 21, was the first modern bassist. He had a big tone and unshakable time, and he was the first bassist capable of "melodic" improvising. He woke the band up rhythmically. Webster was 30 and had been with Ellington briefly, as well as with Andy Kirk, Fletcher Henderson, Cab Calloway, Benny Carter and Teddy Wilson.

The Duke Ellington Band, 1943. Left to right, Otto Hardwicke, Juan Tizol, Harold Baker; Ray Nance, Duke Ellington, Harry Carney, Betty Roché, Rex Stewart, Johnny Hodges, Ben Webster, Chauncey Haughton, Joe Nanton, Wallace Jones, Lawrence Brown and Sonny Greer. (Frank Driggs collection)

("I always had a yen for Ben," Ellington says in his autobiography.) All the big black bands except Ellington's had tenor saxophone stars. Basie had Lester Young and Herschel Evans; Andy Kirk had Dick Wilson; Fletcher Henderson had Coleman Hawkins; Cab Calloway had Chu Berry. But Ellington's major saxophone soloist had been the alto and soprano saxophonist Johnny Hodges. Webster enriched the band tonally, and he brought it new intensity and emotion. In return, Ellington built "Cotton Tail" and "Just A-Settin' and A-Rockin'" around Webster and gave him an invaluable opportunity to sit beside Hodges in the saxophone section and absorb him. Within a year or so, Webster, already on the verge of being first-rate, was the equal of Young and Hawkins.

So the band was complete. On trumpets were Wallace Jones, Rex Stewart and Cootie Williams (replaced late in 1940 by Ray Nance); on trombones Juan Tizol, Lawrence Brown and Tricky Sam Nanton; on reeds Otto Harwicke, Barney Bigard, Ben Webster, Johnny Hodges and Harry Carney; and in the rhythm section Ellington on piano, Fred Guy on guitar, Jimmy Blanton on bass and Sonny Greer on drums.

Ellington's 1940-1942 masterpieces have strong jazz characteristics—improvised or partly improvised solos, jazz timbres (plunger mutes, growls, instrumental tonal peculiarities), and a regular sounded beat. They also have classical characteristics—fixed solos (originally improvised, but which gradually became set), concerto-like forms and complex scoring, some of it rivaling Berlioz's. And they were entirely original in their instrumental combinations and in their odd, often surprising structures. Ellington used the 12-bar blues and the 32-bar AABA song form, but he decorated them with introductions and codas, with interludes and transitions, with key changes, with dissonance.

Much of the time, his materials appeared to dictate his forms. "Sepia Panorama" has an "arch" form. The first chorus lasts 12 bars, the second chorus lasts 16 bars, the third lasts eight and the fourth 12; the fifth chorus repeats the fourth chorus, the sixth repeats the third, the seventh repeats part of the second, and in the eighth we are back at the first chorus. "Concerto for Cootie" has an eight-bar introduction, and the first chorus is 36 bars long (two 10-bar sections and two eight-bar sections). A two-bar transition leads into the second chorus, which is 16 bars. There is an eight-bar recapitulation of the first 10 bars of the first chorus and an eight-bar coda. Ellington, (and, increasingly, Strayhorn) wrote most of the materials. Ellington had considerable help from his sidemen, who would contribute a melody here and a bridge there and who often groused about not getting more credit (to say nothing of royalties).

He also reworked chestnuts like "Chloe" and "The Sidewalks of New York" and occasionally he built a new structure on old chords: "In a Mellotone" was based on "Rose Room" and "Cotton Tail" on "I Got Rhythm." He wrote several different kinds of pieces. There were programmatic or descriptive pieces, like "Just A-Settin' and A-Rockin'," "Harlem Airshaft" and "Dusk." There were tone poems, like "Blue Serge." There were rhythmic exercises, like "The Giddybug Gallop," "Ko-Ko" and "Jumpin' Punkins." There were plain old blues, like

Duke Ellington with Billy Strayhorn, his "alter ego," arranger, composer and number-two piano player, 1951. (Frank Driggs collection)

"Across the Track Blues" and "C Jam Blues." And there were miniature concertos, like "Concerto for Cootie" and "Jack the Bear."

How does one of those concertos go? Here is "Ko-Ko," a minor blues and no relation of Charlie Parker's "Ko-Ko" made five years later. It starts *in medias res*. Sonny Greer gives a couple of quick timpani beats, and Carney goes immediately into a chuffing sustained note in his low register—his house-moving register—and is backed by the trombone section, possibly salted with one trumpet. The introduction lasts eight bars. In the first chorus, which is 12 bars, Juan Tizol plays an ingenious six-note figure that is pursued closely by the reed section in such a way that it sounds like a continuation of Tizol's figure. Tizol starts the sentence and the reeds finish it. In the next two choruses, 12 measures apiece, Tricky Sam Nanton, using a plunger mute, solos against offbeat muted trumpets and the reed section, which plays a sighing three-note figure. Greer punctuates on his tom-toms. In the fourth chorus, also 12 bars, the reeds repeat the figure they used in the first chorus and the trumpet section supplies the "ooh-wahs." Ellington himself surfaces from behind, throwing runs and chords into the air. The 12-bar fifth chorus is climactic The trumpet section plays a repeated long-held note while the saxophone section plays accented fugures and a melody parallel to the trumpets. The dissonance is almost overpowering and the atmosphere of the number is rough and hustling. The piece bullies. It sets out to be abrasive *and* lyrical, and it succeeds.

—W.B.

Charles Mingus

CHARLES MINGUS, the incomparable 49-year-old bassist, composer, bandleader, autobiographer and iconoclast, has spent much of his life attempting to rearrange the world according to an almost Johnsonian set of principles that abhor, among other things, cant, racism, inhibition, managerial greed, sloppy music, Uncle Tomism and conformity. His methods have ranged from penny-dreadful broadsides to punches on the nose. The results have been mixed. They have also been costly, and have landed Mingus on the psychiatric couch and in Bellevue (self-committed), lost him jobs and made him periodically fat ("I eat out of nerves"). At the same time, Mingus' experiences have been steadily distilled into a body of compositions that for sheer melodic and rhythmic and structural originality may equal Thelonious Monk and Duke Ellington. (Their content has been equally fresh, for they have included, in the Ellington manner, everything from love songs to social satire.) These experiences have been reflected in his playing, as well, which long ago elevated him to virtuosic rank. But now Mingus has taken another step. He has written a book about himself: *Beneath the Underdog: His World as Composed by Mingus* (Knopf).

The book is impressionistic and disembodied (it has almost no dates) and has a taste of all the Minguses. It is brutal and dirty and bitter. It is sentimental and self-pitying. It is rude and, in places, unfair (the curt handling of the great Red Norvo). It is facetious and funny. It is awkward and unerringly right, and it is the latter when Mingus' fine ear is receiving full tilt. Duke Ellington's verbal arabesques have never been captured better:

[Juan] Tizol [an Ellington trombonist] wants you to play a solo he's written where bowing is required. You raise the solo an octave, where the bass isn't too muddy. He doesn't like that and he comes to the room under the stage where you're practicing at intermission and comments that you're like the rest of the niggers in the band, you can't read. You ask Juan how he's different from the other niggers and he states that one of the ways he's different is that HE IS WHITE. So you run his ass upstairs. You leave the rehearsal room, proceed toward the stage with your bass and take your place and at the moment Duke brings down the baton for "A-Train" and the curtain of the Apollo Theatre goes

up, a yelling, whooping Tizol rushes out and lunges at you with a bolo knife. The rest you remember mostly from Duke's own words in his dressing room as he changes after the show.

"Now, Charles," he says, looking amused, putting Cartier links into the cuffs of his beautiful handmade shirt, "you could have forewarned me–you left me out of the act entirely! At least you could have let me cue in a few chords as you ran through that Nijinsky routine. I congratulate you on your performance, but why didn't you and Juan inform me about the adagio you planned so that we could score it? I must say I never saw a large man so agile–I never saw anybody make such tremendous leaps! The gambado over the piano carrying your bass was colossal. When you exited after that I thought, 'That man's really afraid of Juan's knife and at the speed he's going he's probably home in bed by now.' But no, back you came through the same door with your bass still intact. For a moment I was hopeful you'd decided to sit down and play but instead you slashed Juan's chair in two with a fire axe! Really, Charles, that's destructive. Everybody knows Juan has a knife but nobody ever took it seriously—he likes to pull it out and show it to people, you understand. So I'm afraid, Charles—I've never fired anybody—you'll have to quit my band. I don't need any new problems. Juan's an old problem, I can cope with that, but you seem to have a whole bag of new tricks. I must ask you to be kind enough to give me your notice, Charles."

The charming way he says it, it's like he's paying you a compliment. Feeling honored, you shake hands and resign.

Mingus' relationship with jazz critics has been generally amiable, and the lumps landed on them in the book are pretty funny. A party is given for Mingus when he first arrives in New York from the West Coast around 1950. No matter that the critics named were never in the same room at the same time in their lives, or that at least two of them were still in college and unpublished. Mingus is talking to Dizzy Gillespie:

"Man, that's a lot of talent, don't you dig it? I see Leonard Feather, he's a piano player. There's Bill Coss and Gene Lees—they sing, I heard. Barry Ulanov must play drums or something, dig, with that Metronome beat. Martin Williams can play everything. I can tell by the way he writes. Put Marshall Stearns on bass and let Whitney Balliett score and John Wilson conduct. Let

all them other young up-and-coming critics dance. How would you like to review that schitt for the Amsterdam News?"

But the best parts of the book deal with Fats Navarro, a brilliant, concise trumpeter who died at the age of 26 in 1950. He tells a young and ingenuous Mingus what it is really like to be a jazz musician:

"Mingus, you a nice guy from California, I don't want to disillusion you. But I been through all that schitt and I had to learn to do some other things to get along. I learned better than to try to make it just with my music out on these dirty gang-mob streets, cause I still love playing better than money. Jazz ain't supposed to make nobody no millions but that's where it's at. Them that shouldn't is raking it in but the purest are out in the street with me and Bird and it rains all over us, man. I was better off when nobody knew my name except musicians. You can bet it ain't jazz no more when the underworld moves in and runs it strictly for geetz and even close out the colored agents. They shut you up and cheat you on the count of your record sales and if you go along they tell the world you a real genius. But if you don't play they put out the word you're a troublemaker, like they did me. Then if some honest club owner tries to get hold of you to book you, they tell him you're not available or you don't draw or you'll tear up the joint like you was a gorilla. And you won't hear nothin' about it except by accident. But if you behave, boy, you'll get booked—except for less than the white cats that copy your playing and likely either the agent or owner'll pocket the difference.

On a Sunday night a week or so before his book was published, Mingus was sitting at the bar of a restaurant on West 10th Street. He was dressed in a conservative dark suit and tie, and he was in the middle state. That is, he was neither thin nor huge. A Charlie Chan beard was arranged carefully around his mouth, and he looked wonderful. A year before, his face had been gray and puffy; he had not played a note for two years, and he was very fat and had a listless, buried air. Now he was sitting at the bar sampling a tall white drink. "Ramos gin fizz," he blurted out. "Milk or cream, white of an egg, orange flower water, lemon juice, gin and soda water. I used to drink 10 at a sitting in San Francisco." Mingus talks in leaping slurs. The words come out crouched and running, and sometimes they move so fast whole sentences are unintelligible. He finished his Ramos fizz and ordered a half bottle of Pouilly-Fuissé and some cheese. He pronounced the name of the wine at a run, and it came out "Poolly-Foos." "We went down to the peace demonstration in Washington this weekend to play, and it was a drag," he said. "They've never had any jazz at these things, and it seemed like a good idea, but we never did play. My piano player didn't show, and my alto sax couldn't make it, so we only had four pieces, and it wouldn't have made any sense going on like that. I went to bed right after I got back this morning. I hadn't been to bed in two nights. I can't sleep at night anyway, but I do all right with a sleeping pill in the day. I even had a wonderful dream just before I got up. I had everything under control. I was on a diet and losing weight all over the place, and I felt so good. But a dream like that is worse than a nightmare. You wake up and the real nightmare starts."

Mingus asked the bartender if he could get some lobster and was told that the kitchen had closed. "Maybe they got some across the street in that steak house," Mingus said. He told the bartender to keep the rest of the wine—that he would be back right after he had eaten. He crossed the street and went down some steps into a dark, low, empty room. Mingus moved lightly but gingerly and, squeezing himself into a booth, ordered lobster tails, hearts of lettuce and another half bottle of Poolly-Foos.

"My book was written for black people to tell them how to get through life," he said. "I was trying to upset the white man in it—the right kind or the wrong kind, depending on what color and persuasion you are. I started it 25 years ago, and at first I was doing if for myself, to help understand certain situations. I talked some of it into tape recorders, and that girl in the white Cadillac in the book, she helped me type it up. But I wrote most of it in longhand in the dark backstage or on buses on huge sheets of score paper. The original manuscript was between 800 and a thousand pages. It went up and down, what with parts of it getting lost. I started looking for a publisher more than 10 years ago. Things hadn't loosened up yet, and a lot of them looked at it and it scared them. It was too dirty, it was too hard on whitey, they said. McGraw-Hill finally bought it, but they put it on the shelf for a long time. Then Knopf got interested and bought it from McGraw-Hill."

Mingus asked the waitress for a glass of water. She was young and blond. "Say, you my same waitress? It's so dark in here you look like you keep changing." Mingus leaned back and smiled his beautiful smile.

"I'm your waitress," she said, putting a hand lightly on his left arm. "Are you Jaki Byard?"

"Jaki Byard? Jaki Byard? He's my piano player. He's a super-star now. I'm glad you my same waitress. Now, bring me that glass of water, please. Then I got hold of Nel King, who wrote a movie I was in, and she put the book in shape. It took her a year and a half. A whole lot of stuff has been left out—stuff about blacks wearing Afros because they're afraid not to, and skin-lighteners, and my wife, Celia. There was a lot about her in there, but she didn't want to be in the book, so I left her out. I wrote it a b c d e f g h at first, but then I mixed up the chronology and some of the locations. Like that party when I first came to New York in the late Forties. It didn't take place at any apartment in the East Seventies but over at the old Bandbox, next to Birdland. The critics were there, and they didn't stop talking once. They kept right on even when Art Tatum and Charlie Parker sat in together for maybe the only time in their lives. It was the most fantastic music I ever heard. Tatum didn't let up in either hand for a second—*whoosh-hum, whoosh-hum* in the left, and *aaaaaaaaarrrrrrrrrrhhhhhhhhheeeeee* in the right—and neither did Parker, and to this day I don't know what they were doing. The passages on Fats Navarro are the best part of the book. I loved Fats, and I could hear his voice in my head the whole time I was writing him down. But that's just my first book. It's not an autobiography. It's just me, Mingus. My next book will be my life in music."

Bassist Charles Mingus wrote complex, original compositions. (Frank Driggs collection)

Mingus finished his lobster tails and wine and went back across the street. He telephoned his manager, Sue Ungaro, and arranged to meet her in 10 minutes at a Japanese restaurant at Twelfth Street and Second Avenue. It was almost 1:00 AM. Mingus emptied his bottle of wine and took a cab across town. The restaurant was shut, and Mrs. Ungaro was nowhere in sight.

"I better walk over to her place, maybe meet her on the way," Mingus said. The street was deserted, but he reached into a coat pocket and took out a big East Indian knife and, removing its scabbard, held it at the ready in his left hand. "This is the way I walk the streets at night around here. I live down on Fifth Street, and we got so much crime I'm scared to be out at night." He passed St. Mark's in the Bowery and headed west.

Mrs. Ungaro was putting some trash in a garbage can in front of her building. She is a pretty, slender strawberry blonde, and she was wearing blue jeans, clogs and a short, beat-up raccoon coat.

"They closed," Mingus said, pocketing his knife. Mrs. Ungaro said she'd still like something to eat. They took a cab to the Blue Sea on Third Avenue and 24th Street. It was closed. Mingus told the driver to make a U-turn, and go down to a small bar-and-grill on 10th and Third. He and Sue Ungaro sat in a semicircular booth under a jukebox loudspeaker. She ordered a hamburger and salad and Mingus asked the waitress, who was wearing false eyelashes and a black knitted see-through pantsuit, for a dish of black olives and some Poolly-Foos.

"Poorly what?" she said, moving her lashes up and down like a semaphore. "I don't know. I'm just helping out tonight, because I've known these people a long time."

The manager, a short man in shirtsleeves with gleaming glasses and a big paunch, said they had Soave Bolla. A half bottle in a straw basket was put in an ice bucket on the table. Mingus scrunched the bottle down in the bucket and piled ice cubes carefully around its neck.

He looked at Sue Ungaro and smiled. "It's been five years, baby. You know that?" She nodded and took a bite of hamburger. "Sue wrote in for the Guggenheim I just got. I want to write a ballet with the money—an operatic ballet. I've had it in my head for years, like I had the book in my head. It'll have to do with Watts, where I was born and raised, and I want Katherine Dunham to choreograph it. I know her very well, and we've talked about it a long time. But getting the Guggenheim wasn't as easy as filling out forms. I had to carry about 50 pounds of music over for them to see. If I don't finish the ballet this year, I'll apply again."

"Charles wants to put together a 17-piece band," Sue Ungaro said. "And he wants to use some of the Guggenheim money, but they won't allow it. It's only for composition."

"If I do finish the ballet, I'll apply anyway so that I can write some chamber music. That's what I started out doing years and years ago, and I want to go back to it. I've been teaching all winter, one day a week, at the State University at Buffalo. The Slee Chair of Music. They invited me, and I've been teaching composition to about 10 kids. They're bright, and they get their work done on time. I used some of my own pieces, showing them how to work with a melody and no chords or sets of chords, and no melody or just a pedal point, to give them a sense of freedom. But I feel sorry about jazz. The truth has been lost in the music. All the different styles and factions went to war with each other, and it hasn't done any good. Take Ornette Coleman." Mingus sang half a chorus of "Body and Soul" in a loud, off-key voice, drowning out the jukebox. It was an uncanny imitation. "That's all he does. Just pushing the melody out of line here and there. Trouble is, he can't play it straight. At that little festival Max Roach and I gave in Newport in 1960, Kenny Dorham and I tried to get Ornette to play 'All the Things You Are' straight, and he couldn't do it."

Mingus took a sip of wine and made a face. "I don't know, this doesn't taste right."

"Maybe it isn't cold enough," Sue Ungaro said.

Mingus fished out his knife, deftly cut the straw basket off the bottle and put the bottle back in the ice. The waitress appeared and said "Everything fine, honey?"

"The wine doesn't taste right. It's not cold enough."

The waitress took three ice cubes out of the bucket and plopped them in our glasses and splashed some wine over them.

"Hey, that'll make it all water," Mingus said, seizing the bottle and jamming it back in the bucket.

"I'm just helping out, sir, like I said."

"She'll make the reputation of this place," Mingus mumbled.

"The Black Panthers have been to see Charles," Sue Ungaro said, "but he won't go along with them."

"I don't need to. I'm a single movement. Anyway, I don't like to see the blacks destroying this country. It's a waste of time. The militants have nothing to sell. And that's what this country does best—sells. Makes and sells thing to the world. But the militants don't sell *nothing*. All the black pimps and black gangsters know this, because they *have* something to sell, like the king-pimp Billy Bones in my book. Man, he made millions of dollars around the world. The black people don't like themselves to begin with. You've got all these variations of color and dialect. You've got terrific economic differences. You never hear anything from the wealthy blacks, but they don't like the militants. Some of them been working at their money 75 years, in real estate or whatever, and they not about to let the militants come and take it away for something called freedom. Hell, what's freedom? Nobody's free, black or white. What's going to happen is there will be one hell of a revolution and it'll be between black and black. Like the big trouble in Watts, when the blacks were ready to shoot the blacks. It all started when a truckload of militants arrived and started throwing bombs into the black stores and such. Well, man, the shop owners—and I grew up with a lot of them—got upset and came charging out with guns, and by this time the truck had moved on and the white cops had arrived and saw all these blacks standing around with guns and started shooting them, and that was it."

Mingus leaned back, out of breath. The manager passed the table and Mingus asked him if he had any fresh fish. The manager went into the kitchen and came back with a handful of cherrystones. Mingus looked surprised. He ordered half a dozen on the shell, and some vintage champagne.

"No vintage," the manager replied. "I got a bunch of vintage in last week and it was dead and I sent the whole mess back. I'll give you regular. Piper Heidsieck."

The clams arrived and Mingus coated each one with lemon juice and cocktail sauce and about a teaspoonful of Tabasco. "Hell, a while back, I took my daughter to Columbia to hear what's-his-name, Eldridge Cleaver, and right away all I heard him saying was mother this and mother that. Well, I didn't want my daughter hearing that. That's vulgarity no matter if the man is right or wrong. I left. I took my daughter and left right away."

Mingus looked relaxed and content. In fact, he looked as if he had finally got the world straightened around to his liking. The talk wandered easily along between jukebox selections, and Mingus and Sue Ungaro discussed astrology (Mingus: "My birth date is four/two-two/two-two. The astrologers have never been able to get over that"), weight problems (Mingus: "Man, I get to this size and it's painful. My arms hurt all the time up here from banging against the rest of me"), the effects on the stomach of too much vitamin C, the sorrows of drug addiction, and the fact that Mingus suddenly has more "visible, taxable" money than ever before in his life.

The lights started to go out. It was almost 4 AM. Mingus went to the men's room, and Sue Ungaro said: "I don't really like Charles' book, and I've told him. I think the sexual parts are too savage, and I think that Charles himself doesn't come through. It's the superficial Mingus, the flashy one, not the real one." Mingus reappeared and the waitress let us out the door. "'Night, now," she said with a couple of semaphores. "It's been a real pleasure servicing you."

Two nights later Mingus opened at the Village Vanguard with a sextet for a week's stand. It included Lonnie Hillyer on trumpet, Charlie McPherson on alto saxophone, Bobby Jones on tenor saxophone, John Foster on piano, Mingus, and Virgil Day on drums. Mingus the musician is a tonic to watch. He becomes a massive receiver-transmitter, absorbing every note played around him and then sending out through his corrective or appreciative notes. The result is a two-way flow which lights up his musicians who, in turn, light up his music.

Whenever he has felt out of sorts in recent years, Mingus has taken to offering lackluster medleys of bebop numbers or Ellington tunes, completely ignoring his own storehouse of compositions. But at the Vanguard he brought out refurbished versions of such numbers as "Celia" and "Diane." They were full of his trademarks—long, roving melodies, complex, multipart forms, breaks, constantly changing rhythms, howling ensembles, and the against-the-grain quality with which he brands each of his performances. Most of them were also done in Mingus' customary workshop manner. When a number would start hesitantly, he would rumble, "No. No, no," and stop the music. Then the group would start again. Sometimes there were three or four false starts. In all, there were half a dozen long numbers in the first set, and they were exceptional. Mingus soloed briefly just once, on a blues number, but everything was there. Dressed in a short-sleeved shirt and tie, he sat on a tall stool and played, and he looked as serene as he had on Sunday.

At the beginning of the following week, Knopf gave a publication party for *Beneath the Underdog*, with music. It was held in a couple of box-like, orange-carpeted rooms in the Random House building on East 50th Street. It was jammed, and Mingus' sextet, with a ringer on bass, was playing "Celia" at close to the 100 decibel level. There were more blacks than whites, and Mingus, again dressed in a dark suit and tie, was talking with a lady of his proportions. It was like seeing Sidney Greenstreet and Eugene Pallette porch to porch. Ornette Coleman, dressed in a glistening black silk mandarin suit, said he had just completed a piece for 80 musicians that sounded just like his playing. Nel King said that Mingus' book had been a lot of work and that perhaps her being a woman was a help in managing his tempestuous moods. Max Gordon, a Mingus supporter from the early days, was standing with Mingus and Sue Ungaro and a tall, slender youth in a beard, straw hat and cowboy boots. Sue was still in her blue jeans and clogs. "Meet my son, Charles, Jr.," Mingus said. He poked Charles, Jr. in the stomach. "*He* doesn't have any weight problem. And look at his beard! I can't grow any more than what I have on my face." Mingus asked his son if he had read his book.

"Listen, I haven't even seen it yet," Charles, Jr. replied. "Besides, I've been working on my play."

A man who had joined the group said that one of the minor but unavoidable axioms of the literary life was that children never read their parents' books. Mingus grunted. Nel King approached and told him she wanted him to meet someone. She asked Mingus before she towed him away how he liked the party.

"It's strange, man," he said.   —W. B.

An abstract of Lester Young. (Art Kane photograph from January 1959 *Esquire*)

Lester "Pres" Young

VERY LITTLE ABOUT the tenor saxophonist Lester Young was unoriginal. He had protruding, heavy-lidded eyes, a square, slightly Oriental face, a tiny mustache, and a snaggletoothed smile. His walk was light and pigeon-toed, and his voice was soft. He was something of a dandy. He wore suits, knit ties, and collar pins. He wore ankle-length coats, and pork-pie hats—on the back of his head when he was young, and pulled down low and evenly when he was older. He kept to himself, often speaking only when spoken to. When he played, he held his saxophone in front of him at a 45-degree angle, like a canoeist about to plunge his paddle into the water. He had an airy, lissome tone and an elusive, lyrical way of phrasing that had never been heard before. Other saxophonists followed Coleman Hawkins, but Young's models were two white musicians: the C-melody saxophonist Frank Trumbauer and the alto saxophonist Jimmy Dorsey—neither of them a first-rate jazz player. When Young died in 1959 he had become the model for countless saxophonists, white and black. He was a gentle, kind man who never disparaged anyone.

He spoke a coded language, about which the pianist Jimmy Rowles has said "You had to break that code to understand him. It was like memorizing a dictionary, and I think it took me about three months." Much of Young's language has vanished, but here is a sampling: "Bing and Bob" were the police. A "hat" was a woman, and a "homburg" and a "Mexican hat" were types of women. An attractive young girl was a "poundcake." A "gray boy" was a white man, and Young himself, who was light-skinned was an "oxford gray." "I've got bulging eyes" for this or that meant he approved of something, and "Catalina eyes" and "Watts eyes" expressed high admiration. "Left people" were the fingers of a pianist's left hand. "I feel a draft" meant he sensed a bigot nearby. "Have another helping," said to a colleague on the bandstand, meant "Take another chorus," and "one long" or "two long" meant one chorus or two choruses. People "whispering on" or "buzzing on"

him were talking behind his back. Getting his "little claps" meant being applauded. A "zoomer" was a sponger, and a "needle dancer" was a heroin addict. "To be bruised" was to fail. A "tribe" was a band, and a "molly trolley" was a rehearsal. "Can Madam burn?" meant "Can your wife cook?" "Those people will be here in December" meant that his second child was due in December. (He drifted in and out of three marriages, and had two children.) "Startled doe, two o'clock" meant that a pretty girl was in the right side of the audience.

Eccentrics flourish in crowded, ordered places, and Young spent his life on buses and trains, in hotel rooms and dressing rooms, in automobiles and on bandstands. He was born in Woodville, Mississippi, in 1909, and his family moved almost immediately to Algiers, just across the river from New Orleans. When he was 10, his father and mother separated, and his father took him and his brother Lee and sister Irma to Memphis and then to Minneapolis. Young's father, who could play any instrument, had organized a family band, which worked in tent shows in the Midwest and Southwest. Young joined the band as a drummer, and then switched to alto saxophone. An early photograph shows him holding his saxophone in much the same vaudeville way he later held it. Young once said that he was slow to learn to read music. "Then one day my father goes to each one in the band and asked them to play their part and I knew that was my ass, because he knew goddam well that I couldn't read. Well, my little heart was broken, you know; I went in crying and I was thinking, I'll come back and catch them, if that's the way they want it. So I went away all by myself and learned the music."

Young quit the family band when he was 18 and joined Art Bronson's Bostonians. During the next six or seven years, he worked briefly in the family band again, and at the Nest Club, in Minneapolis, for Frank Hines and Eddie Barefield. He also worked with the Original Blue Devils and with Bennie Moten, Clarence Love, King Oliver, and in 1934, Count Basie's first band. In an interview with Nat Hentoff, Young recalled playing with Oliver, who was well into his 50s and at the end of his career:

"After the Bostonians, I played with King Oliver. He had a very nice band, and I worked regularly with him for one or two years, around Kansas and Missouri mostly. He had three brass, three reeds and four rhythm. He was playing well. He was old then and didn't play all night, but his tone was full when he played. He was the star of the show and played one or two songs each set. The blues? He could play some nice blues. He was a very nice fellow, a gay old fellow. He was crazy about all the boys, and it wasn't a drag playing for him at all."

Soon after going with Basie, Young was asked to replace Coleman Hawkins in Fletcher Henderson's band, and, reluctantly, he went. It was the first of several experiences in his life that he never got over. Hawkins had spent 10 years with Henderson, and his oceanic tone and heavy chordal improvisations were the heart of the band. Jazz musicians are usually alert, generous listeners, but Young's alto-like tone (he had shifted to tenor saxophone not long before) and floating, horizontal solos sounded heretical to Henderson's men. They began "buzzing on" him, and Henderson's wife forced him to listen to Hawkins recordings in the hope he'd learn to play that way. Young lasted three or four months before going to Kansas City, first asking Henderson for a letter saying that he had not been fired.

Two years later, he rejoined Basie, and his career began. The pianist John Lewis knew Young then: "When I was still very young in Albuquerque, I remember hearing about the Young family settling there. They had a band and had come in with a tent show and been stranded. There was a very good local jazz band called St. Cecilia's that Lester played in. He also competed with an excellent Spanish tenor player and house painter named Cherry. I barely remember Lester's playing. He had a fine, thin tone. Then the family moved to Minneapolis, and I didn't see him until around 1934, when he came through on his way to the West Coast to get an alto player for Count Basie named Caughey Roberts. Lester sounded then the way he does on his first recordings, made in 1936. We had a lot of brass beds in that part of the country, and Lester used to hang his tenor saxophone on the foot of his bed so that he could reach it during the night if an idea came to him that he wanted to sound out."

Young's first recordings were made with a small group from Basie's band. The melodic flow suggests Trumbauer, and perhaps Dorsey, and an ascending gliss, an upward swoop, that Young used for the next 15 years suggests Bix Beiderbecke. Young had a deep feeling for the blues, and King Oliver's blues must have become a part of him. He had a pale tone, a minimal vibrato, a sense of silence, long-breathed phrasing, and an elastic rhythmic ease. Until his arrival, most soloists tended to pedal up and down on the beat, their phrases short and perpendicular, their rhythms broken and choppy. Young smoothed out this bouncing attack. He used long phrases and legato rhythms (in the manner of the trumpeter Red Allen, who was in Henderson's band with him), and

he often chose notes outside the chords—"odd" notes that italicized his solos. He used silence for emphasis.

Young "had a very spacey sound at the end of '33," bassist Gene Ramey recalls. "He would play a phrase and maybe lay out three beats before he'd come in with another phrase." Coleman Hawkins' solos buttonhole you; Young's seem to turn away. His improvisations move with such logic and smoothness they lull the ear. He was an adept embellisher and a complete improviser. He could make songs like "Willow Weep for Me" and "The Man I Love" unrecognizable. He kept the original melodies in his head, but what came out was his dreams about them. His solos were fantasies—lyrical, soft, liquid—on the tunes he was playing, and probably on his own life, as well. The humming quality of his solos was deceptive, for they were made up of quick runs, sudden, held notes that slowed the beat, daring shifts in rhythmic emphasis, continuous motion, and often lovely melodies. His slow work was gentle and lullaby-like, and as his tempos rose his tone became rougher. Young was also a singular clarinetist. In the late Thirties, he used a metal clarinet (eventually it was stolen, and he simply gave up the instrument), and he got a plaintive, silvery sound.

Young bloomed with Basie. He recorded countless classic solos with the band, giving it a rare lightness and subtlety, and he made his beautiful records accompanying Billie Holiday—their sounds a single voice split in two. Late in 1940, Young decided to go out on his own, as Coleman Hawkins had done years before. He had a small group on 52nd Street for a brief time, then went West and put a band together with his brother Lee. The singer Sylvia Syms hung around Young on 52nd Street as a teenager. "Lester was very light," she said, "and he had wonderful hair. He never used that pomade so popular in the Forties and Fifties. He was a beautiful dresser, and his accent was his porkpie hat worn on the back of his head. He used cologne, and he always smelled divine. Once, I complained to him about audiences who talked and never listened, and he said, 'Lady Syms, if there is one guy in the whole house who is listening and maybe he's in the *bathroom*—you've got an audience.' His conversation, with all its made-up phrases, was hard to follow, but his playing never was. He phrased words in his playing. He has had a great influence on my singing, and through the years a lot of singers have picked up on him."

Jimmy Rowles worked with Young when he went West: "I don't know when Billie Holiday nicknamed him Pres—for 'the President'—but when I first knew him the band called him Uncle Bubba. Of all the people I've met in this business, Lester was unique. He was alone. He was quiet. He was unfailingly polite. He almost never got mad. If he was upset, he'd take a small whisk broom he kept in his top jacket pocket and sweep off his left shoulder. The only way to get to know him was to work with him. Otherwise, he'd just sit there playing cards or sipping, and if he did say something it stopped the traffic. I never saw him out of a suit, and he particularly liked double-breasted pinstripes. He also wore tab collars, small trouser cuffs, pointed shoes and Cuban heels.

In 1941, the older guard among musicians still didn't recognize his worth. They didn't think of him as an equal. He was *there* , but he was still someone new. And here's an odd thing. His father held a saxophone upside down when he played it, in a kind of vaudeville way, so maybe Lester picked up his way of holding his horn from that. Whichever, the more he warmed up during work, the higher his horn got, until it was actually horizontal."

The Young brothers played Café Society Downtown in 1942, and after stints with Dizzy Gillespie and the tenor saxophonist Al Sears, Young rejoined Count Basie. He was drafted in 1944, and it was the second experience in his life that he never got over. There are conflicting versions of what happened, but what matters is that he collided head on with reality for the first time, and it felled him. He spent about 15 months in the Army, mainly in a detention barracks, for possession of marijuana and barbiturates and for being an ingenuous black man in the wrong place at the wrong time. He was discharged dishonorably, and from then on his playing and his personal life slowly roughened and worsened.

John Lewis worked for Young in 1951: "Jo Jones was generally on drums and Joe Shulman on bass, and either Tony Fruscella or Jesse Drakes on trumpet. We worked at places like Bop City in New York, and we travelled to Chicago. He would play the same songs in each set on a given night, but he would often repeat the sequence the following week this way: if he had played 'Sometimes

Fifty years before Jean Bach's documentary "A Great Jazz Day in Harlem" was nominated for an Oscar, an arty jazz short, "Jammin' the Blues" was produced by Norman Granz, a young Hollywood film editor who later founded and ran Jazz At The Philharmonic concerts and tours with Lester Young, Coleman Hawkins, Roy Eldridge, Dizzy Gillespie and many other stars. These title frames feature Young. (Frank Driggs collection)

I'm Happy' this Tuesday with a variation on the solo he had played on the tune the week before; then he would play variations on the variations the week after, so that his playing formed a kind of gigantic organic whole. While I was with him, I never heard any of the coarseness that people have said began creeping into his playing. I did notice a change in him in his last few years. There was nothing obvious or offensive about it. Just an air of depression about him.

"He was a living, walking poet. He was so quiet that when he talked each sentence came out like a little explosion. I don't think he consciously invented his special language. It was part of a way of talking I heard in Albuquerque from my older cousins, and there were variations of it in Oklahoma City and Kansas City and Chicago in the late Twenties and early Thirties. These people also dressed well, as Lester did—the porkpie hats and all. So his speech and dress were natural things he picked up. They weren't a disguise—a way of hiding. They were a way to be hip—to express an awareness of everything swinging that was going on. Of course, he never wasted this hipness on dudish people, nor did he waste good playing on bad musicians. If Lester was wronged, the wound never healed. Once, at Bop City, he mentioned how people had always bugged him about the supposed thinness of his tone. We were in his dressing room, and he picked up his tenor and played a solo using this great big butter sound. Not a Coleman Hawkins sound but a thick, smooth, concentrated sound. It was as beautiful as anything I've ever heard."

Young spent much of the rest of his life with Norman Granz's Jazz At The Philharmonic troupe. He had become an alcoholic, and his playing was ghostly and uncertain. He still wore suits and a porkpie hat, but he sat down a lot. When he appeared on "The Sound of Jazz" in 1957, he was remote and spaced out; he refused to read his parts for the two big-band numbers. (Ben Webster, who had been taught by Young's father, replaced him.) When he took a chorus during Billie Holiday's blues "Fine and Mellow," his tone was intact, but the solo limped by. The loving, smiling expression on Billie Holiday's face may have indicated that she was listening not to the Lester beside her but to the Lester long stored away in her head.

The tenor saxophonist Buddy Tate drove down with Young from the Newport Jazz Festival the next year: "I first met Lester when he was in Sherman, Texas, playing alto. A little later, I replaced him in the first Basie band when he went to join Fletcher Henderson. He didn't drink then, and he didn't inhale his cigarettes. He was so refined, so sensitive. I was with him in the second Basie band in 1939 and 1940, and he had a little bell he kept on the stand beside him. When someone goofed, he rang it. After the 1958 Newport Festival, I drove back with him to New York, and he was really down. He was unhappy about money, and said he wasn't great. When I told him how great he was, he said, 'If I'm so great, Lady Tate, how come all the other tenor players, the ones who sound like me, are making all the money?'"

The arranger Gil Evans knew Young on the West Coast in the Forties and in New York at the end of his life. "Solitary people like Lester Young are apt to wear blinders," he said. "He concentrated on things from his past that he should have long since set aside as a good or bad essence. The last year of his life, when he had moved into the Alvin Hotel, he brought up the fact that his father had been displeased with him when he was a teenager because he had been lazy about learning to read music. But maybe his bringing that up at so late a date was only a vehicle for some other, present anger that he was inarticulate about. Sometimes that inarticulateness made him cry. A long time before, when I happened to be in California, Jimmy Rowles and I went to see Pres, who was living in a three-story house that his father owned. We walked in on a family fight, and Pres was weeping. He asked us to get him out of there, to help move him to his mother's bungalow in West Los Angeles. We had a coupe I'd borrowed, so we did—lock, stock and barrel. Those tears were never far away. I was with him in the Fifties in a restaurant near 52nd Street when a man in a fez and a robe came in. This man started talking about Jesus Christ, and he called him a prophet. Well, Pres thought he had said something about Jesus and 'profit.' He got up and went out, and when I got to him he was crying. I had to explain what the man had said. I don't know where he got such strong feelings about Jesus. Maybe from going to church when he was young, or maybe it was just his sense of injustice. He couldn't stand injustice of any kind. He had a great big room at the Alvin, and when I'd go up to see him I'd find full plates of food everywhere. They'd been brought by friends, but he wouldn't eat. He just drank wine. One of the reasons his drinking got so out of hand was his teeth. They were in terrible shape, and he was in constant pain. But he was still fussy about things like his hair. He had grown it long at the back, and finally he let my wife, who was a good barber, cut it. At every snip, he'd say, 'Let me see it. Let me see it,' before the hair landed on the floor. It was amazing—a man more or less consciously killing himself, and he was still particular about his hair."

Tenor saxophonist Zoot Sims, who listened hard to Young in the Forties, also saw some of this harmless narcissism. "We roomed together on a Birdland tour in 1957," he said, "and one day when he was changing and had stripped to his shorts, which were red, he lifted his arms and slowly turned around and said, 'Not bad for an old guy.' And he was right. He had a good body—and a good mind. Lester was a very intelligent man."

Young died at the Alvin Hotel the day after he returned from a gig in Paris. He had given François Postif a long and bitter interview while he was in France, and, perhaps wittingly, he included his epitaph in it: "They want everybody who's a Negro to be an Uncle Tom or Uncle Remus or Uncle Sam, and I can't make it. It's the same all over: you fight for your life—until death do you part, and then you got it made.

—W.B.

Roy Eldridge

SLOWED BY VARIOUS ailments and by the deep fatigue that sooner or later afflicts all brass players, the trumpeter Roy Eldridge gave up playing in public in 1979 at age 74, thereby diminishing American musical life. For the last 10 years of his career, he had been on almost constant view at Jimmy Ryan's on West 54th Street, leading a small swing band and proving, night after night, that his great engines still worked very well.

Joe Muranyi, his longtime clarinetist at Ryan's, said of him, "Roy is complex, but he's very much in touch with his feelings and they'd all come out in his music. They came out when he wasn't playing, too. He liked to act out the same dramas every day. He fought his battles with race, with his playing, with managers over and over. And he and I would have terrible arguments. He'd make me mad as hell by telling me that I didn't sound like a Hungarian clarinet player, that I must be Polish. And when I'd make him mad it was Mt. Vesuvius to the fifth power. A few years ago, he had a heart attack. We had done a gig up in Connecticut not long before that, and after we had set up and were going out for food Roy just sat there on the stand and said to bring him a cheeseburger. Then he said, 'I'm sick and tired of this. What do I need it for?' But even toward the end there was no notable loss in his playing. He could still be fiery. He would start slowly every evening, pacing himself until he got it all together."

Eldridge had a restless career. He played in every size and kind of band from jam groups to Boyd Raeburn's forward-looking big band. He played for the best black bands (McKinney's Cotton Pickers, Fletcher Henderson, Count Basie) and for the best white bands (Gene Krupa, Artie Shaw, Benny Goodman). He led his first band, Roy Elliott and his Palais Royal Orchestra, in Pittsburgh, where he was born, before he was 20. Then he joined Horace Henderson's Dixie Stompers, and in 1929 and 1930 he was with the Nighthawks, Zack Whyte and Speed Webb. He also worked in Milwaukee with Johnny Neal's Midnite Ramblers. He moved to New York in 1930, and he went from Cecil Scott to a famous Elmer Snowden band that included Dicky Wells, Al Sears, Otto Hardwicke and Sidney Catlett and that made a high-jinks short film, "Smash Your Baggage." Hollywood still disguised the few blacks it showed, and everyone in the band was dressed as a Pullman porter. He passed through Charlie Johnson, Teddy Hill and McKinney's Cotton Pickers, and in 1936 joined Fletcher Henderson. He formed his own band the same year and held forth for a long spell at the Three Deuces in Chicago. Angry over racism, he quit music in 1938 and studied radio engineering. By 1939, though, he had put together a new band, which played mostly dance music at the Arcadia Ballroom on Broadway. In 1941, after stints at the Apollo Theatre, Kelly's Stable and the Capital Lounge in Chicago, he went with Gene Krupa, forcing that mundane band to play with joy and fervor. Krupa broke up the band in 1943, and Eldridge gigged around New York and joined Artie Shaw in 1944.

Shaw once talked about him this way: "He was a cute, little, chunky guy, a feisty guy, in many ways a tragic guy. It was very tough for him racially in my band, just as it had been for Billie Holiday when she was with me in the Thirties. With Hot Lips Page, who was in the band in 1941, it was different, because he had the attitude of 'I can't change it, so I'll put up with it'—maybe because he came from the South. When I hired Roy, I told him he

Roy Eldridge and buddy from the Teddy Hill and Fletcher Henderson bands, tenor star Chu Berry, in front of Savoy Ballroom, 1935. (Baron Timmie Rosenkrants/Institute of Jazz Studies photograph)

would be treated like everyone else in the band and that he would be paid very well, because he was the best. I told him that I could handle racial matters when we were on the stand, but that there was very little I could do when we were off. Droves of people would ask him for his autograph at the end of the night, but later, on the bus, he wouldn't be able to get off and buy a hamburger with the guys in the band. He used to carry a gun, and I'd try and discourage him, and he'd tell me that he'd rather take his chances with the police than run up, unarmed, against some crazy. He saw himself as traveling through a hostile land, and he was right. Things came to a head at the San Francisco Auditorium when he arrived late and they wouldn't let him in the main entrance. He was a bitch of a player, and everybody in the band loved him."

Eldridge stayed with Shaw a year, had another band of his own, rejoined Krupa for a short time, and in 1950 went to Europe with Benny Goodman. He stayed on in Paris after Goodman had gone home, returning to New York in 1951 to make a sensational appearance at the Old Stuyvesant Casino down on Second Avenue. He spent much of the Fifties in Norman Granz's Jazz At The Philharmonic. Then he accompanied Ella Fitzgerald for two years. He was with Count Basie in 1966, and he led his own groups and appeared at festivals until he moved into Jimmy Ryan's. He was on the CBS television show "The Sound of Jazz" in 1957. Not long before he became ill, he played at the miniature jazz festival that President Jimmy Carter held on the south lawn of the White House—a gracious affair that included many of Eldridge's peers and descendants.

Eldridge's style was incandescent, lyrical, melancholy, indelible and erratic. He learned the hard way, as he told John Chilton for the liner notes of a Columbia album called "Roy Eldridge—The Early Years." "When I was young I used to go out and look for every jam session going," Eldridge said. "I used to stand out on the sidewalk smoking, listening to the band inside, summing up the opposition. Eventually I'd walk in and try to cut them. All my life, I've loved to battle. And if they didn't like the look of me and wouldn't invite me up on the bandstand, I'd get my trumpet out by the side of the stand and blow at them from there."

He also told Chilton, "The cats in New York were a hard bunch, guys were coming in from all over the country trying to prove themselves, and those who had got there first elected themselves as the judges. The rule seemed to be that you told newcomers the things you didn't like about their playing and not the things you liked. So, Hot Lips Page heard me and said, 'Why are you playing like an ofay?' Well, he knew his stuff, so I took note of that. And Chick Webb, who was guaranteed to speak his mind, said, 'Yeah, you're fast, but you're not telling me any story,' and those words sank right into me. At that time I had this thing about playing as fast as I could all the time. I double-timed every ballad I did, and never held a long note. I was able to run the changes on any song and do nice turn-arounds at the end of each eight bars, but I wasn't developing my solos."

His phrasing and way of building a climax resembled Louis Armstrong's, and he has said that he learned from Rex Stewart and the white cornetist Red Nichols. He has said, too, that he learned much from saxophonists like Coleman Hawkins and Benny Carter, which helps explain the flow and momentum of his playing. He spent time listening to the flashing, mercurial Jabbo Smith in the late Twenties, and Smith's speed and quirkiness must have affected him. And he heard the strange notes and dark sound and laid-back attack that Red Allen used with Fletcher Henderson in 1933 and 1934. All this coalesced into a stunning and original style, which in due course brought forth Dizzy Gillespie.

Eldridge's style comes in two parts. The most celebrated is his up-tempo, upper-register attack, as heard on Gene Krupa's 1941 recording of "After You've Gone." Following some introductory clowning (cheers from the band and quotes by Eldridge from a Sousa march and from "Yankee Doodle"), Eldridge hurtles through three choruses of the song. He does the first more or less straight, and he improvises the next two. Along the way, he plays five exhilarating four-bar breaks. In the first, he falls through three registers, his fingers and lips releasing notes the way a dog shakes off water; he rockets up and down his horn in the second and third, producing avalanches of notes somewhere between arpeggios and glissandos; in the fourth he mixes giant intervals and teeming arpeggios; and in the fifth he connects descending steplike notes with racing staccato passages.

The record is dazzling showing off; it moves on the rim of chaos. Eldridge settles to earth in his slow and medium-tempo ballads and blues. His gruff, dense tone expands, his improvisational skills blossom, his delicate vibrato comes into view, and the emotion always present in his playing pours out. There is a strong melancholy strain in Eldridge, and it imbues all his ballads and blues. His blues are monumental, and so are some of his ballads (consider the 1953 Verve recording of "The Man I Love" and his Krupa "Rockin' Chair"). But sometimes his emotions engulfed him. His sporadic stage fright would cause this, and so would situations—a roomful of listening peers, say—that he could not control. At such times, he would work so hard and grow so excited that he would end up caroming around his highest register and sounding almost mad. But even then he was majestic. Eldridge was a fine scampish jazz singer, with a light, hoarse voice and a highly rhythmic attack. He sang the blues much in the manner of Hot Lips Page, and his nonsense vocals ("Saturday Night Fish Fry,""Knock Me a Kiss") rocked.

Eldridge lived with his wife, Vi, and his only child, Carole, in a small two-story house in Hollis, at the back of Queens, not far from Belmont Park and Nassau County. His house was in a sea of small houses, each afloat on its patch of green, each moored to several trees. Eldridge was not much over five feet. Compact, bristling, cheerful, beamy, he fit the nickname—Little Jazz— given him long ago by Otto Hardwicke. His hair was graying, he wore Harry Truman glasses and his teeth remained the most beautiful in the business.

Eldridge's living room had a thick greenish rug, a fireplace with a mirror over it, a television set, a sofa, two wide-shouldered leather chairs, a picture window that looked out on the street, and a stairway to the second floor. A kitchen was visible beyond the stairway, and to its left, a dining room. In a small alcove-den between the dining room and the front door were some of Eldridge's trophies—a *Down Beat* award for placing first in the 1946 trumpet poll, an Esky statuette from *Esquire* in 1945, a certificate of appreciation from Mayor John Lindsay, a letter of appreciation from President Carter for playing at the White House. On a table covered with family photographs he displayed a card that Vi gave him. Headed "How to Know You're Growing Older," it listed these hints:

> You get winded playing chess.
> You join a health club and don't go.
> You look forward to a dull evening.
> Your back goes out more than you do.

One afternoon, Eldridge sat on a low stool in front of his picture window and talked about the present and the past. He did not particularly relish being interviewed, partly because, like most of the surviving musicians of his generation, he was interviewed-out, and partly because he was a proud man who did not like giving away things of value unless he was sure they would be treated the right way. He looked steadily out the window as he talked, registering each car and truck and human being that passed, and occasionally commenting ("Man, look at that old cat all bent over! At least I can walk standing up straight"). He spoke the way he sang, and he laughed a lot. There were long pauses between some of the things he said, and he jumped all around the landscape of his life.

"New York is mean," he said, "but I wouldn't live anywhere else. When I was on the road I searched Europe and South America for the perfect place to live. No place had the right feel—not even Copenhagen, which is my favorite European city. Of course, Europe has changed. They met you with flowers in Scandinavia in the Fifties. Now it's like going to Newark.

"Vi and I have been married since 1936. Her maiden name was Viola Lee. Her father was Chinese. She was a hostess at the Savoy Ballroom. I carried both Vi and Carole, who's a legal secretary, over to Europe one year on tour, and were they glad to get back! Doing one-nighters, you see the airport, the road to the hotel, the place where the concert is, the place you eat at after the concert, the hotel, and, the next morning, the road back to the airport. Near the end, I'd hear them saying in the next room, 'Only four days to Christmas,' then 'Only two days to Christmas'—Christmas being the day we were scheduled to fly home.

"We've been in this house 27 years. It was nicer around here when we first moved out from New York. There was a butcher, a drugstore, a theatre. I've had two or three heart attacks in the past six years, and I've quit playing. I've also got some kind of emphysema. I don't miss the music anymore. I've had enough fun and praise and ovations to keep me. I played 50 years, and that was long enough. Anyway, I found out the main doors were always locked. The color thing. I also found out I'd never get rich.

"At first, after I got sick, I'd play along with the television commercials all evening, but I don't do that anymore. I used to play the piano and drums, but I gave my piano away because it got wet down in the cellar, and I still haven't gotten around to putting the drums Gene Krupa gave me back in shape. When I stopped playing, I fell into another slot. I didn't have to wear a watch, I didn't have to break my back. There's so much to do around here I don't have the time to do it.

"Playing was my life. Before I went onstage, I would sit in my dressing room and run over in my mind what I was going to do. But when I got out there I didn't try and make the B-flat or whatever I was thinking of, because I'd go right into a void where there was no memory, nothing but me. I knew the chords and I knew the melody, and I never thought about them. I'd just be in this blank place, and out the music would come.

"It wasn't always easy. Riding up on that stage at the Paramount Theatre with the Krupa band scared me to death. When the stage stopped and we started to play, I'd fall to pieces. The first three or four bars of my first solo, I'd shake like a leaf, and you could hear it. Then this light would surround me, and it would seem as if there wasn't any band there, and I'd go right through and be all right. It was something I never understood.

"I'd go all over from the late Twenties to the Forties looking for people to challenge on trumpet. One occa-

Roy Eldridge often sat in on his second instrument, the drums. (Institute of Jazz Studies photograph)

sion broke my heart. It happened in 1930. I already knew Rex Stewart, and he came into Small's Paradise, where I was with Elmer Snowden's band, and said he'd meet me later at Greasy's, an after-hours place. Gus Aiken and Red Allen showed up, and a lot of guys from the Henderson band. They were great agitators at cutting sessions. At these sessions, we used to stomp. That means that eight bars before your solo you'd stomp your foot to let the cat who was finishing his solo know that you were going to come in. Rex and I got to battling and exchanging choruses at Greasy's, and after he finished a chorus I stomped him and screamed a G. At the end of my chorus, he stomped me back and screamed a B-flat. I'd never heard the note he hit, and he had played something I couldn't play. I brooded all the next day. He had hit that note, but he hadn't played up to it or come down from it. I found the note and worked on it until I could play up to it and down from it, and the next time we met I showed it to him.

"A couple of years before that, I had a run-in with Jabbo Smith in Milwaukee. We met at a place called Rails, and Jabbo used my horn. We played fast and slow. I could play fast all over, but when the tempo got down it wasn't my stick. The crowd thought I had cut Jabbo, and he didn't talk to me for two weeks, but I didn't fool myself. I knew he had cut me. A session I enjoyed a lot more around the same time took place in Detroit. When I went into this club to sit in, the band was off and the stand was empty except for a girl sitting there. I asked her where the trumpet player was, and she said, 'I'm the trumpet player.' Her name was Doll Jones. The next set, she started out and my mouth gaped. I couldn't believe it. We jammed until three o'clock in the afternoon.

"Coleman Hawkins and I were very tight and very good together. I dug him, and he dug me. He told me that he first heard me on records when he was in Europe in the late Thirties, and that he'd never heard anyone play the trumpet like that. He was used to the best of everything. If a new camera came out, he had to have it. The same with binoculars or a watch. Coleman had class.

"I first met Lester Young in Baltimore in the mid-Thirties when he was with Fletcher Henderson. I met him jamming. I used to pick him and Jo Jones up in Chicago when they were with Basie and had finished work. Lester loved to jam, and that was where we hit it.

"I loved Big Sid Catlett. He was so smooth. He had that weight without being noisy. Webb was the best drum soloist I ever heard.

"When Ben Webster was sober, he was the nicest cat you ever met, but when he was drinking he'd turn rough. Sometimes he'd slap me or something like that, and I'd end up chasing him down the street, big as he was."

Eldridge stopped talking, reared back, and shouted at the ceiling, "Vi! Hey, Vi! You want the heat up? It's cold in here." He lowered his voice. "I have to watch the cold now, with this emphysema. I listen to all the medical shows in the morning, and they say don't eat chicken, don't eat veal, don't eat this, don't eat that. They look at the dinosaurs—they ate nothing but greens. And I say, 'Where are they now?' "

Vi Eldridge came down the stairs. She was pretty and medium-sized. Eldridge asked her again if she wanted more heat, and she said, "How can you tell?" She turned up the heat and asked Eldridge if he wanted anything to eat or drink. He said no, and she went upstairs.

Eldridge looked sharp left out his window. "I wonder if those cats are stripping that car or fixing it," he said. "They've stripped the tires off of my station wagon, nothing else. You have to have a car out here, or you're smothered. Sometimes I drive over into Nassau, but I don't go into New York much anymore. It's expensive going places now, and they don't always know who you are. Anyway, all my old clothes are too big.

"I grew up on the north side of Pittsburgh. My brother Joe was two and a half years older. My mother played some piano and had the kind of ear where after she came home from the movies she could repeat exactly what she'd heard the pianist in the pit do. And I'd accompany her on my little drum, which I took up at six. She was a nice-looking woman. She was from somewhere around Winston-Salem.

"My father was from Petersburg, Virginia. He was my height, but heavier built, and darker. He had a lot of brothers. He was a contractor, and he was good with houses. He didn't drink or smoke. He was religious. I'd fight at the drop of a hat, and somebody was always coming to the house and telling him, 'Your son hit my boy aside the head with a rock.' After the man had gone, my father would say, 'What's the matter with you, boy? You act like a savage.'

"We lived near the Pennsylvania Railroad, and he made the top of our house into a dormitory where the railroad men could pay and stay. He also set up a shoeshine stand for my brother and me. And he had a restaurant downstairs that my mother and a cousin from North Carolina ran. My father was a good businessman.

"Then we moved up to Irwin Avenue. The house was on a hill, and you could look over the north side. My father ended up leaving me about six houses, but I was always traveling, and what with bad tenants and the like, I lost them. After grammar school, I went to David B. Oliver High. Pittsburgh was a funny place. We had to sit in the peanut gallery at the movies, but the schools weren't segregated.

"I played drums in the local drum-and-bugle corps. The day of a parade, I'd be up at six waiting for the sun to come up and give me enough heat so I could get my snare head tuned right. I started on trumpet because one day when we were out at the cemetery they handed me a bugle and told me to play 'Taps.' I was shaking like this. My brother got my parents to give me a trumpet. I had a good ear, and anything I heard I could play. My brother taught me to read in 1928 when I was with Horace Henderson, and by the time I was with Fletcher Henderson in 1936 I was able to handle all those difficult keys Fletcher wrote his arrangements in.

"My mother died when I was about 11. I got kicked out of the ninth grade. I wasn't interested in schoolwork, and I refused to play in the band. I'd tap out drum riffs all day on my desk. I was supposed to go back to school the next fall, but I got a gig with a touring company and took off. I didn't know hardly anything—how to work the spit valve, how to care for the horn. I didn't tell my father I got the job, and I didn't take any clothes. I just went."

—W.B.

Thelonious Monk

WHEN NATHAN ZUCKERMAN fishes for approbation in Philip Roth's *The Ghost Writer*, the great Lonoff tells him he has "the most compelling voice I've encountered in years, certainly for somebody starting out. I don't mean style. I mean voice: something that begins at around the back of the knees and reaches well above the head."

Voices like that are rare in any art, but when one turns up in the jazz world it often has an unusually comprehensive and immediate effect. I'm referring to the kind of musician with a voice so startling—a grasp so sure—that the whole music seems to stop in its tracks to confront the interloper, and emerges enhanced and fortified. This was certainly the case with Armstrong, Young, Parker and Coleman. But not with Thelonious Monk, who conducted his first record session at 30, organized his first working band at 40, and dropped from sight at about 55. Although a small coterie of musicians (notably Coleman Hawkins, Mary Lou Williams, Dizzy Gillespie, Charlie Parker and Bud Powell) esteemed him from the beginning, he labored in solitude for much of his most creative period. His records were ignored, his compositions pilfered, his instrumental technique patronized, his personal style ridiculed. Yet no voice in American music was more autonomous and secure than Monk's, and no voice in jazz relied more exclusively on jazz itself for its grammar and vision.

The controversy about Monk must be difficult for younger listeners to comprehend. One can readily appreciate why Schoenberg and his disciples or the jazz avant-garde of the Sixties caused dissension. Those musics were conceived as attacks and practically demanded rejoinders. Monk's music is more accurately compared to Stravinsky's early ballets, which, though new and daring for the time, proved accessible to the general public long before intransigent critics saw the light. Monk isn't merely accessible; he's almost gregarious in his desire to entertain, as long as the listener is willing to be entertained on Monk's terms. By this, I

don't mean to suggest that Monk's music is lightheaded or lighthearted, though on occasion it can be both, but that everything he did was designed to heighten the listener's response to melody, rhythm and harmony. His tools were traditional, his craftsmanship impeccable. Monk relished swing and the blues and the freedom to do with them as he pleased (his motto was "jazz is freedom"); he pursued his muse with dauntless concentration, impressive faith and an almost childlike glee. This, after all, was the musician who more than anyone else transformed the minor second from mistake to resource.

Immersing oneself in Monk's art is both an exhilarating and dispiriting experience—the former because his music is eternally fresh, the latter because so much else seems tame and trite by comparison. I thought I knew his Blue Note recordings pretty well, but rummaging through the treasure box that is *The Complete Blue Note Recordings of Thelonious Monk* (Mosaic MR4 101), I find that even the most familiar pieces unveil new mysteries and reveal new charms. One obvious reason is that this four-record box, comprising the six sessions he conducted for the label between 1947 and 1952, plus a middling 1957 session under the leadership of Sonny Rollins, includes no less than 14 previously unreleased performances. Eleven are alternate takes, but don't for a moment think that they are merely flawed warm-ups with slightly different embellishments or changes in tempi. In almost every instance, they afford us the chance to hold familiar gems to the light and discover new refractions of Monk's genius; his work on some of the alternates—including "Nice Work If You Can Get It" and "Skippy"—is actually superior to that on the master versions. The remaining discoveries (all from 1952) are a mildly amusing reading of an obscure Fred Ahlert melody ("I'll Follow You") and two takes of a previously unknown Monk original, "Sixteen," that reharmonizes "Ja-Da" much in the same way "In Walked Bud" reharmonizes "Blue Skies." Although Monk never officially recorded the tune, he recycled a key lick from his tumbling, all-in-one-breath, first-take solo five months later for his improvisation on "Little Rootie Tootie." Some years later, Sonny Rollins employed similar changes for "Doxy," and one can't help but wonder if they were a lesson from the master.

The Blue Note years capture Monk in the throes of youthful assertion, training musicians of varying abilities in the exigencies of a music unlike but indebted to the hopped-up modernism of the age. They remind us, as indeed all of Monk's work does, that he was the quintessential New York jazzman. A proudly chauvinistic resident of West 63rd Street—where a circle is now named in his honor—for most of his life (his family moved there from North Carolina when he was six), Monk lived and breathed the sounds of the city as surely as Louis Armstrong was nurtured by New Orleans. It's there in everything he wrote and played—the clangor and ambition; the nostalgia and irreverence; the influences of the church, big bands, Tin Pan Alley, Harlem stride, modernism. He embraced it all. Yet despite a teen age sojourn at Juilliard, he knew less of the European tradition than most of his contemporaries, particularly Parker and Gillespie; Quincy Jones once credited this combination of self-absorption and willful ignorance with Monk's ability to avoid "contrived" experiments.

Monk's modernism may once have seemed difficult to comprehend and remains extremely difficult to play, but it was never self-conscious. Michael Cuscuna, co-partner with Charlie Lourie in the Mosaic venture, wisely devotes much of his copious notes to musicological comments by such as Gunther Schuller, Ran Blake, Steve Lacy and Martin Williams. Listening through their ears, we can perhaps better enjoy the harmonic and rhythmic innovations that inform these performances, but our appreciation of complex Monkian neologisms in no way vitiates our ability to listen ingenuously, too. Monk delights the brain, but he also animates the heart and viscera.

His first masterpiece, appropriately called "Thelonious," was recorded at the close of his first session, and was greeted by *Billboard* as "a controversial jazz disking worked out on a one note riff." Though only a prelude to the more accomplished work to come, it merits close inspection. I don't know a better example of the way a musician can draw extensively on the jazz past and come up with something indigenous and wonderful. A first listening tells us nothing if not that the composition and execution are pure Monk, and something new in jazz in 1947. Yet the materials continuously summon ghosts from the past. For starters, there is the rhythmic/melodic concept that governs the entire piece—a hammering, repeated theme that appears to be confined to one note, though it is really built on three. The antecedent I'm reminded of is the first of Louis Armstrong's two choruses on "Muggles" (1928). Armstrong constructed the entire episode by ping-ponging two notes, A and C, and then climactically springing up an octave to high C. Monk works just as exclusively with F and B-flat, increasing tension with B-flat octaves, only he sustains this motif for the entire performance.

Monk announces his rhythmic intentions with an introduction by piano and drums. The theme is voiced on piano while the winds (in their sole contribution to the piece) play descending arpeggios—not functionally unlike the vamp for reeds at the beginning of Ellington's "East St. Louis Toodle-oo" (1927). Ellington is more explicitly suggested in the theme's unusual structure: AABA with a 10-bar release, plus two-bar interlude between choruses. The unchanging interlude may also remind us of the kind of blues fillips Jimmy Yancey often employed as transitions between choruses (cf. the 1939 "How Long"). The eight bars of B-flats that end the first improvised chorus recall not only Armstrong but the king of the one-note ride, Lester Young, especially since the sequence begins a measure ahead of time (a favorite Lestorian ploy). The second chorus, however, opens with stride piano out of James P. Johnson (albeit with Monkian minor seconds), and concludes with an au courant rhythmic lick that contemporaries called "Salt Peanuts" (after Gillespie's record) but that older fans may have remembered from Armstrong's "I'm a Ding Dong Daddy." And the final chorus climaxes with a series of triplets à la Count Basie in a performance that any fool knows is 100 percent Monk. I don't suggest that Monk was much interested in sprinkling his music with homages or clues; the lesson here is that Monk found in jazz all he needed to elaborate his own devious fantasies. By contrast, a good many deliberate glorifications of the jazz tradition sound fabricated and coy.

Monkian revelations proliferate in these recordings. How did he think of so many odd notions that sound so unalterably right in performance—such as the single measure of boogie woogie bass in the bridge of his gorgeous ballad, "Ruby, My Dear," or the introduction to "In Walked Bud" that is nothing more than a cascading arpeggio that caroms into the oddly accented theme with algebraic precision (Art Blakey's press rolls in this piece have the same effect), or the two measures of whole-tone phrases right before the first improvised turnback on "Off Minor"? Blakey, of course, requires more than parenthetical mention as one of Monk's finest collaborators. You can almost hear him hearing the pianist, so deftly and empathically does he shift dynamics, bearing down when appropriate, floating the rhythm with unfaltering exactness. The other major voice here belongs to Milt Jackson, whose unperturbed grace inspired Monk to some of his most outlandish conceits, such as the erupting sevenths on "Misterioso" that might have been turned into a new tune, in the manner of "Evidence." There are memorable turns by other players as well, but it's Monk who consistently steals the show, whether he's doubling the bass line behind the trumpet solo on "Suburban Eyes" or closing an eight-bar solo on "All the things You Are" with blues licks or clipping chords (raising all his fingers but one) and pounding minor seconds on "Introspection" or playing havoc with 4/4 by displacing the melody accents of "Criss Cross" or making his sole comment on the cool school with the melodious "Let's Cool One" or voicing ripe alto sax on only the third and eleventh bars of "Round Midnight" or orchestrating tritones on "Skippy" or playing with waltz meter on "Carolina Moon."

Thelonious Monk at the Beehive in Chicago, spring 1955. (Frank Driggs collection)

This is music that pleases first time out, but I wonder if it ever gives up all its secrets. Perhaps the biggest surprise this box will have for veteran Monk enthusiasts is the alternate to "Well You Needn't." Apparently, he hadn't absolutely determined the way the piece should be played when he arrived at the studio; after he recorded the master, he tried a version with a slight change in thematic accents—the result is practically a new piece.

The Mosaic production is exemplary in all important aspects, but I have two quibbles. First, there is much talk in the notes of still unreleased takes, some of them described in detail, which means they exist. I'm willing to believe Cuscuna when he calls them tedious (though it's hard to believe they are entirely dispensable), but I wish he'd use more caution in calling his collections "complete"; eight years ago (when he collated *The Complete Genius* for Blue Note), "complete" didn't allow

for the 14 new performances in this set, and who knows what it will mean a few years hence. Second, there is a splendid discography that solves many puzzles (including the seemingly deliberate errors on Columbia's 1966 *Misterioso*) but pointlessly ignores live recordings that weren't originally intended for commercial release on the grounds that they aren't "legitimate." By what logic are discarded takes from the Blue Note vaults legitimate, while the 1941 Jerry Newman tapes from Minton's, which have either been widely available for 37 years or issued responsibly by Xanadu in the Seventies, aren't? Record producers should be moral, upstanding citizens and the scourge of bootleggers, but discographers should just be scholarly. There are also a few typos, of which "In Walked Dud" is the most egregious. This limited edition (7,500 copies world-wide) was created for Mosaic Records of Santa Monica, California.

—G.G.

Coleman Hawkins

COLEMAN HAWKINS and Lester Young—the emperors of the tenor saxophone and the inventors of so much regal, original music—were opposites. Hawkins was a vertical improviser who ran the chord changes and kept the melody in his rearview mirror. Young was a horizontal improviser, who kept the melody beside him and cooled the chord changes. Hawkins had a voluminous, enveloping tone. Young had an oblique, flyaway sound. Hawkins played so many notes in each chorus that he blotted out the sun. Young handpicked his notes, letting the light and air burnish them. Hawkins played with ferocious, on-the-beat intensity. Young seemed to be towed by the beat. Hawkins was handsome, sturdy and businesslike. Young was slender, fey and oracular. Hawkins had a heavy voice, and he spoke rapidly and articulately. Young had a light voice and talked elliptically, in a funny, poetic language of his own. Hawkins appeared to grow bigger and denser when you looked at him. Young verged on transparency.

But the two were not totally dissimilar. Hawkins eventually destroyed himself with alcohol, and so did Young, although he did the job quicker. (Hawkins died at the age of 64 in 1969, and Young at the age of 49 in 1959.) Both were assiduous dressers, with Hawkins being something of a fashion plate. Both were consumed by their music, and have countless musical descendants.

Hawkins invented the tenor saxophone in the way that Richardson invented the novel: he took an often misunderstood instrument and made it work right for the first time. The saxophone, like the tuba, had been used for comic effects and in marching bands, and it was regarded—half brass, half reed—as a hybrid. It took Hawkins 10 years to figure out completely the instrument's capabilities. He hit upon using an unusually wide mouthpiece and hard reed, and by 1933 he had developed a tone that had never before been heard on a saxophone. (There were saxophone virtuosos before Hawkins, but they had a facile tone and concentrated on creamy glissandos and dazzling arpeggios.) His tone had the edgelessness of cellos and contraltos. It filled the mind with images of fire-lit mahogany, of august spaces, of great elms. Hawkins talked (when he talked—he was taciturn) the way he played: crowding his words together and steadily gaining momentum.

Here he is on an autobiographical recording made in the Fifties for Riverside. He is discussing his style: "It changed automatically through different things that I heard. It always shows in your music. I mean, it just comes spontaneously. I mean, you don't have to practice it. I never practiced anything like that, you know. I never practiced any particular thing to learn a style or anything like that. I never did in my life. I find myself playing a lot of things, changing them around and playing them completely different than what I would perhaps have played them a year before. But that just came through, I mean, different things I've heard. You know, I've heard it and I remembered it, you know what I mean? The next night, I perhaps didn't remember it, but maybe six months later it would show up in the music … That's what used to happen. That's why the style used to change all the time. And I tell you something else I used to do. I was the only one—there wasn't anybody else doing this. I used to go out on these road trips with Fletcher [Henderson]. Every time we came in after a road trip, I always had me some new things. And you know where I used to find them? In these little clubs and places, in all these little towns we used to go in and play . . . I've never stopped, you know; I'm still doing the same thing today. I hear every musical organization of any interest that there is."

And here he is, on the Riverside record, talking about the effect of New York on newly arrived country-mouse musicians: "This place makes all musicians sound funny when they come around. When they first come here—I don't care what they were in their hometowns—when they first come here, they get cut. They get cut every time. They have to come here and learn all over again, practically. Then when they come back they're all right, or if they stay here they'll develop to be all right."

Hawkins walked quickly, in an erect, the-meeting-will-now-come-to-order fashion. He did not smile much; he was a reserved man, surrounded by lawns of reticence. But reserved people often conceal hellions. Hawkins loved to play jokes on his friends, and he loved to drive fast. The trombonist Sandy Williams told Stanley Dance, in "The World of Swing," "I remember coming with him and Walter Johnson from Philly once, and he had it up to 103 miles an hour. That was the first time I ever did over a hundred an hour, but Hawk was a good driver. 'Hell, I don't want to kill myself,' he'd tell you right quick. 'What are you worried about?'" Hawkins had no showmanship, and when he played he closed his eyes and held his horn to the right of him, almost at port arms.

Hawkins was born in 1904, or perhaps earlier, in St. Joseph, Missouri. He was the second child of Cordelia Coleman and Wil Hawkins. (Their only other child, a girl, died in infancy.) He liked to tell interviewers that he was born at sea while his parents were returning from a European vacation—he was a great leg-puller and a good mythologist. His father was an electrical worker who was killed accidentally in the Twenties, and his mother was a schoolteacher who lived to be 95. (A grandmother reached 104.) He took up the piano when he was 5, studied cello for several years, and was given a tenor saxophone when he was 9. By the time he was 13 he was full-grown, and his parents had sent him to Chicago, where he lived with friends and went to high school. He also heard King Oliver and Louis Armstrong and Jimmie Noone. He is supposed to have attended Washburn College, in Topeka, but there is no proof he did. In 1921, he was working at the Twelfth Street Theatre in Kansas City, where he was heard by the blues singer Mamie Smith, whose accompanists included the Ellington trumpeter Bubber Miley and the reedman Garvin Bushell. Bushell told Nat Hentoff, in *The Jazz Review*, "We played the Twelfth Street Theatre, and that's where I first met Coleman Hawkins. They had added a saxophone to play the show with us in the pit. He was ahead of everything I ever heard on that instrument. It might have been a C-melody he was playing then. Anyway, he was about 15 years old—I remember that because one night we went to his mother's house in St. Joseph and asked her to let him go with us, and she said, 'No, he's only a baby; he's only 15.' He was really advanced. He read everything without missing a note. I haven't heard him miss a note yet in 37 years. And he didn't—as was the custom then—play the saxophone like a trumpet or clarinet. He was also running changes then, because he'd studied the piano as a youngster."

Hawkins joined Mamie Smith's Jazz Hounds in 1922, and Fletcher Henderson's first band in 1923. He stayed 11 years. The Henderson band—powerful, erratic, undisciplined—was the first big swing band and the model for almost every big band of the thirties. It was also an academy for such first-rate jazz musicians as Louis Armstrong, Rex Stewart, Red Allen, Roy Eldridge, Joe Thomas, Jimmy Harrison, Sandy Williams, Benny

Coleman Hawkins at the Fiesta Danseteria on 42nd Street near Broadway in New York, 1940. (Frank Driggs collection)

Morton, J. C. Higginbotham, Dickie Wells, Keg Johnson, Benny Carter, Ben Webster, Lester Young, Chu Berry, John Kirby, Walter Johnson and Sidney Catlett.

Rex Stewart, in his *Jazz Masters of the Thirties*, recalls Hawkins in the early Thirties: "As usual, on hitting a town, we all went to look the burg over, and it so happened that I found myself with Coleman in a department store. He went to the cosmetic counter and bought several bars of very expensive soap. Hawk's remark that this was the year's supply and a great bargain made me wonder how he could figure that six bars of soap would last him a whole year. But the next morning in the hotel, I found out. First, out came a pair of ornate washcloths, then the special soap, then some ordinary soap. One cloth was for the special soap, the other for the ordinary, and never the twain should meet. The fancy soap was daintily applied to a corner of washcloth number one. That was for his face and around his eyes only. Then, the ordinary soap, applied to the other cloth, was used on his body."

Stewart went on to say, "Another facet of Mr. Saxophone's character is his frugality . . . This is not to imply that Hawk is cheap; it's just that he is cautious. Before he got over his mistrust of banks, it was common for him to walk around with $2,000 or $3,000 in his pockets! One time, he carried with him his salary from an entire season of summer touring, about $9,000. When we became stranded, for some reason or other, Hawk laughed while showing his roll. But he wouldn't give a quarter to see the Statue of Liberty do the twist on the Brooklyn Bridge at high noon."

In 1934, Hawkins, tired of Henderson's lackadaisical ways as a leader and a businessman, and curious about the high-class things he had heard about Europe, wired the British bandleader Jack Hylton, was offered a job and took a six-month leave of absence. He remained abroad five years, and it may have been the happiest time of his life. He was one of the first great jazz soloists, and he was treated like royalty wherever he went. He played in England and Wales, then settled on the Continent, where he worked in Belgium, Holland, Switzerland, Denmark and France. He recorded with English and Dutch and French and Belgian musicians, among them Django Reinhardt and Stéphan Grappelli, and with such Americans as Benny Carter, Tommy Benford and Arthur Briggs.

According to Chris Goddard, in "Jazz Away Home," Briggs once gave this picture of Hawkins in Paris: "He was such a wonderful person. I couldn't believe that anyone could drink so much alcohol and that it would have so little effect on him. When we were working together in Belgium . . . he would drink a bottle of brandy a day . . . He would be featured at the tea dance. He did three numbers so most of the time he was free in the baccarat room. He didn't gamble. He'd just be at the bar. And when I sent someone to fetch him to play he'd come on as straight as ever. I never knew him to practice . . . He didn't talk much. But he had wonderful taste. I remember him paying 20 dollars for a pair of socks. He was crazy about beautiful shirts in silk and things like that. He would dress like a prince. I think Europe was a rest cure for him."

Hawkins returned from Europe in July 1939. In October, he recorded (as an afterthought) his celebrated "Body and Soul" for Victor, and early in 1940 he put together a big band. Hawkins' playing passed through four phases in his life, and he was about to enter his third and best period. His neophyte period had lasted until the late Twenties. During that time, he had a hard sound, and his rhythmic attack was aggressive and staccato and congested. He even used slap-tonguing, a device that had originated in New Orleans and that resembled the sound of a ratchet.

He entered his second phase in the early Thirties. His tone filled out, he abandoned much of his staccato attack, and he developed a rich vibrato. He began playing slow ballads like "It's the Talk of the Town," "Out of Nowhere" and "Star Dust." Jazz had been a rough-and-ready, shouting, realistic music; Hawkins proved it could be romantic, and changed it forever. When he came home, his always imperious confidence intact, he went out on the town and was adulated every place he stopped. But he must have felt some nervousness, and the uncanny popular success of the Victor "Body and Soul," which consists of two unvarnished, uninterrupted choruses of improvisation, certainly cheered him. He did not record between 1940 and 1943 (a musicians' union recording ban was part of the reason), but from 1943 to

1947 he recorded more than 100 numbers, some of them as brilliant as any jazz recording.

Bob Wilber remembers him on 52nd Street in the early Forties: "We'd go to Kelly's Stable to hear Coleman Hawkins and he'd come out in a gray pin-striped suit. I guess we were expecting the extraordinary but all that happened was his piano player said, 'What you want to play, Hawk?' and Hawkins said, 'Body,' meaning 'Body and Soul,' which was his big thing then. After that, he'd do one of his riff tunes based on the chords of 'I Got Rhythm' or something like that, and you wouldn't see him again for a couple of hours."

His playing had reached its peak. His slow numbers were distinguished by his great welcoming tone, his almost discursive vibrato, and the seigneurial new melodies he imposed on improvisations. His up-tempo numbers were headlong. He poured through the chords, restructuring them as he went. He never paused to breathe, and he built a rampaging momentum, transposing to his horn with great speed everything he heard in his head. His rare missed notes immediately vanished in the surrounding perfection. His improvisations were rivaled in density, daring and sheer strength only by Art Tatum's. (Hawkins had first heard Tatum in the early Thirties, and Tatum had made a strong impression.)

Hawkins began working Norman Granz's Jazz At The Philharmonic tours in the late Forties, and when he settled down again in the Fifties something had happened to his style. He had entered his final period. At times he was exceptional, but there were increasing signs of unsteadiness. His vibrato fell away or became quavery. His tone hardened, recalling the sound he had in the late Twenties. He began using alarming shrieks and cries—Lear sounds. The bursting melodic invention withered, the great rhythms faltered.

Hawkins' big band was not a success and lasted less

"Body and Soul," cut by Coleman Hawkins in 1939, is arguably the most famous jazz record ever made. (Institute of Jazz Studies photograph)

than a year. For a time, he played and lived in Chicago, where he met a white woman named Delores Sheridan. They were married in 1943 in New York, and they had three children—Colette, Rene and Mimi. The rest of his career was spent with Jazz At The Philharmonic or with small groups generally made up of Hawkins and a rhythm section. He suffered some neglect in the early Fifties but came to the fore again in the mid-Fifties and remained more or less in view until the last year or two of his life. He had for a long time been a renowned eater, but his drinking slowly supplanted food. He eventually drank steadily and ate almost nothing. He became thin and careworn, and he grew a patriarchal beard, perhaps as a sort of disguise. He sometimes sat down on a chair when he played.

Not long after his death, his old friend Roy Eldridge talked about him. "Coleman was a first-class cat all the way down the line," Eldridge recalled. "He was the old school. He never traveled economy, and, of course, he was like a genius on his horn. I guess I knew him as well as anybody. I got my first job—for 12 dollars a week, in 1927—through him, by copying his solo, note for note, off Fletcher Henderson's record of 'Stampede.' And I was the first person near him after he came back from five years in Europe in 1939. I had a Lincoln and he had a Cadillac, and we followed each other to gigs—double things like that. He was a person people were afraid to talk to. If anything went wrong on a job, they wouldn't go to him, they'd always come to me. He was proud, but he wasn't cold. And he had a sense of humor. He just stayed away from cats he didn't like. People said he didn't like Lester Young, who was supposed to be his great rival. Man, I remember Coleman and I sat up all one night with Lester in the Fifties, when we were with Jazz At The Philharmonic, trying to find out why Lester was up so tight. We never did.

"The last five years, Coleman was sick, and he just about quit eating" Eldridge said. "All he had eyes for, when he ate at all, was Chinese food, like Lester. But I'd call him in the evening and tell him what I was cooking. I'd tell him such-and-such, and he'd say, 'That sounds pretty good. I'll have to come out and get me some.' The next day, I'd call again, and he'd forgotten everything. Coleman always had money, and he always spent it the right way. He'd have a Leica and a Steinway and three-hundred-dollar suits, but before anything else he always laid out $600 a month to take care of his rent and his wife and children. I often wondered if he had a little income of his own, but I never knew, because money was one thing we didn't discuss. Just a while ago, I went out with Coleman when he wanted to look at a Rolls-Royce to buy, and I said to him, 'You'd look ridiculous riding around in that.' So he bought a Chrysler Imperial. Eight thousand in cash. I don't think he got to put more than a thousand miles on it."

In the Fifties and Sixties, Hawkins often worked with younger musicians, like the drummer Eddie Locke, the pianist Tommy Flanagan, and the bassist Major Holley. They recently spoke of Hawkins. Flanagan said, "He was a very humorous man. He'd tell stories at great length in that bass voice of his. It was always bigger than anyone else's voice. It reminded me of his horn. He was at home with every kind of music. A master musician."

Says Locke, "He opened my ears to classical music. I believe that he incorporated that in his music. That separated him from other saxophone players. He played jazz, but it was classical-jazz. He loved the piano, and he always had piano players visiting him—guys like Joe Zawinul and Monk. Monk loved Coleman. He was a different person around him. Nothing weird or strange, just straight conversation."

Holley reminisces, "He was a very knowledgeable man. He'd amaze you with the things he would tell you that didn't pertain to music. He knew about the assembly of automobiles—I could tell, I had worked in a factory. He knew about art. He knew about flowers. He had impeccable taste in clothes. He was a connoisseur of wine. He was a culinary expert. When he did a stew, it was like European cooking—a whole potato, a whole carrot. If he invited you over to eat, he would be put out if you didn't come. He played the piano, and he could do things that full-time players were hard-pressed to do. He had learned circular breathing, which was why he could play those very long lines. I once saw him pick up a cello and play it very well after not touching one for 40 years. He was a master at setting up comedy, a master jokesman. He would ask a whole bunch of us to his apartment on Central Park West—maybe Tommy Flanagan and Roland Hanna and Lew Tabackin and Zoot Sims. He'd play classical records by the hour, and maybe get into Chopin, and then suggest that Roland Hanna play one of the Chopin études we had just heard, and, of course, by this time Hanna had consumed a fair amount of brandy—and, well . . . Sometimes Hawkins would call me and I'd answer the telephone and all I'd hear would be him shaking a glass of ice in it and laughing in the background, and he'd hang up. He was very private and very shy. He had great concern for people, and he did a lot of stuff he never talked about. When he went out on the road he would visit some musician he knew in prison, whether he knew him well or not. Or he would go to see his mother in St. Joe. He had rules, he had morals. He had the sort of courtesy that has to be taught you when you're a kid. He was always interested in young people and in getting his ideas across to them; had a great ambition to play for younger people. We worked together for two or three years. He was my friend, but I would have liked to know him better. I didn't really get to understand him. We didn't have enough time."

—W.B.

Louis Armstrong at sunset. (Art Kane photograph from January 1959 *Esquire*)

On the Road with Louis Armstrong

by Milt Hinton

In his book BassLine (Temple University Press, 1988, written with his friend David Berger) Milt Hinton tells of one night when he was filling in briefly for Armstrong's regular bass player. (He was too much in demand in the New York studios to stay on the road regularly.) Here's Milt's story:

I WENT OUT with Louis' band, and for a while we did mostly one-nighters. Cozy Cole was still there, along with Trummy Young on trombone. Barney Bigard was still on clarinet and Marty Napoleon on piano. At one of those early gigs something incredible happened.

It was an outdoor concert in Washington, D.C., near one of those big malls right on the Potomac River. The stage and dressing rooms were set up on a barge docked at the edge of the river and the audience sat on the long, wide grass bank in front of it. I remember we had to walk down a long ramp to get into the barge so we could change into our tuxedos and get set up.

In addition to us (Louis' sextet) Lionel Hampton's and Illinois Jacquet's bands were on the program. Jacquet was scheduled to play first from 6:00 to 7:00, and Hamp would follow from 7:00 to 8:00. Then after an intermission, Louis would come out and do the finale.

We worked in New Jersey the night before and had driven down from Jersey in a private bus, getting in at 5:30, an hour and a half before show time. There were over a thousand people in the audience on the grass, but no sign of Jacquet's band.

We unloaded our suitcases and instruments and moved all our stuff over to the barge. By the time we'd changed into our tuxedos, it was 6:30. Jacquet should have gone on at 6:00, but he still hadn't arrived. To make matters worse, Hamp hadn't got there yet, either.

Standing backstage, we could tell the audience was getting restless. Every couple of minutes they'd start applauding and chanting, "Start the show," and "We want music!" You couldn't blame them. It was more than half an hour since it should have started. They'd *seen* us go backstage, but nothing was happening. You couldn't blame them for getting impatient.

About 15 minutes later (it was now 6:45) one of the producers came back to Frenchy, our road manager, and asked if Louis would go on first. Louis was a star—*the* star—but he didn't care about billing or protocol. He was usually understanding and cooperative, so he said "OK, we'll do it, we'll go on first."

So we went out and started playing. After waiting so long the audience gave us an unbelievable reception. They applauded every solo, and when we finished a tune they'd stand up and cheer and stomp for two or three minutes. They went nuts for Pops and our music.

We played for about an hour, then took our bows. But the people wouldn't let us off the stage. They screamed for encores, and we kept doing them. Louis knew there was no act to follow us, and he was content to just stay out there and keep everyone happy until help arrived.

Finally, during our fifth or sixth encore, we saw a bus pull up and unload. As soon as Pops knew it was Jacquet's band, he told us, "This time when we finish, walk off, and stay off."

As soon as we finished, we headed for the dressing rooms and changed. Then we packed our instruments and hung around backstage talking to some of the guys from Jacquet's band.

Trying to follow a performer like Louis really put Jacquet in a difficult position. To make matters worse, the audience knew he'd been set to play first and had kept them waiting. So when he came out on stage, he got a very lukewarm reception.

Jacquet had a lot of good musicians with him, very professional. He started with a couple of standards, but got almost no response from the crowd. He even featured the drummer, but that didn't seem to rouse the audience either. Finally Jacquet figured he had nothing to lose, so he called "Flying Home," the tune he'd made famous with Hampton's band many years before.

It took a couple of minutes before the audience recognized his big hit tune and started to react. By then Jacquet was doing his famous tenor solo, and he gave it everything he had, building, honking, screaming, and even dancing while he played on. All the moves, chorus after chorus of "Flying Home." By the time he finished, he had the audience in the palm of his hand, the same as Louis had them an hour before.

The audience screamed for an encore, and Jacquet did another two choruses of "Flying Home." But right in the middle of this, Hampton's bus pulled in. Hearing someone else do his tune, and the one *he* was best known for (his theme in fact) and seeing the fantastic crowd reaction must have made him furious.

Backstage we all saw what was going on and knew Hampton would want to somehow outdo Jacquet. Pops was watching, and he got interested, too. I remember we were all set to get on the bus, but he turned to a couple of us and he said, "Wait, we have to see this."

Jacquet finished, and after the stage got set up for Hampton, Lionel and his band came out. He began with "Midnight Sun," one of his famous ballads, but after Louis' performance and Jacquet's great finale the audience was in no mood for it. He did "Hamp's Boogie Woogie," and a couple more numbers. He even played drums and he sang, but he still didn't get much of a reaction.

I was standing in the wings with Louis and a couple of the other guys, and we could see how hard Hamp was working. But time was running out. He looked frustrated and desperate and *he* finally called "Flying Home."

The band started playing, but there wasn't much response from the audience. They'd just heard a *great* version of *that* tune! But Hamp wouldn't give up. He put everything he had into his solo, starting out soft, then building up to a crescendo. When he finished, sweat was dripping off every part of him, and a handful of people cheered. He was finally beginning to get to them.

I guess Hamp sensed he *was* making some headway with the crowd. So while the band kept rocking he went over to Monk Montgomery in the back who was playing Fender bass, and told him, "Gate, you jump in the river on the next chorus. I'll give you an extra ten."

Monk must have agreed, because when the band got to the next crescendo, Hamp raised his mallets, and Monk jumped right back over the railing into the water. The crowd went crazy!

The band kept playing, and a few minutes later Monk came back up on the stage dripping wet. He started back to his bass. But Hamp walked over to him and said, "Another ten if you do it again."

Monk made it back to his bass and played another chorus. Then when the band came back to the same crescendo again and Hamp raised his mallets up in the air again Monk went back over the railing into the river again! By this time the people were in a frenzy, and Hamp knew he'd accomplished what he'd set out to do.

Pops turned to us and said, "Start up the bus. We can go now." ●

Charles Graham, center, and trumpeter Ruby Braff, right, hanging out with Louis Armstrong at his home in 1960. (Lucille Armstrong photograph)